Master Point Press • Toronto

ERIC KOKISH & MARK HORTON

CLOSE

ENCOUNTERS

BRIDGE'S GREATEST MATCHES

BOOK 2: 2003 TO 2017

Master Point Press
214 Merton St. Suite 205
Toronto, Ontario, Canada
M4S 1A6 (647)956-4933
info@masterpointpress.com

Websites: www.masterpointpress.com
                 www.teachbridge.com
                 www.bridgeblogging.com
                 www.ebooksbridge.com

Library and Archives Canada Cataloguing in Publication

Kokish, Eric, author
        Close encounters : bridge's greatest matches / Eric Kokish and Mark Horton.
Contents: Book 2: 2003-2017.
Issued in print and electronic formats.
ISBN 978-1-77140-045-9 (book 2 : softcover).--ISBN 978-1-55494-641-9 (book 2 : PDF).--
ISBN 978-1-55494-686-0 (book 2 : HTML).--ISBN 978-1-77140-885-1 (book 2 : Kindle)

        1. Contract bridge--Tournaments--History. 2. Contract bridge--Bidding.
3. Contract bridge--Defensive play. I. Horton, Mark, author II. Title.

GV1282.6.K65 2018   795.41'58   C2018-902754-1
                                                      C2018-902755-X

Canada   We acknowledge the financial support of the Government of Canada.
           Nous reconnaissons l'appui financier du gouvernement du Canada.

Editor   Ray Lee
Copy editor/interior format   Sally Sparrow
Cover design   Olena S. Sullivan/New Mediatrix

1 2 3 4 5 6 7   21 20 19 18
Printed in Canada at Webcom

Publisher's Note

Close Encounters was a long time coming — indeed, it began life as a totally different book. After initial discussions, the authors departed to their respective continents, and began to work. Both have been writing about top-level bridge for decades, and their files contain a wealth of fascinating material. Three or four years later, when the manuscript finally arrived, it was about twice the length I had envisaged — but it would have been tragic simply to discard half of it. The solution was to divide it into two books, one of which you are holding as you read this. After further lengthy discussion, we decided on a simple approach to this — we would break it into two books chronologically. That way the reader could see something of the evolution of theory and practice in top-level bridge over the decades, and even follow the fortunes of some of the players who are recurring characters in the narrative.

Close Encounters I covered the twentieth century, beginning with the Blue Team era, and ending with the dramatic Venice Cup final in Paris in 2001. This second book deals with the past twenty years, starting with an account of the 2003 Bermuda Bowl, a match that featured perhaps the most bizarre finish in the history of bridge. It ends with the most recent World Championship final in Lyon in 2017, which was decided by slam bidding on the final two deals. Inevitably, the Nickell team features prominently in this book — but then they have been the preeminent force in world bridge for the last thirty-odd years.

Ray Lee
Master Point Press

Forewords

After surviving the emotional roller coaster of the first book, you're about to be exposed to some of the center-court matches of the young millennium. As you might imagine, choosing from among many worthy candidates was a challenge, and we could easily have presented some different matches or some additional ones. The truth is that we initially sent only one very long book to the publisher, but soon learned that it would have to be divided into two volumes to make the project viable. That reality spawned a protracted discussion about the best way to create books of relatively equal length before settling on chronological order as the criterion. That has left us with only four chapters in Book 2 while Book 1 covered seven matches somewhat less comprehensively, but we're hopeful that you will find the depth and intimacy of our coverage satisfying.

I confess without regret that I sometimes shed a tear during the playing of national anthems, some sports events and certain movies, and just looking back at some of the matches we've written about in *Close Encounters* — the most poignant remains the Brazil-USA semi-final in the 1985 Bermuda Bowl (covered in Book 1) — has had the same effect for me. I hadn't considered before writing these books that I would be hoping, perhaps subconsciously, that readers might experience similar reactions, but now I guess that amounts to a further confession.

It goes without saying that there will always be dramatic high-level matches with the issue in doubt until the very end, so if these books prove popular, we can't rule out a future *Close Encounters, Book 3*.

Eric Kokish, Toronto, Canada, 2018

Bridge matches can be frustrating affairs, especially if a vast amount of your time is taken up by watching them unfold. It's tricky to entertain your audience as a VuGraph commentator or journalist if the deals are uncooperative. (One famous author of my acquaintance refuses to write up deals that end in 1NT.) However, every once in a while, one is lucky enough to be in the right place at the right time to witness the most dramatic events unfold.

This second volume of *Close Encounters* continues the in depth reporting of bridge matches from the twentieth and twenty-first centuries that are entertaining, instructive, emotional — choose your own adjective and it will not be out of place. Once again we have chosen contests that will have you metaphorically sitting on the edge of your seats.

These unbelievably exciting matches are instructive in so many ways, but most of all they are a testament to the skill and nerves of the participants.

Mark Horton, Sutton Benger, UK, 2018

Acknowledgements

Tracking down information and photographs is never easy, sometimes impossible. We could not have managed without the assistance of the ACBL, the USBF, Bridge Winners, BBO, Nikos Sarantakos and the VuGraph Project, *The Bridge World*, *Bridge Magazine* (RIP), *Le Bridgeur*, *Bridge d'Italia*, *International Popular Bridge Monthly* (RIP), Tim Bourke, Francesca Canali, Wolf Klewe, Tracy Yarbro, Jeff Rubens, Simon Fellus, Richard Fleet, Gabriel Chagas, Benito Garozzo, Sami Kehela, Sally and the late Raymond Brock, Brian Senior, Zia Mahmood, Peter Hasenson and so many of the players who appear in action in these books.

Contents

1. 2003 The Count in Monte Carlo

In 2003, the World Championships returned to Monaco for the third time, the principality having previously hosted the Bermuda Bowl in 1954 and both the Bermuda Bowl and Teams Olympiad (in consecutive two-week slots in May) in 1976, the only time in history that two World Championships were held in the same year. (The year 2000 was an anomaly: the official 2000 World Championship — the Olympiad — was staged in the fall in Maastricht, Netherlands, but the 1999 Bermuda Bowl, which had been awarded to Bermuda, was deferred until January 2000 to commemorate the Golden Anniversary of the first edition of the event in 1950.)

Monte Carlo is an expensive town. USA 1, my guys*, are bunking at the Hotel de Paris, together with the Hermitage around the corner the two brightest five-star joints in the constellation, steps from the Casino and the so-called Carré d'Or (the Golden Square), which have featured in several movies. My wife Beverly, for some time the active player in our family, is here with me because she's playing for Canada in the Venice Cup, so this hotel treat feels a lot like a honeymoon. We have a spectacular view from our balcony, which is a valuable perk for couples like us with only one smoker. Ah, this is the life!

The WBF has not done badly for its staff this time, many of whom are housed in Le Mirabeau — marginally less luxurious (its restaurant boasts only *one* Michelin star) — and located on the route of the annual Formula One Grand Prix. Among the movies featuring motor racing and Monte Carlo is *Monte Carlo or Bust!* — a comedy film based on the Monte Carlo Rally. It follows the adventures of the contestants as they race across Europe and use all possible means in an attempt to win. No relation to bridge, then.

---

* Primary author Eric Kokish.

Day One. We're tired. We contemplate room service. Sticker shock: 47 Euros for a cheeseburger ($56 at current exchange rates!). Fries are included with that, however. We resign ourselves to seeking alternatives.

Day Two. We come down for breakfast *inclus* and are guided gently to a gorgeous garden café with an equally gorgeous spread of delectables. Soft music in the background. Bliss.

Day Three. All smiles, we come down for breakfast *inclus* and are guided rather brusquely to an ugly, uncomfortable room (if that is possible in the Hotel de Paris!) with terrible acoustics, where we are told by the particularly snooty maître d' that this is (the trough) where the bridge players (he sneered) will be fed. The poor quality, limited-options breakfast with abominable service is not the stuff of honeymoons, and skipping breakfast becomes a serious consideration. Did anyone read the fine print in the (slightly discounted room rate) contract negotiated by the WBF?

But Monte Carlo has beautiful vistas everywhere, ideal for short walks in all directions. The Café de Paris across the square is one of our frequent haunts, and early on, we find a nearby restaurant — Rampoldi — which becomes our go-to dinner destination. This is in no small measure due to the ambience and joyful service, but also due to a consistently perfect *steak au poivre*, seductive langoustines, immaculate *carré d'agneau* and sinful desserts, which include the fabulous Paris-Brest, last enjoyed by Beverly in Deauville in 1983 and missed ever since.

But I digress. We're here for the Bermuda Bowl.

Italy (Maria Teresa Lavazza, npc: Lorenzo Lauria, Alfredo Versace, Norberto Bocchi, Giorgio Duboin, Fulvio Fantoni, Claudio Nunes with Massimo Ortensi, coach) finds its form early in the round robin, builds a big lead, then coasts home despite an ominous loss (by 39 IMPS, 6-24 VP) to USA 1 in the last round. The Italians have every reason to believe that this is their year, their chance to win the title for Italy for the first time since 1975. In the 128-board final, Italy will face USA 1 (Sidney Lazard, npc: Nick Nickell, Dick Freeman, Bob Hamman, Paul Soloway, Jeff Meckstroth, Eric Rodwell with Eric Kokish, coach), the team that finished second by nearly a full match to Italy in the round robin. These traditional rivals are widely regarded as the world's best teams.

Thanks to that lopsided round robin win over Italy, USA 1 will start with a 13-IMP advantage, carrying forward one-third of the 39-IMP margin (had the Italians won that match, they would have carried forward *half* of the IMP difference, thanks to their superior overall finish in the round robin).

Bocchi-Duboin (variable notrumps) have scrapped much of their artificiality and can now pass a 1♣ (2+ cards) opening, as can Lauria-Versace, who have been operating from an ostensibly natural base (strong notrump) for years. All Fantoni-Nunes' opening one-level bids are forcing, 14+ HCP, and their weak notrump openings could include any 5-4 apart from major two-suiters. Their high-frequency two-bids are constructive (about 9-13 with one- or two-suited unbalanced hands) and often create scenarios leading to decisions that would not be faced at the other table. All three Italian pairs play five-card majors.

Hamman-Soloway (four-card majors, some canapés into the minors, medium notrumps) and Meckstroth-Rodwell (five-card majors, mini-notrump when logical, strongish otherwise) play very different strong-club systems, with Nickell-Freeman employing mainstream natural methods, five-card majors and strong notrump. It is going to be interesting to see whether the forcing club, limited opening bids and four-card major openings will be a factor. It was not so many years ago that these were Italian staples, but now it is the Americans who have embraced these methods.

Some of the innovative Italian competitive methods are threatening to become quite popular in the expert community, but in this match their opponents will not be using them and there may be some swing potential in this area, one way or the other. Another feature to look for will be the two challenging Brown Sticker conventions fielded by Lauria-Versace: a 2♡ opening to introduce a weak two in one of the majors and a 2♠ opening to indicate either a 'bad' three-bid in one of the majors or 10-15 HCP, 6/4 in the minors. In contrast, Meckwell's contribution to this genre is a relatively-benign 2♠ opening to show a 'bad' preempt in clubs or any diamond preempt. Although Meckstroth-Rodwell have earned a reputation for light openings and responses leading to hyper-thin game contracts, they are nowhere near as aggressive as Lauria-Versace when it comes to initial defensive actions. By comparison, the other four pairs in the final would have to be labeled conservative, although in an absolute sense that is not the case.

Segment One (Boards 1-16)

Keep in mind the 13-IMP carryover enjoyed by USA 1.

Board 1. Neither Vul.

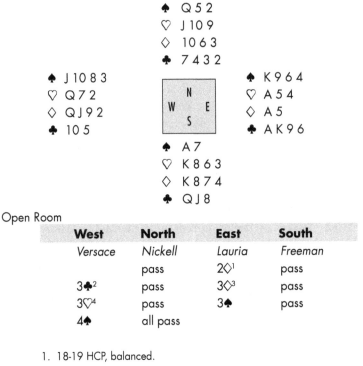

```
              ♠ Q 5 2
              ♡ J 10 9
              ◇ 10 6 3
              ♣ 7 4 3 2
♠ J 10 8 3                   ♠ K 9 6 4
♡ Q 7 2          N           ♡ A 5 4
◇ Q J 9 2     W     E        ◇ A 5
♣ 10 5           S           ♣ A K 9 6
              ♠ A 7
              ♡ K 8 6 3
              ◇ K 8 7 4
              ♣ Q J 8
```

Open Room

West	North	East	South
Versace	Nickell	Lauria	Freeman
	pass	2◇¹	pass
3♣²	pass	3◇³	pass
3♡⁴	pass	3♠	pass
4♠	all pass		

1. 18-19 HCP, balanced.
2. Puppet Stayman.
3. No five-card major.
4. Four spades.

Freeman leads the ♣Q against Lauria, who wins the ace, cashes the ♣K and ruffs a club, establishing his nine. On the lie of the cards, a trump finesse would make life easy for him, but instead he passes the ◇Q to the king. Freeman exits in the same suit to the ten and ace, tucking declarer in hand. Lauria advances the ♣9, ruffing his winner in dummy when South parts with the ♡6. He cashes a diamond to discard a heart, then passes the ♠J to the ace. Freeman has no good answer, but he saves the overtrick by exiting with his remaining diamond to let Nickell ruff dummy's winner. Lauria loses a heart for +420.

West	North	East	South
Rodwell	*Fantoni*	*Meckstroth*	*Nunes*
	pass	1♣[1]	pass
1◇[2]	pass	1NT[3]	all pass

1. Strong, artificial.
2. Negative.
3. 17-18.

It's not often that an aggressive pair, playing a strong club system against silent opposition, will miss a game that is reached by their counterparts playing a natural system, less often still that the pair is Meckstroth-Rodwell. That is not to say that 4♠ is a particularly good contract, not vulnerable, but on the lie of the cards declarer must take a series of wrong views to fail.

Against 1NT, Nunes leads a heart, and declarer wins in hand and plays the ♠K. Nunes takes that with the ace and continues with the ♡3 to dummy's queen. Fantoni takes the third spade and switches to the ♣7, but Meckstroth wins and plays the ◇A and another diamond. Nunes wins the king and cashes his hearts, +120, a 7-IMP gain for Italy.

Jeff Meckstroth

Board 2. N-S Vul.

```
                    ♠ 7 6 4
                    ♡ K J 9 7 6
                    ◇ K Q 8
                    ♣ 10 3
   ♠ 10 9 8 5 2                      ♠ A K J 3
   ♡ A Q 8 2          N              ♡ 10
   ◇ A 10 6       W       E          ◇ 9 7 4
   ♣ 5               S              ♣ K Q J 8 7
                    ♠ Q
                    ♡ 5 4 3
                    ◇ J 5 3 2
                    ♣ A 9 6 4 2
```

Open Room

West	North	East	South
Versace	Nickell	Lauria	Freeman
		1♣[1]	pass
1♠	pass	3♠	pass
4♣[2]	pass	4♡[3]	pass
4♠	pass	5♣[4]	pass
6♠	all pass		

1. 2+ clubs.
2. First- or second-round club control.
3. First- or second-round heart control, no diamond control.
4. First- or second-round club control, slam-suitable non-minimum.

Lauria-Versace climb all the way to 6♠. Lauria, hoping for the especially-valuable ♣A and not a shortness control, aggressively goes past game lacking diamond control because of his strong trumps. Versace, expecting a bit more, commits to slam on the strength of his first-round controls in diamonds and hearts and a fifth spade, but perhaps 5◇ would be enough at his fourth turn. Although partnership style and individual judgment are key elements in this disaster (Versace believes he bid too much, looking for perfect cards), this combination is simply a difficult one for the 'economical' Italian control-showing style. With this deal as the catalyst, Lauria-Versace would soon revise their methods: 3NT would show a high-card club control, 4♣ a shortness control. With the diamond lead clearly indicated on the auction, Versace has no chance in 6♠, and goes two down after winning the first diamond, cashing one high trump and leading the ♣K from dummy. Freeman wins the ace and the defenders take two diamonds, +100.

West	North	East	South
Rodwell	Fantoni	Meckstroth	Nunes
		1◊[1]	pass
2♠[2]	pass	4♠	all pass

1. 2+ diamonds, 10-15.
2. 5 spades/4+ hearts, game-invitational.

Rodwell is also held to ten tricks on the lead of the ◊K, +420, 11 IMPs to USA, ahead 24-7.

Board 8. Neither Vul.

```
              ♠ A 10 9 7 5
              ♡ A 7
              ◊ A K 7 3 2
              ♣ 7
  ♠ 6 3                      ♠ J 2
  ♡ K 10 8 6        N        ♡ 9 5 4 3 2
  ◊ Q 9 8 6 4    W     E     ◊ J 5
  ♣ Q 10            S        ♣ A 9 8 4
              ♠ K Q 8 4
              ♡ Q J
              ◊ 10
              ♣ K J 6 5 3 2
```

Open Room

West	North	East	South
Versace	Nickell	Lauria	Freeman
pass	1♠	pass	2NT[1]
pass	3◊[2]	pass	3♡[3]
pass	4♣[4]	pass	4♠
all pass			

1. Forcing spade raise.
2. Extra values, undisclosed singleton.
3. Which?
4. Clubs.

Freeman, who would have responded 2♣ had his suit been better, opts for an artificial game-forcing raise. After Nickell shows both a short suit and extra values, Freeman learns that he is facing club shortness, and settles for game, expecting Nickell to make another move if slam were a good proposition.

Nickell gives it plenty of consideration, but finally passes. Lauria leads the ♡2 (low from an odd number), and Versace covers in case his partner has underled the ace. Although Nickell misguesses clubs when Lauria follows low to the first round, he wins the heart return in dummy, ruffs a club, goes to the ♠K, ruffs a club, crosses to the ♣Q, and can claim, establishing clubs, for +480.

Closed Room

West	North	East	South
Rodwell	Fantoni	Meckstroth	Nunes
pass	1♠	pass	2♣[1]
pass	2◇	pass	2♠
pass	3◇	pass	3♠[2]
pass	4♣[3]	pass	4◇[4]
pass	4♡[5]	pass	4♠
pass	5◇[6]	pass	6♠
all pass			

1. Game-forcing: natural, or spade support, or balanced.
2. Denies a heart control, stronger than an artificial 3NT.
3. Club control, implies heart control.
4-5. Control-showing.
6. First-round diamond control, odd number of keycards.

Although 6♠ is hardly lay-down, it's worth bidding. Nunes' 2♠ leaves Fantoni in the dark about the number of spades he holds, a crucial piece of information. In that context, Fantoni does well to bid on over 4♠; when he shows three keycards and significant extra values, Nunes, with strong trumps and playing strength, is obliged to commit to slam. Meckstroth shortens the play by leading the ♣A. He continues clubs, Fantoni playing the jack and ruffing away the queen. When he tests trumps and they divide 2-2, he has the rest: +980, 11 IMPs to Italy, 18-25.

To have a legitimate chance to defeat 6♠, East must lead a trump, then duck when declarer leads a club towards dummy. If declarer misguesses, putting in the jack, West leads a second trump and with both minors lying badly for declarer, the slam will fail.

Board 9. E-W Vul.

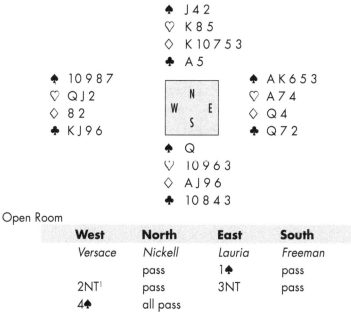

```
                  ♠ J 4 2
                  ♡ K 8 5
                  ◇ K 10 7 5 3
                  ♣ A 5
    ♠ 10 9 8 7              ♠ A K 6 5 3
    ♡ Q J 2          N       ♡ A 7 4
    ◇ 8 2        W       E   ◇ Q 4
    ♣ K J 9 6        S       ♣ Q 7 2
                  ♠ Q
                  ♡ 10 9 6 3
                  ◇ A J 9 6
                  ♣ 10 8 4 3
```

Open Room

West	North	East	South
Versace	Nickell	Lauria	Freeman
	pass	1♠	pass
2NT¹	pass	3NT	pass
4♠	all pass		

1. Three-card limit raise or lesser four-card raise.

Freeman leads the ♡10, and Nickell, holding the supporting ♡8, covers dummy's queen to allow the defenders to continue hearts from either side. Although that seems like a sensible idea, with a threatening club holding in dummy, it may well cost the defenders their best chance to set the contract. Lauria wins the ♡A, cashes the ♠A, and leads a club to the king and ace. Nickell drives out the ♡J, but Lauria runs the ♠10, draws the last trump, plays a fourth round of trumps (diamond discards) and plays the ♣Q followed by a club to the nine for an excellent +620.

Even if North withholds the ♡K at Trick 1, 4♠ can be made with some very good views by declarer. When the ♡Q wins, he must cash the ♠A and lead a club to the jack. Declarer can always force a club entry for the spade finesse (by finessing the nine: it doesn't help South to put up the ten to block the suit because there's a fourth-round trump entry to the West hand). Once declarer credits South with a singleton spade, this line becomes less far-fetched.

As it happens, an apparently unfortunate initial club lead would leave declarer with no real chance, North taking the ace and returning the suit.

West	North	East	South
Rodwell	Fantoni	Meckstroth	Nunes
	1NT	dbl	pass[1]
pass[2]	rdbl[3]	pass	2♣[4]
dbl	2◇[5]	pass[6]	pass
2♠	pass	3♠	all pass

1. Non-forcing, but opener passes only with 4-3-3-3.
2. 6+ HCP (2♣ would have been artificial and weak).
3. Two places to play or no strong five-card suit.
4. Scramble, more or less natural.
5. Typically four or five diamonds plus four hearts or four spades.
6. Forcing.

When Fantoni-Nunes extricate themselves from 1NT doubled (Fantoni's strategy might have landed him in a 3-3 heart fit: he bids too quickly), which might have made, Meckstroth-Rodwell find their spade fit, but are not able to stop at the two-level with any confidence. As Fantoni's aggressive opponents would not have anything in reserve when they stop short of game, he starts with the ♠2.

Rodwell, declaring from the short side, wins dummy's ace, and reads the trump position correctly. He calls for the ◇Q, and Nunes wins to switch to the ♡3 (queen, king, ace). A club goes to the king and ace, and Fantoni cashes the ◇K before exiting with a second club. That picks up the suit for declarer, who wins with the nine, passes the ♠10, and claims, +170. Rodwell would rely on the bidding to play clubs correctly if it were to come to that. That looks like a good result for USA, but Italy gains 10 IMPs and takes the lead for the first time in the match, 28-25.

Board 13. Both Vul.

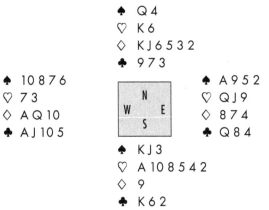

```
              ♠ Q 4
              ♡ K 6
              ◇ K J 6 5 3 2
              ♣ 9 7 3
♠ 10 8 7 6              ♠ A 9 5 2
♡ 7 3          N        ♡ Q J 9
◇ A Q 10    W   E      ◇ 8 7 4
♣ A J 10 5     S       ♣ Q 8 4
              ♠ K J 3
              ♡ A 10 8 5 4 2
              ◇ 9
              ♣ K 6 2
```

Open Room

West	North	East	South
Versace	Nickell	Lauria	Freeman
	pass	pass	1♡
dbl	2◇	2♠	all pass

Nickell shows his diamonds directly, his suit quality limited by his failure to open a weak 2◇. He has no reason to act over Lauria's 2♠, but that contract can't be beaten legitimately, and Lauria has a shrewd idea about the lie of the red suits. He wins the opening lead of the ◇9 with dummy's ace and plays two rounds of trumps. Nickell wins, and plays the ♡K, then a heart to the ace. With the ♣K onside, the defense has only the high trump and a late diamond trick to come. Freeman actually switches to the ♣K, but nothing matters: +110.

Closed Room

West	North	East	South
Rodwell	Fantoni	Meckstroth	Nunes
	pass	pass	2♡[1]
dbl	pass	2♠	all pass

1. 9-13, 5+ hearts, unbalanced.

It is merely happenstance that Nunes has a sixth heart for his two-level opening (the partnership approach with unbalanced hands not quite strong enough for a 'usually 14+' one-bid). Rodwell risks a takeout double and Meckstroth devalues his heart holding to settle for 2♠. Randomly deprived by the bulky opening of the information about the diamond suit, Meckstroth puts in the ◇Q at Trick 1. Fantoni has reason to assume that 'unbalanced' means that the diamond lead is a singleton, and so returns the suit-preference ◇J. Nunes ruffs, plays the ♡A and a heart to the king, gets another diamond ruff, and gives Fantoni an overruff in hearts. Now a fourth round of diamonds promotes the ♠K for two down before Meckstroth can catch his breath: -200. That's 7 more IMPs to Italy, extending the lead to 12, 37-25.

Board 14. Neither Vul.

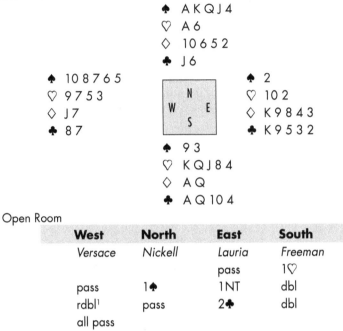

```
              ♠ A K Q J 4
              ♡ A 6
              ◇ 10 6 5 2
              ♣ J 6
   ♠ 10 8 7 6 5              ♠ 2
   ♡ 9 7 5 3                 ♡ 10 2
   ◇ J 7                     ◇ K 9 8 4 3
   ♣ 8 7                     ♣ K 9 5 3 2
              ♠ 9 3
              ♡ K Q J 8 4
              ◇ A Q
              ♣ A Q 10 4
```

Open Room

West	North	East	South
Versace	Nickell	Lauria	Freeman
		pass	1♡
pass	1♠	1NT	dbl
rdbl[1]	pass	2♣	dbl
all pass			

1. Equal length in the minors.

Nickell-Freeman would surely reach 6NT, but when Lauria comes into the live auction with his minor two-suiter, the Americans seize the opportunity to extract a significant penalty. Against 2♣ doubled, Freeman leads the ♡K, which holds, then continues the ♡4 to the ace. Two rounds of spades force Lauria to ruff, and a low diamond goes to the queen. Freeman continues with the ♡8 to emphasize his interest in an uppercut, and Nickell duly ruffs with the jack. Lauria accurately discards a diamond, but then ruffs the high-spade continuation with the ♣3, overruffed with the four. Now Freeman can drive out the ♣K, and when he wins the ◇A, he draws the last trump and claims, down six, -1400. Although it is not easy to see, Lauria could have saved a 7-IMP trick by ruffing with the ♣5 rather than the ♣3.

	West	North	East	South
	Rodwell	*Fantoni*	*Meckstroth*	*Nunes*
			pass	1♡
	pass	2♠¹	pass	3♣
	pass	3◇	pass	3NT
	pass	4NT	pass	6NT
	all pass			

1. 5+ spades, forcing to game.

Although Fantoni-Nunes reach the par contract, the auction is not comfortable for them: North is obliged to go past 3NT with a good 15-16 HCP because South's range for his sequence is 14-18 HCP. That would have propelled them to 4NT with a combined 29-count on a different deal, but here everything goes smoothly. Nunes takes the lead of the ♠7 with the ace and leads the ♣J, which Meckstroth covers: +1020.

That is 9 IMPs to USA, within 3 now at 34-37.

Board 16. E-W Vul.

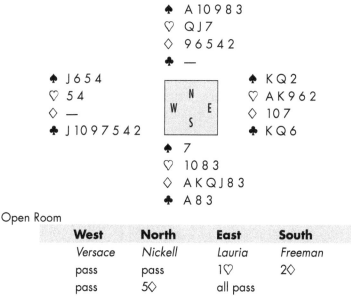

```
              ♠ A 10 9 8 3
              ♡ Q J 7
              ◇ 9 6 5 4 2
              ♣ —
♠ J 6 5 4              ♠ K Q 2
♡ 5 4           N      ♡ A K 9 6 2
◇ —          W   E     ◇ 10 7
♣ J 10 9 7 5 4 2   S   ♣ K Q 6
              ♠ 7
              ♡ 10 8 3
              ◇ A K Q J 8 3
              ♣ A 8 3
```

Open Room

West	North	East	South
Versace	*Nickell*	*Lauria*	*Freeman*
pass	pass	1♡	2◇
pass	5◇	all pass	

Despite the ominous-looking heart lead, 5◇ proves unbeatable, thanks to the layout of the trump suit: West can't ruff the third round of hearts.

Closed Room

West	North	East	South
Rodwell	Fantoni	Meckstroth	Nunes
pass	pass	1♣*	pass
1◇*	1♠	1NT	dbl¹
3♣	pass	3NT	pass
4♣	all pass		

1. Fantoni: 'No agreement: I suppose points and spade support.'

Nunes has no way to show a strong overcall on the first round over Meck-stroth's strong club, and is not willing to take his chances with a tactical 3◇. Passing turns out well for him when he can double 1NT, a contract he can defeat (although Fantoni can't pinpoint his hand type). It gets even better for him at his next turn when his opponents are in 3NT, but Nunes likes that too much to double it. Now, when Rodwell retreats to 4♣, Nunes hasn't really shown his hand yet and decides to pass, in effect wagering that 4♣ will go down more often than a diamond contract will produce at least ten tricks. Had diamonds been 1-1, 4♣ would have failed while 4◇ would have produced +130, but on the actual layout, the range of possibilities is much wider. Nunes gets his spade ruff, but that merely holds 4♣ to four, +130. Meanwhile, the same diamond division produces eleven tricks in diamonds in the Open Room, so Nunes pays the maximum price for his decision. USA gains 11 IMPs to end their losing session on a high note. Italy wins the set 43-32, but the Americans are still ahead in the match, 45-43.

Take a short break from this tense match to consider the same Board 16 in the Bermuda Bowl Bronze Medal playoff:

West	North	East	South
Groetheim	Wildavsky	Aa	Doub
pass	pass	1♣*	pass
1◇*	2♣¹	all pass	

1. Hearts and clubs, or spades and diamonds.

And so it comes to pass that Doug Doub and Adam Wildavsky of USA 2 play their 11-card-fit 5◇ game in their 3-0 club fit. Those nasty Norwegians are unkind enough not to double. Thus is coined the definitive title for a 3-0 fit: 'Doubious' or 'Doubian'. I lean towards 'Doubskyan'.

Although something similar probably happens somewhere in the world every day, the related episode I can't help but recall took place sometime in the 1960s. Harold Guiver, a Los Angeles expert who was one of the great characters in bridge, was in the passout seat against opponents who had clearly lost their way and were about to play a contract with very few trumps. Giving them hope, Harold, a diminutive fellow, stood up on his chair to suggest he was about to make the world's soundest penalty double. But then, timing it perfectly, he smiled and said, 'Ah, they're such nice guys — I'm passing!' That story has made the rounds for generations, but it has aged well.

Segment Two (Boards 17-32)

The Americans field the same foursome, but for Italy, Bocchi-Duboin replace Lauria-Versace.

Board 20. Both Vul.

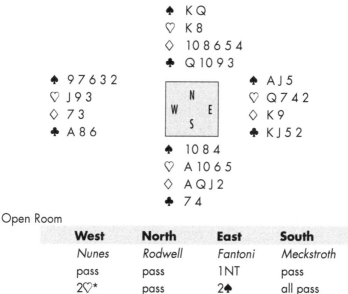

Open Room

West	North	East	South
Nunes	*Rodwell*	*Fantoni*	*Meckstroth*
pass	pass	1NT	pass
2♡*	pass	2♠	all pass

Fantoni's weak notrump forces Nunes to choose between a pass and a transfer to spades, an issue that is best resolved by adopting a consistent strategy. Here, Nunes lands his side in the more promising strain. Meckstroth leads the ♣7 (eight, nine, jack). With trumps as they are, Fantoni can make his contract legitimately by playing ace and another trump and eventually finessing the ♡9. Instead, when he exits with a low spade, the defense can prevail by taking a heart ruff, but Rodwell returns the ◇8 to the king and ace. On the ◇J, Rodwell follows with the six, an accurate 'standard' remainder-count card, but in this case Meckstroth needs a suit-preference signal so he can switch confidently to a low heart. The partnership uses upside-down suit preference, so it may be that Meckstroth reads the ◇6 as a request to stay off hearts, for he reverts to clubs. Fantoni wins in dummy, picks up trumps, and leads a heart to the nine: +110.

Closed Room

West	North	East	South
Nickell	Bocchi	Freeman	Duboin
pass	pass	1♣	pass
1♠	pass	1NT	all pass

Although East's first two bids describe the same balanced range as Fantoni's opening bid, West's decision over 1NT is different here: East has not raised spades, a live option with three-card support, and might have been stuck for a rebid with 1=4=3=5 shape. Nickell passes, and Freeman is left to struggle in a fragile contract. South leads the ♡5 (attitude), and when Bocchi wins the ♡K (deuce from Freeman), he switches to the ◇4, also attitude. The king loses to the ace and the defenders take five diamonds, two hearts and a spade for two down: -200. Freeman has discarded two spades and a club from both dummy and the closed hand and, although Duboin accurately switches to a spade to the king and ace when Freeman leads a heart to build a trick, the spades are blocked so the defenders can't come to a ninth winner. Still, that is 7 IMPs to Italy, back in front, 53-49.

Board 21. N-S Vul.

```
              ♠ A Q 9 7 6
              ♡ 10 8
              ◇ 6
              ♣ A 10 9 8 2
♠ 5 4                           ♠ J 10
♡ Q J 5          N              ♡ A K 9 7 6 3
◇ K Q 4 3 2    W   E            ◇ J 9 8
♣ 7 6 5          S              ♣ K Q
              ♠ K 8 3 2
              ♡ 4 2
              ◇ A 10 7 5
              ♣ J 4 3
```

West	North	East	South
Nunes	Rodwell	Fantoni	Meckstroth
	1♠	2♡	3♠[1]
pass	4♠	all pass	

1. 7-9, 4+ spades.

Against Rodwell's 4♠, Nunes, who hasn't raised hearts, follows to the lead of the ♡A with the five, playing reverse (primary) attitude and (secondary) count signals. Fantoni cashes the ♡K and Nunes follows with the jack, convincing Fantoni that he started with jack-five doubleton. Assuming that he could kill declarer's impending discard from dummy on the ♡Q, Fantoni continues with the ♡6, which presents Rodwell with the opportunity to discard a club from dummy and ruff in hand, thus avoiding the possibility of a misguess in clubs. That provokes an Italian groan in the VuGraph theater, but a few moments later, that anguish turns into a roar of delight when declarer discards a diamond from dummy, draws trumps and takes two losing finesses in clubs to go one down: -100.

The Daily Bulletin's report on this deal described discarding a club from dummy and ruffing in hand as 'a cast-iron way to make 4♠', but that isn't precisely true. As there would be handling charges if trumps were 3-1, declarer would have to decide how many trumps to draw and whether to leave the trump king in dummy. And then he'd also have to decide whether to pass the ♣J *before* playing the ♣A. Running the jack would lose to a singleton honor with East, while cashing the ace would lose to king-queen fourth or fifth with West (the likelihood that East would lead or shift to a small singleton club would also have to be factored into the equation). In practice, it would nearly always be best to lead the ♣J and rise with the ace, because West would cover the jack if he held both honors.

When an opponent hands you a surprising gift, as Fantoni does here, it's usually wise to ask yourself whether he knows more about the hand than you do. Although Rodwell has reason to believe that Fantoni has simply misread the heart position and has not cleverly created a losing option for declarer, he does not want to pass up a 75% line for his contract (two club finesses). Rodwell feels that taking the tempting ruff-and-discard might create some complications or subject him to a potentially nasty guess and lead him to defeat when the simple high-percentage line would have seen him home. Although he will be widely criticized for rejecting the club discard from dummy, there is surely more to the play than the naysayers may have noticed.

Closed Room

West	North	East	South
Nickell	Bocchi	Freeman	Duboin
	1♠	2♡	2NT[1]
3♡	4♢[2]	pass	4♠
all pass			

1. Limit raise with four trumps.
2. Intended as shortness; interpreted as natural by South.

Freeman leads the ♡A, and when Nickell follows with the queen, Freeman continues with a suit-preference three to the jack. The club return is ducked to the king and Freeman exits with a trump. Bocchi eventually leads the ♣J to the ace to make his contract, +620. He bases his play on his view that Nickell would not be keen to lead from the ♣Q with the jack in dummy. So 12 IMPs to Italy, 65-49.

Should Freeman win the first club with the queen, then? How curious! While it surely seemed attractive to Freeman to put his partner in with the ♡J, directing him to lead a club, perhaps that approach should have been rejected in favor of a passive trump switch. Had East cashed the ♡K and exited with a trump, declarer might have gone wrong. What is certain is that Freeman was unaware of Bocchi's diamond shortness. Upon being queried about 4♢, Bocchi had made a 'scooping' gesture with his hands, convincing Freeman that 4♢ was just a normal descriptive continuation. Whether he should have sought a more definitive answer, or whether Bocchi should have made certain that Freeman understood the explanation, is the stuff that TDs and Appeals Committees consider more often than you might think, but the issue dies at the table. Had Freeman known that dummy's diamonds were not a threat, the more passive defensive strategy would have had considerable appeal. Even if Bocchi were 6=2=1=4, when the club switch from West's side might have seemed important, declarer would not have been able to eliminate diamonds and pass a club to East at a point when he retained a trump in both hands.

Board 22. E-W Vul.

```
              ♠ K 9 6 5 3 2
              ♡ J 10 3
              ◇ —
              ♣ Q J 9 8
  ♠ 10 4                      ♠ J
  ♡ K Q 9 7 4       N          ♡ A 5
  ◇ A 6 5       W       E      ◇ Q J 10 9 7 4
  ♣ 10 4 2          S          ♣ A K 5 3
              ♠ A Q 8 7
              ♡ 8 6 2
              ◇ K 8 3 2
              ♣ 7 6
```

Open Room

West	North	East	South
Nunes	Rodwell	Fantoni	Meckstroth
		1◇¹	pass
1♡²	2♠	pass	3♠
dbl³	pass	5◇	all pass

1. 14+, 5+ diamonds or 4-4-4-1.
2. 0-9, 4+hearts.
3. Maximum, takeout.

Against Fantoni's 5◇, Meckstroth cashes the ♠A, on which is played the four, deuce (encouraging) and jack. Meckstroth switches to the ♡2, hoping to kill the suit by leading it twice, but Fantoni wins the ace, passes the ◇J, and continues with the king-queen of hearts, discarding a club. When the suit divides 3-3, Fantoni discards another club on a high heart. Meckstroth can ruff, but Fantoni is able to neutralize the ◇K, +600.

Closed Room

West	North	East	South
Nickell	Bocchi	Freeman	Duboin
		1◇	pass
1♡	1♠	2◇	2NT¹
3◇	4♠	5◇	pass
pass	5♠	dbl	all pass

1. Limit raise or better.

Bocchi boldly competes to 5♠, which is down only three, -500 (Freeman cashing the ♣AK before switching to ace and another heart), so Italy somewhat scarily gains 3 IMPs, extending its lead to 19 IMPs, 68-49.

Board 24. Neither Vul.

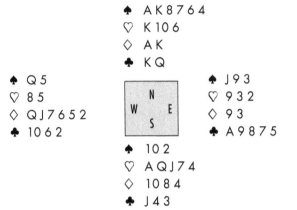

```
              ♠ A K 8 7 6 4
              ♡ K 10 6
              ◇ A K
              ♣ K Q
  ♠ Q 5                        ♠ J 9 3
  ♡ 8 5            N           ♡ 9 3 2
  ◇ Q J 7 6 5 2  W   E         ◇ 9 3
  ♣ 10 6 2          S          ♣ A 9 8 7 5
              ♠ 10 2
              ♡ A Q J 7 4
              ◇ 10 8 4
              ♣ J 4 3
```

Closed Room

West	North	East	South
Nickell	Bocchi	Freeman	Duboin
pass	1♠	pass	1NT
pass	2♣[1]	pass	2◇[2]
pass	3♡[3]	pass	4♣[4]
pass	4◇[5]	pass	4♡
pass	4NT	pass	5♣
pass	5◇[6]	pass	6♡[7]
all pass			

1. Gazzilli: forcing, either natural and limited, or most strong hands.
2. Artificial, game-forcing opposite the strong type.
3. Six spades and three hearts, expected to be 18-20.
4. Artificial slam try for hearts.
5. Diamond control.
6. Asking for the ♡Q.
7. Yes, but no side king.

Reaching 6♡ is superb for North-South. This is an excellent combination for Bocchi-Duboin's methods, although Bocchi has a bit in reserve. When Duboin tries for slam facing 18-20, Bocchi knows enough to take charge. Freeman leads ace and another club, but Bocchi, playing from the short side, wins the king, draws trumps and ruffs out spades for +980.

West	North	East	South
Nunes	Rodwell	Fantoni	Meckstroth
pass	1♣*	pass	1♠[1]
pass	2♣[2]	pass	2♥[3]
pass	3♥	pass	4◇[4]
pass	4♥	all pass	

1. Hearts, positive.
2. Spades.
3. No spade support, minimum.
4. 'Last Train' — a mild slam try for hearts.

To a certain extent, Meckstroth-Rodwell are in an even better position than their counterparts, with 3♥ a slam try facing a known minimum lacking spade support, and 4◇ conveying an interest in cooperating while denying a useful spade honor or a club control. North also knows that South can't have a high-card control in diamonds. While that information points to South's slam interest being based on strong trumps, South has not jumped to 5♥ to indicate such a holding, admittedly a big bid on such modest values with only five hearts. Although RKCB would tell North what he needs to know about the trump suit, he takes an uncharacteristically conservative position by settling for 4♥. While it might seem incredible that one of the world's best pairs should miss a seemingly straightforward slam bid at the other table using Blackwood, it's the sort of disaster that can only befall an expert partnership, one that relies on trust and judgment as much as science. Meckstroth wins the diamond lead in dummy, draws trumps and starts spades, but must lose the ♣A or his third diamond: +480. Italy gains 11 IMPs.

With the session running out, Italy has run off 45 IMPs without reply following the Americans' 4-IMP gain on the first deal of the set. The score is 88-49, Italy.

Board 30. Neither Vul.

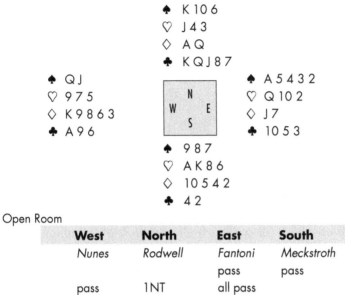

```
                ♠ K 10 6
                ♡ J 4 3
                ◇ A Q
                ♣ K Q J 8 7
  ♠ Q J                        ♠ A 5 4 3 2
  ♡ 9 7 5          N            ♡ Q 10 2
  ◇ K 9 8 6 3   W     E         ◇ J 7
  ♣ A 9 6          S            ♣ 10 5 3
                ♠ 9 8 7
                ♡ A K 8 6
                ◇ 10 5 4 2
                ♣ 4 2
```

Open Room

West	North	East	South
Nunes	Rodwell	Fantoni	Meckstroth
		pass	pass
pass	1NT	all pass	

Rodwell, in 1NT, gets a spade lead to the jack and king, and leads the ♣K, West winning to cash the ♠Q before switching to diamonds. When the queen holds, Rodwell cashes two clubs and gets the good news, crosses to the ♡A, returns to the ◇A to finish the clubs and exits with a spade to Fantoni's ace, forcing him to lead from the ♡Q, +180. This is a strongly indicated play, as West would have opened 1NT in third seat if he had the ♡Q in addition to the honors he's already shown.

Eric Rodwell

Closed Room

West	North	East	South
Nickell	*Bocchi*	*Freeman*	*Duboin*
		pass	pass
pass	1♣[1]	pass	1◇[2]
pass	1♡[3]	all pass	

1. Natural or balanced 15-17.
2. 4+ hearts.
3. Three hearts and 15-17 balanced, or an unbalanced minimum with four hearts.

One of the best parts of Bocchi-Duboin's transfer-response structure is the ability to show three-card major-suit support without raising the level, as here, where they can stop safely in 1♡ on a mildly tempting combination. Freeman leads the ◇J, which runs to the queen. Nickell takes the ♣K with the ace and switches to the ♠Q, which is covered. Freeman takes the ace and reverts to diamonds, but Bocchi plays three rounds of trumps. Freeman wins and crosses to the ♠J, and Nickell can cash the ◇K. Instead, he plays a club and declarer takes the rest: +140. 1 IMP to USA, 51-88. Although Nickell *could* have saved an IMP, Rodwell's play *actually* saves one.

IMPs of this type are exchanged remarkably frequently, even in the highest-quality matches, particularly when the players are tired and under stress. We tend to think of them as inconsequential, an unavoidable operating cost. A player who knows he is tired tends to believe he should not expend too much effort trying to make or prevent a twelfth trick on a deal like this, as he may incur a hidden cost later, when he needs that energy to make or defeat a game or slam. But it's surprising how often those 1-IMP swings can make a significant difference.

Board 31. N-S Vul.

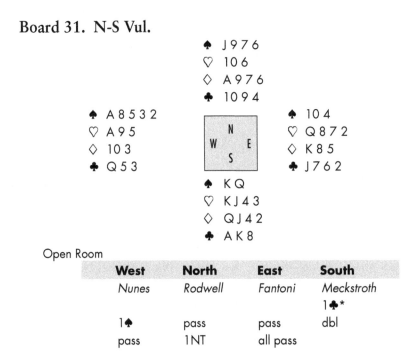

```
                  ♠ J 9 7 6
                  ♡ 10 6
                  ◇ A 9 7 6
                  ♣ 10 9 4
  ♠ A 8 5 3 2                      ♠ 10 4
  ♡ A 9 5          N               ♡ Q 8 7 2
  ◇ 10 3       W      E            ◇ K 8 5
  ♣ Q 5 3          S               ♣ J 7 6 2
                  ♠ K Q
                  ♡ K J 4 3
                  ◇ Q J 4 2
                  ♣ A K 8
```

Open Room

West	North	East	South
Nunes	Rodwell	Fantoni	Meckstroth
			1♣*
1♠	pass	pass	dbl
pass	1NT	all pass	

Meckstroth, who usually opens 2NT with 19 HCP, does well to rate his hand as only 18 and open a forcing 1♣. Meckstroth-Rodwell double low-level overcalls of their strong club with 6-7 HCP, so they are on firm ground when they stop in 1NT. Nunes ducks two rounds of spades, and Rodwell plays a diamond to the ace, then a diamond towards dummy. Fantoni wins the king and Rodwell unblocks the queen. East shifts to the ♣2, ducked to the queen, and Nunes clears spades while he retains the ♡A; Rodwell settles for eight tricks, +120.

Closed Room

West	North	East	South
Nickell	Bocchi	Freeman	Duboin
			2◇¹
pass	3♣²	pass	3◇³
pass	3♡⁴	pass	3NT
all pass			

1. 18-19 balanced.
2. Modified Puppet Stayman.
3. At least one four-card major.
4. Four spades, fewer than four hearts.

The stakes are much higher in the Closed Room, where Duboin declares 3NT after Bocchi commits to game on the strength of his wealth of intermediates. Nickell leads a spade to the ten and king, then ducks the ♠Q. Duboin crosses to the ◊A and drives out the ♠A, parting with a heart after Freeman releases the ♡2. Nickell switches to the ♣3 to the jack and king, and Duboin drives out the ◊K. Freeman returns a club and, when Duboin ducks that to the queen, Nickell returns a spade, and so is able to take his long spade when he gets in with the ♡A. Duboin is one down, -100. That is excellent defense by Nickell, and USA gains 6 IMPs, to trail 57-88.

Nick Nickell

Can 3NT be made legitimately? Even on the defense put up by Nickell-Freeman, declarer can prevail. He must win the second club, and when he leads the fourth round of diamonds to dummy, West is squeezed in an uncommon way. If he releases a spade, declarer cashes the ♠9 and exits with a club to collect the ♡K at the end; if instead he blanks the ♡A to keep the long spade, declarer leads a heart to the jack and ace, and West must give him the ♠9 after cashing the ♣Q.

Italy wins the second segment convincingly, 45-14, and after one quarter of the final, leads by 29, 88-59.

Segment Three (Boards 33-48)

Although Italy dominated the previous set, there were some late signs that the American ship had righted itself. Hamman and Soloway make their first appearance in the final in Segment Three, replacing Nickell and Freeman. Lauria and Versace come back in for Italy, taking the places of Fantoni and Nunes.

Board 36. Both Vul.

```
              ♠ A 8 5 2
              ♡ K 10 6 4 3
              ◇ Q
              ♣ 10 5 3
♠ 9                          ♠ K Q J 10 7
♡ A Q 7 5          N         ♡ J 9
◇ A 9 7 6 4    W     E       ◇ K 8 5 2
♣ K Q 8            S         ♣ 7 4
              ♠ 6 4 3
              ♡ 8 2
              ◇ J 10 3
              ♣ A J 9 6 2
```

Open Room

West	North	East	South
Hamman	Bocchi	Soloway	Duboin
1♡	pass	1♠	pass
2◇[1]	pass	3◇	pass
3NT	all pass		

1. Possible canapé.

East-West belong in game, vulnerable, with 3NT the most logical choice. Hamman and Soloway get there on an ostensibly natural sequence, Hamman's 2◇ rebid making no statement about the relative lengths of his suits or their quality. Bocchi would like better intermediates in hearts to lead the suit bid on his right, a flaw that becomes apparent when dummy's ♡9 takes the first trick. Hamman plays on spades, Bocchi taking the first to switch to a club. When Duboin wins the ♣A, declarer has ten tricks, +630. With the black aces switched, 3NT would need some racing luck.

West	North	East	South
Versace	Rodwell	Lauria	Meckstroth
1◇	1♡	dbl[1]	pass
2◇	pass	2♠[2]	pass
2NT	pass	3◇	all pass

1. Four or five spades.
2. Not forcing, but a strong suit.

Lauria-Versace's innovative (for the times) competitive methods in this situation usually work very well. Here, although they have a pretty good picture of their respective strengths and hand types, Lauria feels he lacks the controls to raise notrump, while Versace doesn't see where the tricks will come from, so pulls in a notch and stops short of game. Rodwell leads a club against 3◇, and Meckstroth wins to switch to the ♡8. Versace wins the ♡A, discards the ♡J from dummy on the third club, plays ace-king of trumps, and concedes a spade: +130, but 11 IMPs to USA, 71-88.

Board 37. N-S Vul.

```
              ♠ Q 7
              ♡ A K 10 9 6 3
              ◇ K Q 6
              ♣ J 4
♠ A 6 5 2                    ♠ K J 9 3
♡ Q              N           ♡ 4
◇ J 8 4 3    W     E         ◇ A 10 9 7 5
♣ A 6 5 3        S           ♣ K 10 7
              ♠ 10 8 4
              ♡ J 8 7 5 2
              ◇ 2
              ♣ Q 9 8 2
```

West	North	East	South
Hamman	Bocchi	Soloway	Duboin
	1♡	dbl	3♡
3♠	all pass		

West	North	East	South
Versace	Rodwell	Lauria	Meckstroth
	1♡	dbl	3♡
dbl	pass	3♠	pass
4♠	all pass		

Neither North gives his opponents a fielder's choice by bidding a somewhat tempting 4♡ with the marked ten- or eleven-card heart fit. Versace's choice of actions over 3♡ proves more effective than Hamman's when he can raise 3♠ to 4♠, knowing of the 4-4 fit. With potential duplication in hearts and weak spades, Hamman isn't sure he wants to be in 4♠ opposite a minimum with four spades, so he settles for 3♠, which he deems an accurate value bid. Soloway considers raising, but with a high-card minimum and facing a potentially modest hand at this vulnerability, decides not to stretch.

Hamman makes four after Bocchi, trying to beat three, starts with two rounds of hearts (Duboin plays the deuce at Trick 1). Hamman discards a club from dummy, ruffs in hand, and leads a diamond, putting in the ten when Bocchi follows low. Hamman cashes the ♠K and then calls for the ◇A, aiming to keep control if spades are 4-1. Duboin ruffs and might well play yet another heart, but he switches to a club. Hamman wins the ace, cashes the ♠A to draw the remaining trumps, and concedes a diamond, +170.

It's not clear how Lauria would handle 4♠ after a heart to the king and a club switch, but in the event Meckstroth leads his singleton diamond. Lauria takes the queen with the ace, plays ace and another trump, and can safely draw trumps and concede a diamond, losing only a slow club trick in addition: +420, 6 IMPs to Italy, 94-71.

Board 48. E-W Vul.

```
                    ♠ 9 7
                    ♡ A 3 2
                    ◇ 10 5
                    ♣ A J 10 7 6 5
 ♠ 10 6                              ♠ A 3 2
 ♡ J 10 7          N                 ♡ Q 5 4
 ◇ A J 9 8 2    W     E              ◇ K Q 6 4 3
 ♣ 9 8 3          S                  ♣ Q 4
                    ♠ K Q J 8 5 4
                    ♡ K 9 8 6
                    ◇ 7
                    ♣ K 2
```

Open Room

West	North	East	South
Hamman	*Bocchi*	*Soloway*	*Duboin*
pass	pass	1◇¹	1♠
2◇	3♣	pass	3♠
all pass			

1. 3+ diamonds, limited.

Hamman's single raise doesn't generate any momentum for North-South, as raising to 3◇ might do, but since 3♠ is invitational, Bocchi really owes Duboin a raise. Hamman leads the ♡J and Duboin wins with dummy's ace, plays a trump to the queen, and the ♠K to Soloway's ace. After the return of the ♡Q, declarer finishes with eleven tricks when the ♣Q capitulates, +200.

Closed Room

West	North	East	South
Versace	*Rodwell*	*Lauria*	*Meckstroth*
pass	2♣¹	pass	2◇²
pass	3♣³	pass	3♠
pass	3NT	pass	4♠
all pass			

1. 6+ clubs, limited.
2. Artificial inquiry.
3. Minimum.

It is easy to make 4♠ on the lie of the cards even if the ♣Q does not drop, as the hearts are 3-3, but the trick is to bid it. Once Rodwell opens the North hand, Meckstroth is not going to stop short of game, and he chooses the right strain, doing well to overrule Rodwell's best-guess stab at 3NT. Although there have been many excellent developments in this area, there will always be certain auctions of this type to give the Precision 2♣ opening a bad name. The lead and early play mirror events in the Open Room, but when Lauria wins the trump ace, he switches to the ◇K, gets a count card from Versace, and returns the ♡4. Meckstroth takes the king, plays a couple of high trumps, then takes the high clubs, felling the queen, leaving 3-3 hearts as a backup position, +450. That is 6 IMPs to USA, but Italy wins the session, 21-20. After 48 boards the overnight Italian lead is 30 IMPs, 109-79.

Segment Four (Boards 49-64)

Sidney Lazard stays with Meckstroth-Rodwell and Hamman-Soloway, while Maria Teresa Lavazza gives Bocchi-Duboin the morning off, bringing back Fantoni-Nunes.

Board 49. Neither Vul.

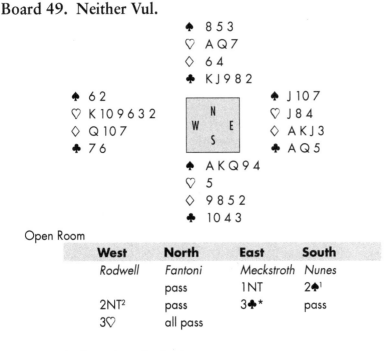

```
                    ♠ 8 5 3
                    ♡ A Q 7
                    ◇ 6 4
                    ♣ K J 9 8 2
   ♠ 6 2                          ♠ J 10 7
   ♡ K 10 9 6 3 2        N        ♡ J 8 4
   ◇ Q 10 7         W         E   ◇ A K J 3
   ♣ 7 6                 S        ♣ A Q 5
                    ♠ A K Q 9 4
                    ♡ 5
                    ◇ 9 8 5 2
                    ♣ 10 4 3
```

Open Room

West	North	East	South
Rodwell	Fantoni	Meckstroth	Nunes
	pass	1NT	2♠[1]
2NT[2]	pass	3♣*	pass
3♡	all pass		

1. 5+ spades and a 4+ minor.
2. Lebensohl.

It takes a diamond lead to defeat 3♡, and Fantoni, whose silence in the auction seems odd, finds it, starting with the four, low from two small. Rodwell wins the ace in dummy — five from Nunes (which looks less than definitive, whatever it means), seven from hand — and leads the ♡J, putting up the king. On the diamond continuation, Nunes plays the nine, suit preference, as Rodwell wins in hand to lead a low trump. Fantoni goes in with the queen, and leads the ♠5 to the ♠Q; Nunes gives him a diamond ruff without cashing a second spade. It makes no difference here: -50. With 3♠ eminently beatable, Fantoni's decision to defend 3♡ is vindicated.

Closed Room

West	North	East	South
Versace	Hamman	Lauria	Soloway
	pass	1NT	2♠
4♣¹	4♠	5♡	pass
pass	dbl	all pass	

1. Hearts.

The real action is in the Closed Room, where bold bidding by Hamman and Soloway reaps a substantial harvest. A North-South contract of 4♠ doubled is a favorite to go down at least two, even without an early club ruff, as declarer would have significant handling charges. However, Lauria, sniffing out spade shortage in Versace's hand, takes the push to 5♡ because he thinks all his cards are working. That is true, but Versace has about a spade and a quarter more than Lauria anticipates and his hand is particularly awful for his bidding. Hamman's double makes Lauria's decision look even worse, but after two high spades and a club shift (Hamman's second spade is suit preference for clubs) Lauria does not have to suffer the ignominy of a third undertrick in the form of a diamond ruff: -300, 6 IMPs to USA, 85-109.

The next deal isn't nearly as good for Lazard's troops...

Bob Hamman

Board 50. N-S Vul.

```
              ♠ A Q 3
              ♡ Q J 10 3 2
              ◇ —
              ♣ A 10 7 6 4
  ♠ 10 9 6 5 4          ♠ 8 7 2
  ♡ 6 4          N      ♡ A K 5
  ◇ J 10 7 6 4  W   E   ◇ Q 9 8 5 3 2
  ♣ 3           S      ♣ 2
              ♠ K J
              ♡ 9 8 7
              ◇ A K
              ♣ K Q J 9 8 5
```

Open Room

West	North	East	South
Rodwell	Fantoni	Meckstroth	Nunes
		pass	1♣[1]
pass	3♣[2]	3◇	4♣
5◇	pass	pass	6♣
6◇	pass	pass	dbl
all pass			

1. Forcing, 14+ natural, or 15+ balanced.
2. 10-14(15), game forcing: 5+ clubs and another 5+-card suit.

Rodwell thinks it likely that after Fantoni's forcing pass of 5◇ Nunes would not bid 6♣ with the 'wrong' hand, an opinion bolstered by the belief that a passed-hand overcall would most often be at least somewhat lead-directing. As a result, he convinces himself that it would be reasonable to save in 6◇, as the sacrifice figures to be relatively inexpensive if Meckstroth's diamonds are good and he has a reasonable spade holding. Minus 1100 is not the result he has in mind, but all the defenders' tricks are in top cards and there is no escaping five down.

Closed Room

West	North	East	South
Versace	Hamman	Lauria	Soloway
		1◇	1NT
3◇	5NT[1]	pass	6♣
pass	pass	dbl	all pass

1. Pick a slam, starting with clubs and hearts.

Whatever you might think of the North-South auction to reach a very low percentage 6♣ (it has a single-dummy chance without a heart lead: declarer eliminates everything and leads a heart, hoping for a singleton honor in either hand), there is no denying that this is a very difficult combination, especially where East-West are making loud noises in diamonds. North would normally expect much less duplication in diamonds, although Hamman has a bit of information in that department thanks to Soloway's 1NT overcall.

Versace thinks that there might be a spade ruff coming, so South gets out for one down, losing two heart tricks but no heart ruff, -200. That's a big 16 IMPs to Italy, ahead now by 40, 125-85.

Board 51. E-W Vul.

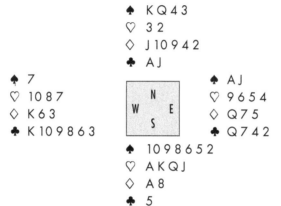

```
            ♠ K Q 4 3
            ♡ 3 2
            ◇ J 10 9 4 2
            ♣ A J
♠ 7                        ♠ A J
♡ 10 8 7        N          ♡ 9 6 5 4
◇ K 6 3      W   E         ◇ Q 7 5
♣ K 10 9 8 6 3  S          ♣ Q 7 4 2
            ♠ 10 9 8 6 5 2
            ♡ A K Q J
            ◇ A 8
            ♣ 5
```

Open Room

	West	North	East	South
	Rodwell	Fantoni	Meckstroth	Nunes
				1♠[1]
	pass	2◇[2]	pass	2♡
	pass	2♠	pass	2NT[3]
	pass	3♣[4]	pass	3♠[5]
	pass	4♣[6]	pass	4◇
	pass	4♠[7]	pass	4NT[8]
	pass	5♣[9]	pass	5◇[10]
	pass	6♠	all pass	

1. Forcing: 5+ spades, 14+ HCP.
2. Natural, game-forcing.
3. Minimum.
4. Relay.
5. Six spades and four hearts.
6. Club control, stronger than an artificial 'mild try' 3NT.

7. Nothing extra, no heart control.
8. Heart control and an even number of keycards (Turbo).
9-10. First-round controls.

That it can be dangerous to look for perfect cards is illustrated in this room where Fantoni-Nunes milk their assets for all they are worth, and then some.

Fantoni could start with 2♣ to segue into relay mode, or he could start with a support-showing (very wide-ranging) 2NT, but he prefers to force to game immediately by showing his long suit. Having agreed spades and discovered that Nunes is 6-4 with a minimum, it would be more prudent to issue a mild slam try of 3NT than the more serious control-showing 4♣, but he really likes his potential opposite 6-4. When Nunes carries on over 4♣ (usually at least four controls and fillers), momentum carries them to 6♠, Fantoni hoping for diamond shortness. After a heart lead and continuation (by Meckstroth upon winning the first spade), Nunes crosses to the ♠K and leads a low diamond to his eight. One down, -50.

Closed Room

West	North	East	South
Versace	Hamman	Lauria	Soloway
			1♠
pass	4♠	all pass	

The North hand is somewhat peculiar facing a limited opening bid of 1♠ as there are a variety of minimum hands with shortage in diamonds that produce a superb 6♠, yet it's possible that even game will be too high opposite a poor mesh. Hamman thinks it practical to settle for game, taking the least informative route to 4♠. Versace leads the ♡7. Declarer loses a diamond and the ace of trumps: +450, 11 IMPs to USA, 96-125.

Board 53. N-S Vul.

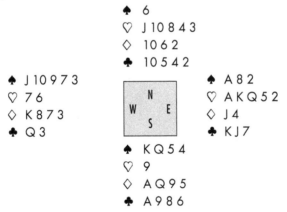

```
              ♠ 6
              ♡ J 10 8 4 3
              ◇ 10 6 2
              ♣ 10 5 4 2
♠ J 10 9 7 3              ♠ A 8 2
♡ 7 6          N          ♡ A K Q 5 2
◇ K 8 7 3   W     E       ◇ J 4
♣ Q 3          S          ♣ K J 7
              ♠ K Q 5 4
              ♡ 9
              ◇ A Q 9 5
              ♣ A 9 8 6
```

Open Room

West	North	East	South
Rodwell	Fantoni	Meckstroth	Nunes
	pass	1♣*	pass
1◇*	pass	1♡¹	dbl
rdbl	2♣	dbl	all pass

1. 4+ hearts, possibly a canapé.

South describes his hand well with a second-round takeout double of 1♡. That would work very well if the West and North hands are interchanged, but on the actual division of the high cards, East-West are presented with a winning option of redoubling 1♡ and then doubling 2♣. Rodwell starts the ball rolling in that direction, prompting Meckstroth to finish the job although he lacks a fourth trump.

Meckstroth leads the ♡K. The partnership plays standard count at Trick 1 when the opening lead shows the ace-king, but with a singleton in dummy, (reverse) suit preference is often the priority. Rodwell plays the six. Meckstroth doesn't much care for the strong dummy that includes a fourth trump, but he focuses on the task at hand and switches accurately to the ♣7, ducked to the queen. A second trump goes to the king and ace, and Fantoni, hoping to elicit some help from the defense, exits with a third trump. Rodwell discards the ♠3, which doesn't mean much in this situation but suggests that declarer won't be able to take too many tricks in the suit. Meckstroth switches to the ◇J, covered by the queen and king, and Rodwell switches back to hearts: ten, queen... and Fantoni discards a spade from dummy. Meckstroth can cash the ♠A to set the contract, but he has bigger things in mind, and reverts to diamonds. Fantoni's ten is a disappointment, and Meckstroth covers the ♡J with the ace. Fantoni ruffs, cashes two diamonds to discard a spade as Meckstroth carefully discards spades. When Fantoni ruffs the ♠K in his hand, Meckstroth follows with the ace, but that is of no use to declarer, who cashes the ♡8, and presents the four, his last card. Meckstroth scoops that up with his five for one down, -200.

I am reminded of a deal once defended by Canadian Hall of Famer Bruce Elliott, who doubled 7♡ holding two aces, and accurately led a trump. Sure enough, both his aces would have been ruffed, but as the play went, he eventually discarded both those aces and held on to the ◇6, which took the last trick. Beaming brightly, he addressed his partner, Shorty Sheardown, with these immortal words: "Y'see Shorty, I knew I had 'em!"

Well, maybe you had to be there.

West	North	East	South
Versace	Hamman	Lauria	Soloway
	pass	1♡	dbl
pass	2♣	dbl[1]	3♣
dbl[2]	pass	3NT	all pass

1. Takeout.
2. Takeout.

In this room, Soloway's raise to 3♣ is not music to Hamman's ears, and if Lauria passes Versace's takeout double, Italy will be well-placed to gain significantly. When he converts to 3NT, the Americans are off the hook, and need only defend normally to set the contract. Soloway leads the ♣A, catering to a singleton honor in the West hand, a good idea that yields no reward this time. Hamman gives count with the five, and Soloway continues the suit, the queen winning. The ♠J runs to the queen and Soloway clears clubs. Lauria takes his hearts and eventually scores only the ♠A and a diamond trick for two down, -100 and 7 IMPs to USA, 103-125.

Board 54. E-W Vul.

```
                    ♠ J 5 4 3
                    ♡ 2
                    ◇ 6 5 4 2
                    ♣ Q 9 8 6
    ♠ Q 10 8 6 2               ♠ A 7
    ♡ Q 8 7 6         N        ♡ K 10 3
    ◇ K J        W       E     ◇ A 10
    ♣ J 10            S        ♣ A K 7 5 3 2
                    ♠ K 9
                    ♡ A J 9 5 4
                    ◇ Q 9 8 7 3
                    ♣ 4
```

West	North	East	South
Rodwell	Fantoni	Meckstroth	Nunes
		2NT	pass
3♣[1]	pass	3NT[2]	all pass

1. Modified Puppet Stayman.
2. No four- or five-card major.

Meckstroth's 2NT opening, ostensibly 19-21 (indeed, his raw point-count of 18 is worth about 21, based on his strong, long suit and prime values) silences Nunes and deprives him of the opportunity to learn of Fantoni's decided preference for diamonds over hearts. Meckstroth's 3NT bid is a bit safer than it looks, as responder would have started with a transfer holding five hearts and four spades.

With nothing sufficiently convincing to dissuade him from leading his strongest suit, Nunes leads the ♡4. Dummy's six holds, and Fantoni covers the second club honor from dummy. Now Meckstroth can conveniently concede a club on the third round, Nunes discarding first the ♡5, then the ♢3. Fantoni switches to a spade, ducked to the king, and Meckstroth has ten tricks, +630.

If South leads a diamond, declarer can win in dummy, run the ♣J, clear the club suit, win the diamond continuation, and cash two clubs, squeezing South in three suits.

Closed Room

West	North	East	South
Versace	Hamman	Lauria	Soloway
		1♣[1]	2NT[2]
dbl	4♢	dbl	pass
4♠	pass	5♣	all pass

1. 2+ clubs.
2. Diamonds and hearts.

As 3NT is the only game that East-West might make, the best that Lauria-Versace can do when North jumps to 4♢ is double and collect 300 points. Lauria can't double for penalty, but is able to convey extra values, normally with a bias towards takeout. Although his sequence suggests a somewhat flexible strong 5♣ bid, his side is too high. Soloway leads a diamond, won in dummy. Hamman covers the first club from dummy, and later, when Lauria crosses back to his hand with the ♢A to clear trumps, Hamman switches to a spade (Soloway had helpfully discarded the ♢Q on the second trump), avoiding all defensive complications. One down, -100, and 12 IMPs to USA, just 10 behind now at 115-125.

Board 55. Both Vul.

```
                    ♠ K 9
                    ♡ A K 7 2
                    ◇ K Q 10 6
                    ♣ J 5 3
     ♠ Q 8 7 2                      ♠ J 10 3
     ♡ 8 6 4 3          N           ♡ Q J
     ◇ 7            W       E        ◇ J 9 8 5 4
     ♣ K Q 8 4          S           ♣ 10 6 2
                    ♠ A 6 5 4
                    ♡ 10 9 5
                    ◇ A 3 2
                    ♣ A 9 7
```

Open Room

West	North	East	South
Rodwell	Fantoni	Meckstroth	Nunes
			1NT
pass	2♣*	pass	2♠
pass	3NT	all pass	

Rodwell leads the ♣4 against Nunes, who goes with the odds unsuccessfully by playing low from dummy. He wins the third club and runs the ♡9 to the jack. Meckstroth switches to the ♠J, which Nunes takes with dummy's king. He cashes the ♡A; when the queen drops, he has nine tricks, +600.

Closed Room

West	North	East	South
Versace	Hamman	Lauria	Soloway
			1♠
pass	2◇	pass	2NT
pass	3NT	all pass	

Versace leads the ♡6 against Soloway's 3NT, ducked to the jack. Lauria returns the ♡Q, which pleases declarer considerably. Soloway crosses to the ♡10, returns to the ◇K, and cashes the ♡K, discarding a spade. Versace revokes, discarding a spade. As declarer goes about his business, leading a club towards the jack in the process, Versace hangs on to that wretched ♡8. After taking his nine winners, Soloway exits with a club and Versace's last card is the ♡8, which is now a 'phantom' winner.

Alfredo Versace

So where's the interest in this deal?

When play is completed, Soloway calls for the Director, but Hamman asks to speak to Soloway privately, with the Director at the table. Moments later, they state that they would like to have the deal scored as +600, and do not wish to accept the revoke penalty. The Director accepts that request, but returns ten minutes later and explains that the penalty cannot be waived. North-South are awarded one extra trick for +630, and the board is scored this way. 1 IMP to USA, 116-125.

Unfortunately, that is the wrong ruling. As West had taken a trick with the revoke card, albeit at Trick 13, the Laws stipulate a two-trick penalty, and the board should be scored as North-South +660. The severity of this penalty is usually so disproportionate to the damage done that it ought to be addressed by the Laws Commission, but under the prevailing rules, there was nothing to be done about it. The precise timing of the first overture to the officials relating to this second overtrick has not been confirmed, but what is clear is that the Chief Tournament Director himself did not know about it until after the medals were presented at the Victory Banquet. Apparently, there was another scoring error that had been brought to the attention of the staff, and they had dealt with it. However, an inquiry about this 'revoke' IMP was misunderstood to be a further reference to the other error, and the honest reply was that the staff were aware of it and that it had been taken care of. As the posted score continued to reflect a 1-IMP gain to the Americans rather than 2 IMPs, we shall continue to report it that way.

Board 57. E-W Vul.

```
                    ♠ 9 8 6
                    ♡ A Q 3
                    ◇ 8 7
                    ♣ A 9 7 6 4
    ♠ K Q 7 4                      ♠ A J 10 2
    ♡ J 10 5 4        N            ♡ 7 2
    ◇ A K 4       W       E        ◇ J 10 9 5
    ♣ 10 8            S            ♣ K J 2
                    ♠ 5 3
                    ♡ K 9 8 6
                    ◇ Q 6 3 2
                    ♣ Q 5 3
```

Open Room

West	North	East	South
Rodwell	Fantoni	Meckstroth	Nunes
	pass	pass	pass
1◇[1]	pass	1♠	pass
2♠[2]	pass	4♠	all pass

1. 2+ diamonds, 10-15.
2. Four-card support.

Nunes knows very little about the deal, and expects Meckstroth to have a more distributional hand for his bidding. He elects to attack with the ♣3, hardly unreasonable, but although he finds his partner's primary length and a prime asset, that is worst for the defense. Fantoni wins the ♣A and plays the ♡A, looking for guidance. However, when Nunes encourages with the six, Fantoni finds himself with a new problem: if he continues with the ♡3, his queen will ruff out on the next round if declarer has only two hearts, but if he continues with the ♡Q, Nunes might sensibly overtake with the king to play a third heart for him to ruff... which is what happens at the table. When dummy's ten wins the third heart trick, Meckstroth draws trumps and claims, +620.

Meckstroth was going to make 4♠ even on a trump return at Trick 2: he wins in hand and plays a heart, wins the second spade in hand, and plays a second heart. When North wins and leads a third trump, South is squeezed in three suits and declarer can score either the ♣J (on a club discard) or the long card in the red suit that South discards. Fantoni switched to the ♡A because he did not know whether to continue clubs or try to cash out in hearts, so the 'solution play' in hearts — switching to the queen — was not really on his radar.

Closed Room

West	North	East	South
Versace	Hamman	Lauria	Soloway
	pass	pass	pass
1♣[1]	pass	1◇	pass
1♡	pass	1♠	pass
2♠	pass	4♠	all pass

1. 2+ clubs.

Soloway has every reason to lead trumps, Hamman's well-known aversion to this strategy notwithstanding, and that leaves declarer with an uphill struggle. He wins in hand to lead a heart to the jack and queen, and Hamman continues trumps, then clears the suit when he regains the lead on a second heart play by declarer. Soloway discards a club, as he must, Lauria winning in hand to pass the ◇J. Two further rounds of diamonds reveal the bad news about the ◇Q. At this point it would not help Lauria to guess clubs correctly as Soloway would gain the lead in clubs on the second round and force dummy with the ◇Q; Hamman would get the ♣A in the end. In practice, Lauria leads a club to the jack and loses a second club trick for one down, -100.

Perhaps at double dummy, declarer could get home. After the third trump, he crosses to dummy with a diamond, plays a club to the king and exits with a club. South wins and tries a second diamond, but declarer wins in hand and ruffs his remaining club in dummy, squeezing South between the red suits in the process. But even this remote possibility can be avoided if North returns a third heart rather than a third trump.

In the end, 12 IMPs to USA, back in the lead after a long hiatus, 129-125.

Board 58. Both Vul.

```
              ♠ A Q 10 9
              ♡ 10 7 6 5 2
              ◇ 3
              ♣ 9 7 6
  ♠ J 5 3                      ♠ 7 4
  ♡ A J           N            ♡ 9 3
  ◇ 6 5 4      W     E         ◇ A J 9 8 7 2
  ♣ A K 5 4 2     S            ♣ J 10 3
              ♠ K 8 6 2
              ♡ K Q 8 4
              ◇ K Q 10
              ♣ Q 8
```

Open Room

West	North	East	South
Rodwell	Fantoni	Meckstroth	Nunes
		pass	1♣¹
pass	1◇²	2◇	2♡
2NT	3◇³	pass	3♡
all pass			

1. Forcing: 14+ natural or 15+ balanced.
2. 0-9 HCP, 4+ hearts.
3. Artificial game try, nothing specific.

The very soft South hand looks more like a weak notrump, but Nunes treats it as full value, 15+. Curiously, his partnership stops in 3♡ while his counterparts, whose range is 14-16, reach the no-play game. West leads the ♣A, then plays two more rounds after East follows low-jack. Nunes ruffs the third and leads the ♡Q. Rodwell wins with the ace to switch to a diamond. There is nothing left for the defenders to do; +140. Had Rodwell played a fourth club, Nunes would have discarded dummy's diamond. East would uppercut with the nine, but declarer could overruff, establishing West's jack, or discard a spade and draw West's jack after regaining the lead, securing the contract.

Closed Room

West	North	East	South
Versace	Hamman	Lauria	Soloway
		pass	1NT
pass	2♣*	pass	2♡
pass	3♡	pass	4♡
all pass			

In 4♡, Soloway crosses to the ♠Q at Trick 4 and leads a trump to the king and ace. Versace switches to a diamond. That is -100, and 6 IMPs back to Italy, putting an end to the Americans' 44-IMP run, and reclaiming the lead, 131-129.

Board 59. Neither Vul.

```
              ♠ 9
              ♡ A Q 8 6 2
              ◇ 10 7
              ♣ A K 6 4 3
♠ K Q 5 4 3              ♠ J 7 2
♡ J 7            N      ♡ 9 3
◇ K 8 3 2    W     E    ◇ J 6 5 4
♣ Q J            S      ♣ 8 7 5 2
              ♠ A 10 8 6
              ♡ K 10 5 4
              ◇ A Q 9
              ♣ 10 9
```

Open Room

West	North	East	South
Rodwell	Fantoni	Meckstroth	Nunes
			1NT
2◇[1]	dbl[2]	pass	2♡
pass	3◇[3]	pass	3♠
pass	4♣[4]	pass	4◇
pass	4♡	all pass	

1. Diamonds and a major.
2. Takeout.
3. Either (a) stopper ask, (b) looking for spade fit, or (c) slam try in hearts.
4. Slam try in hearts with a club suit.

Fantoni can't show his hearts directly due to system constraints, but then enjoys the benefit of knowing immediately that his partner has four hearts. His multi-meaning 3◇ cuebid doesn't get him much useful information, but in the partnership style, Nunes, with five controls for his 12-14 notrump, owes his partner another move after the 4♣ slam try. Nunes takes thirteen tricks after Rodwell's helpful diamond lead, but +510 is an uncertain result with 6♡ makeable.

Closed Room

West	North	East	South
Versace	Hamman	Lauria	Soloway
			1NT
pass	2◊*	pass	2♡
pass	2♠[1]	pass	3♡[2]
pass	4♣	pass	4◊*
pass	4♠[3]	pass	4NT[4]
pass	5♣[5]	pass	5◊[6]
pass	5♠[7]	pass	6♡
all pass			

1. Artificial game force.
2. Four-card support.
3. RKCB for hearts.
4. Three keycards, or none.
5. Asks for the trump queen.
6. Denies the trump queen.
7. Control-showing; guarantees that all keycards and the trump queen are accounted for, shows the ♣K and grand slam interest opposite *both* third-round club control and an extra king (if only third-round club control were needed, North would have bid 6♣ over 4NT).

The heart slam is excellent for North-South as it has very good play even with the diamond finesse wrong, and if it's played by South, a diamond lead might give declarer an easy ride when both trumps and clubs divide unevenly.

One key to the successful Hamman-Soloway sequence is Soloway's decision to open a 14-16 notrump on his well-stuffed 13-count, which allows Hamman to use a comfortable structure, knowing he is facing a balanced hand. In the end, Soloway knows he does not have what he needs for seven. Declarer wins the spade lead and draws two rounds of trumps with the ace and king, and can establish dummy's long club. He can't avoid a diamond loser and settles for +980. 10 IMPs to USA, new leaders once again, 139-131.

Board 60. N-S Vul.

```
                    ♠ J 10 9 2
                    ♡ Q 8 6 3
                    ◇ 6
                    ♣ K 7 6 4
      ♠ A                           ♠ K 7 6 3
      ♡ K J 10 9 7      N           ♡ A
      ◇ A 8 2       W       E       ◇ K J 10 5
      ♣ 10 9 8 5        S           ♣ A Q J 2
                    ♠ Q 8 5 4
                    ♡ 5 4 2
                    ◇ Q 9 7 4 3
                    ♣ 3
```

Open Room

West	North	East	South
Rodwell	Fantoni	Meckstroth	Nunes
1♡	pass	2♣	pass
3♣[1]	pass	4♠[2]	pass
5◇[3]	pass	6♣	all pass

1. Four-card support, spade shortness.
2. RKCB for clubs.
3. Two keycards, no ♣Q.

Meckstroth responds 2♣ to establish a game force and avoid a potentially awkward fourth-suit sequence, and uses an RKCB surrogate once he learns of Rodwell's distributional features. Blackwood looks slightly optimistic to me, with a poor mesh in the majors and only eight combined trumps, but it has the advantage of precluding a later guess about the number of combined keycards; it's likely that a slower route would work well too. In 6♣, Meckstroth gets a diamond lead from Nunes, and does not put in dummy's eight. He takes North's six with the jack, crosses to the ♠A, leads the ♣5 to his queen, and ruffs a spade. Fantoni covers the ♣9, so Meckstroth wins the ace, goes to the ♣10, comes to the ♡A, draws the last trump, crosses to the ◇A to discard a spade on the ♡K, and loses a diamond in the end for +920.

West	North	East	South
Versace	Hamman	Lauria	Soloway
1♡	pass	2♣[1]	pass
2♡	pass	2NT	pass
3♣[2]	pass	3NT	all pass

1. Natural, or balanced.
2. 11-13: 5+ hearts and four clubs, or six hearts and three clubs.

For the second deal in succession, Italy misses a good slam bid at the other table, but this time it is Lauria-Versace who stop short.

Lauria, facing a minimum, settles for 3NT, which could be the winning decision opposite many hands unsuitable for slam. He gets a diamond lead and, like Meckstroth, does not play dummy's eight, so North's six forces the ten. He crosses to the ♠A, runs the ♣10, leads a club to the queen, cashes the ♡A, returns to the ◊A, cashes the ♡K to discard a spade and finesses in clubs again, but loses the last two tricks, +460. Lauria could take twelve tricks easily enough by cashing the ♡A at Trick 2, crossing to the ◊A, knocking out the ♡Q, using the ♠A to reach dummy's hearts, discarding the ♣Q or ♣J on a heart, passing the ♣10 and taking another club finesse in complete safety. It's easy to see why his heart wasn't in it, however. That's another 10 IMPs to USA, ahead now by 18, 149-131. As it happened, Lauria's lost overtrick does not cost his side an IMP.

Board 64. E-W Vul.

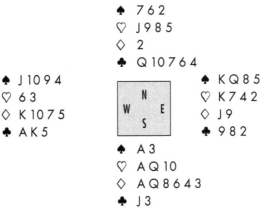

```
              ♠ 7 6 2
              ♡ J 9 8 5
              ◊ 2
              ♣ Q 10 7 6 4
  ♠ J 10 9 4              ♠ K Q 8 5
  ♡ 6 3          N        ♡ K 7 4 2
  ◊ K 10 7 5   W   E      ◊ J 9
  ♣ A K 5         S       ♣ 9 8 2
              ♠ A 3
              ♡ A Q 10
              ◊ A Q 8 6 4 3
              ♣ J 3
```

Open Room

West	North	East	South
Rodwell	Fantoni	Meckstroth	Nunes
1◇*	pass	1♡	2◇
pass[1]	pass	2♠[2]	pass
3♠	all pass		

1. Denies as many as three hearts.
2. Four hearts and four spades, non-forcing.

Nunes overcalls at the two-level, and by doing so can retire comfortably from the proceedings (1NT would have been natural). As Meckstroth's reopening 2♠ denies the strength for a competitive double, Rodwell's raise is very aggressive, and this time he is punished for seeking the brass ring. Against 3♠, Nunes leads the ♣J, a mildly dangerous choice that works well enough. Fantoni encourages with the four, but Meckstroth conceals the deuce, so Nunes can't be sure of the club situation. He wins the first round of trumps and switches to ace and another diamond. Meckstroth ducks and Fantoni takes his ruff, exiting with the ♣Q. Meckstroth wins, draws the remaining trumps, discards his club loser on the ◇K, and loses two heart tricks for one down, -100.

Closed Room

West	North	East	South
Versace	Hamman	Lauria	Soloway
1◇	pass	1♡	1NT
pass	pass	dbl	2◇
dbl	all pass		

Against opponents who open and respond aggressively, it's difficult to say anything negative about Soloway's 1NT overcall, West's known four-plus diamonds (he would open 1♣ with 4=4=3=2) notwithstanding. He pays dearly for it, however, when Lauria has enough to double 1NT, prompting Versace to double 2◇. West cashes two high clubs and switches to the ♠J. Soloway takes the ♠A, and exits in the same suit, Lauria winning to lead the ◇J. Soloway follows low, but covers the continuation of the ◇9 with the queen, retaining a major tenace when Versace wins the king. Soloway ruffs the spade continuation, and plays the ◇A and another diamond. Versace has a safe spade exit, so Soloway has to lose to the ♡K for two down, -300. Italy gains 9 IMPs to end a disastrous session on a positive note.

The Italians started the session with a 30-IMP lead and had extended it to 40 after the second deal, but then the momentum changed dramatically, and the Americans won the set, 77-31. At the halfway mark, USA leads Italy by 16 IMPs, 156-140. Would this continue to be a match of pronounced runs, like their quarterfinal match in the Paris Bermuda Bowl in 2001, or would the teams stay close the rest of the way, trading blows until only one team remained standing?

Segment Five (Boards 65-80)

There are still 64 boards to play. With USA ahead by 16 IMPs, Sidney Lazard replaces Hamman and Soloway with Nickell and Freeman. Bocchi and Duboin return for Italy, taking the places of Fantoni and Nunes.

Board 66. N-S Vul.

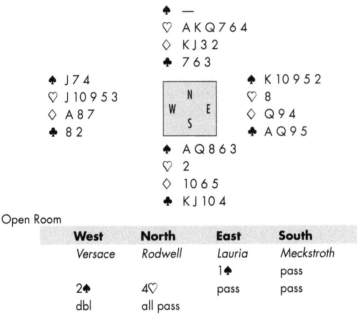

Open Room

	West	North	East	South
	Versace	Rodwell	Lauria	Meckstroth
			1♠	pass
	2♠	4♡	pass	pass
	dbl	all pass		

East leads the ♠10, dummy's queen winning. Rodwell discards diamonds on the ♠AQ, and starts trumps, Versace splitting his equals from the top. When Lauria shows out, discarding a spade, Rodwell leads a club to the jack and then a diamond. Versace rises with the ace and arranges his club ruff, and Rodwell still has a trump to lose; just one down, -200.

West	North	East	South
Nickell	Bocchi	Freeman	Duboin
		1♠	pass
2♠	3♡	pass	3NT
dbl	pass	pass	4♣
pass	4♡	pass	pass
dbl	all pass		

Duboin's ambitious decision to bid 3NT is really just a guess, and he thinks better of it when Nickell doubles. We can see that his 4♣ is a gamble that Bocchi, void in spades, will produce adequate club support, but Bocchi judges that Duboin will not have long, strong clubs as he did not overcall 1♠ with 2♣ with enough strength to bid 3NT over the wide-ranging 3♡. Bocchi retreats to 4♡ although he knows Nickell's double is bound to be based on a strong heart holding.

After the same opening lead, Bocchi doesn't fare as well after discarding two clubs on the ♠AQ. He leads a diamond to the jack and queen, ruffs the spade continuation, cashes two high trumps and leads a diamond to the ten and ace. With diamonds 3-3, he gets out for two down, -500. So 7 IMPs to USA, now ahead 168-140.

Board 68. Both Vul.

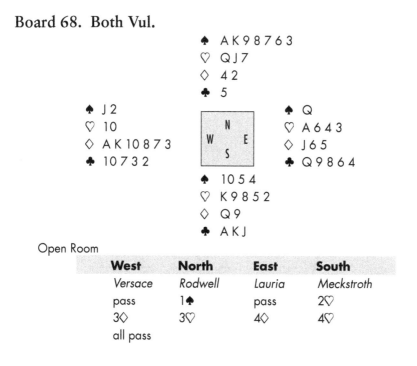

Open Room

West	North	East	South
Versace	Rodwell	Lauria	Meckstroth
pass	1♠	pass	2♡
3◇	3♡	4◇	4♡
all pass			

Although at single dummy it seems that a major-suit game might run into a ruff in the other major and fail as a result, in practice the eight-card fit is perfectly safe. Versace needs a seventh diamond for a vulnerable opening three-bid in his methods, and although he comes in at the three-level, the natural start afforded to Meckstroth-Rodwell gives them a chance to reach the more fortunate game. Rodwell's decision to raise hearts works very well, as Meckstroth is not inclined to go back to spades with weak three-card support.

Lauria, after boldly raising to the four-level, follows to the first diamond with the jack, hoping to direct a spade shift. That is a nice idea in isolation, but Versace can hardly hold the ♣K after failing to open the bidding, so if Versace switches at Trick 2, the second diamond trick and the link to obtain the spade ruff will disappear on a high club. Versace wisely cashes the ◇K, Lauria's six denying the ♣A (else he'd play the missing ◇5), and continues with a third diamond. That is also a good idea, but it proves futile when Meckstroth takes the ruff in hand and plays on trumps. Lauria takes his ace on the third round and exits with a club, but Meckstroth wins, draws the last trump and claims when he leads the ♠10, collecting both the queen and jack, +620. (Meckstroth, aware that Lauria was trying to direct a spade switch, had every reason to fear that the suit was 3-0, but if that were so, Versace would split his honors and strand him in dummy.)

If Versace finds the particularly peculiar switch to a club at Trick 3, Meckstroth will have to cash exactly *one* high spade to extract East's 'flight square' (another term the world of bridge owes to Terence Reese) before leading the third round of trumps. Then, when Lauria finally takes the ace, he cannot tuck declarer in dummy to concede a spade ruff. Had all those things happened, this deal would have been one of the most beautiful in the history of the World Championships.

Closed Room

West	North	East	South
Nickell	Bocchi	Freeman	Duboin
2◇	2♠	3◇	4♠
all pass			

Nickell's natural weak 2◇ (a fossil in most world championships these days, but still an effective weapon) and Freeman's gentle raise result in East leading a diamond against 4♠. West takes two tricks in the suit, switches to the ♡10, and scores a heart ruff for one down, -100 and 12 IMPs to USA, extending the lead to 38, 180-142.

Board 70. E-W Vul.

```
                    ♠ K J 3
                    ♡ Q 8 3
                    ◇ A K 5
                    ♣ K Q 4 3
    ♠ 5 2                              ♠ 7 6 4
    ♡ A J 7 2          N              ♡ K 6 5 4
    ◇ 9 6 4 2      W       E          ◇ Q J 7
    ♣ A J 7            S              ♣ 10 9 8
                    ♠ A Q 10 9 8
                    ♡ 10 9
                    ◇ 10 8 3
                    ♣ 6 5 2
```

Open Room

West	North	East	South
Versace	*Rodwell*	*Lauria*	*Meckstroth*
		pass	pass
pass	1♣*	pass	1◇*
pass	1NT[1]	pass	2♡*
pass	2♠	pass	3NT
pass	4♠	all pass	

1. 18-19 balanced.

On this layout, 4♠ needs some good luck, but the luck is there, and game can be made. Rodwell wins Lauria's trump lead in dummy and calls for the ♡9, which runs to the king. Lauria switches to the ♣10, and when Versace wins the ace, he switches to a diamond. Rodwell wins the ace, draws trumps, and leads the ♡10, so he can build a heart trick, and doesn't need the 3-3 club break, +420.

Closed Room

West	North	East	South
Nickell	*Bocchi*	*Freeman*	*Duboin*
		pass	pass
pass	2◇[1]	pass	2♡[2]
pass	2♠	pass	3♣[3]
pass	4♠	all pass	

1. 18-19 balanced.
2. Transfer.
3. 5-3-3-2 with five spades.

Freeman gets off to the best lead against Bocchi — the ♢Q. Declarer wins, crosses to a trump and leads a club to the king, apparently on the winning track. However, he goes back to dummy and this time tries a heart. Nickell makes him pay for that by rising with the ace to return a diamond, and now Bocchi can't avoid the loss of a diamond, two hearts and a club for one down: -50. Another 10 IMPs to USA, ahead now by 48, 190-142.

Board 71. Both Vul.

```
                    ♠ K Q 7 5 4 3
                    ♡ —
                    ♢ 9 8 5
                    ♣ K J 7 6
  ♠ J 8 6                           ♠ A 10 9
  ♡ K J 7 3          N              ♡ A Q 9 5 4 2
  ♢ Q 10 3      W         E         ♢ A J 7 2
  ♣ A 10 2          S              ♣ —
                    ♠ 2
                    ♡ 10 8 6
                    ♢ K 6 4
                    ♣ Q 9 8 5 4 3
```

Open Room

West	North	East	South
Versace	Rodwell	Lauria	Meckstroth
			pass
pass	2♠	dbl	pass
2NT[1]	pass	3♡[2]	pass
4♣[3]	pass	4♢[4]	pass
4♡	all pass		

1. Artificial positive.
2. Strong.
3-4. Control-showing.

Although these days the North hand is widely deemed suitable for a vulnerable weak two-bid, it's not a particularly comfortable action, even in third seat: the suit is internally weak and the hand is a fine dummy for two other strains, the void adding to that potential. Rodwell's 2♠ may have talked his opponents out of slam but that is the wrong thing to do this time, as East-West end up +650.

Closed Room

West	North	East	South
Nickell	*Bocchi*	*Freeman*	*Duboin*
			pass
pass	1♠	2♡	pass
4♡	pass	4♠¹	pass
5♣²	pass	5♡	pass
6♡	all pass		

1-2. Control-showing.

Bocchi's 1♠ opening fares much better than Rodwell's 2♠ when Freeman takes a more optimistic approach, logically expecting missing diamond honors to be with North. Even allowing for a shaded opening in third position, slam is excellent at single dummy, but with the ◇K wrong, the virtue in bidding 6♡ proves to be its sole reward. The result is -100, 13 IMPs to Italy, reducing the deficit to 35, 155-190.

Board 72. Neither Vul.

```
              ♠ K Q 2
              ♡ Q 5 2
              ◇ K Q 10 3
              ♣ 9 5 4
♠ J 10 9 8 3              ♠ A 7 5 4
♡ A J 9 4        N        ♡ 10 7
◇ 9 4        W       E    ◇ J 8 6
♣ 8 2           S        ♣ A 10 7 6
              ♠ 6
              ♡ K 8 6 3
              ◇ A 7 5 2
              ♣ K Q J 3
```

Open Room

West	North	East	South
Versace	*Rodwell*	*Lauria*	*Meckstroth*
pass	1◇¹	pass	1♡
1♠	dbl²	2NT³	3◇⁴
all pass			

1. 2+ diamonds, 10-15.
2. Three-card heart support.
3. Limit raise in spades.
4. Intended as non-forcing, and interpreted correctly.

Versace's topless 1♠ overcall would not be found in anyone's textbook, but it's standard policy in Italy to overcall in spades if the mere thought of doing so enters your mind, even in a nightmare. That creates an untested scenario for the Americans over Lauria's artificial raise, and it's not difficult to make the cases for 3◊ (in effect a new suit, as 1◊ doesn't mean much) being forcing or non-forcing (no double of 2NT). The bottom line is that Rodwell and Meckstroth are on the same virtual page this time and come to rest in 3◊, their best spot on the lie of the cards (if the ♠A were with West, however, 3NT would be a respectable contract). Even facing what would most often be 11-13 balanced, it looks odd for South to commit to diamonds and a partial when North could be (say) 3=3=2=5 with little or no wasted strength in the opponents' spade suit. For example, 5♣ would be a lot better than 3◊ opposite:

$$ ♠Jxx \quad ♡Axx \quad ◊Kx \quad ♣Axxxx $$

and Rodwell would not correct 3◊ to 3♡ as he would expect at least five diamonds opposite. Lauria leads the ♠A, which enables declarer to pitch a couple of hearts from dummy after drawing trumps, so Rodwell chalks up a lovely +130.

Closed Room

West	North	East	South
Nickell	Bocchi	Freeman	Duboin
pass	1NT	pass	2♣*
pass	2◊*	pass	2♠[1]
pass	2NT[2]	pass	3♣[3]
pass	3NT[4]	pass	4♣[5]
pass	4♠[6]	pass	5♣[7]
all pass			

1-3-5. Inquiry.
2. Minimum.
4. 3=3=3=4 or 3=3=4=3.
6. 3=3=4=3 with a spade control, no heart control.
7. Error: believing North to be 3=3=3=4.

If you open the two-control North hand, as most players would nowadays, it won't come as a surprise to you that partner carries your side to game with an opening bid of his own... or that you can't make it. Perhaps that's a bit harsh, because 3NT would be worth bidding at single dummy, even not vulnerable. We all have our biases about opening hands like North's in first or second position, neither vulnerable, especially in a minor suit that could be as hopeless as two low cards; mine is (probably too strongly) in favor of passing.

Both pairs avoid 3NT, the most promising game contract on their poor mesh, but a systemic error by Duboin lands him in 5♣ with only seven combined trumps. He gets out for just one down after the lead of the ♠J to the king and ace and a switch to the ♡10, Nickell playing ace and jack when Duboin follows low. Declarer wins in dummy to play a trump to the king, and crosses to the ◇K and ◇Q to lead towards his remaining trump honors. Freeman takes his ace on the third round to revert to spades, but Duboin discards a heart and can cross back to the ◇A to extract East's last trump, -50, 5 IMPs to USA, now ahead by 40, 195-155.

If you are from the 'glass half-full' school, you will see this deal in a positive light, as it clears up some systemic issues for both North-South pairs.

Board 73. E-W Vul.

```
              ♠ A 4
              ♡ A 9 6
              ◇ 2
              ♣ A K 10 9 8 7 5
  ♠ Q J 7 6 5 2              ♠ K 8
  ♡ 7 5 3          N         ♡ K Q 10 8 2
  ◇ Q 10 4 3    W     E      ◇ A 9 8 6
  ♣ —              S         ♣ 4 3
              ♠ 10 9 3
              ♡ J 4
              ◇ K J 7 5
              ♣ Q J 6 2
```

Closed Room

West	North	East	South
Nickell	Bocchi	Freeman	Duboin
	1♣	1♡	1♠[1]
dbl[2]	2♡[3]	pass	3♣
3♡	3♠[4]	pass	4♣
pass	4◇[5]	pass	5♣
all pass			

1. Values, fewer than four spades.
2. Spades.
3. Game force with clubs or perhaps both minors.
4. In principle, asks for spade stopper.
5. Diamond control, converts 3♠ to control-showing.

Nickell not only shows his spades, but also voluntarily supports hearts at the three-level, giving us some idea of his respect for a vulnerable one-level over-call. As Bocchi knows that Duboin would not be able to bid 3NT without a spade stopper of his own, he is, in effect, willing to commit to at least 5♣, and his follow-up 4◇ shows controls in *both* pointed suits. As 5♣ turns on the lead, it would have been better on this layout to shoot out 3NT. Freeman leads the ♡K, which would have been the random winning choice had Bocchi's majors been reversed. Declarer wins the ♡A, draws trumps and leads his diamond. Freeman ducks, but Bocchi calls for the king and so makes his contract, +400.

Open Room

West	North	East	South
Versace	Rodwell	Lauria	Meckstroth
	1♣*	1♡	dbl[1]
1♠	2♣	dbl[2]	3♣
4♠	5♣	all pass	

1. 6+ HCP, no five-card suit if 8+.
2. Takeout.

Versace not only shows his spades, but when Lauria doubles 2♣ for takeout, suggesting his actual pattern, he also jumps to game, as all five of his points are working, perhaps as a two-way gambit. Although 4♠ can be set with a red-suit lead, it's certainly not out of the question that it would be made. (A heart lead and continuation from North can produce a third-round ruff, while on a diamond lead, declarer must put up the ace, after which a low heart switch from North upon winning the ace of trumps ruins declarer's timing.) In any case, it is natural for Rodwell to continue to 5♣. Here, however, Lauria leads the ♠K, the winning choice. Rodwell wins the ace and leads the ◇2. Lauria again makes the winning decision by rising with the ace to play a spade. Rodwell can't avoid a heart loser, so goes one down, -50. That's 10 IMPs to Italy, cutting the deficit to 30, 165-195.

Board 79. N-S Vul.

```
              ♠ 10 4
              ♡ A Q 9 2
              ◇ Q 9 5
              ♣ J 10 7 4
♠ A Q J 6                      ♠ K 3
♡ 7 5            N             ♡ 8 6 3
◇ K J 10 6 4  W   E           ◇ A 8 7 2
♣ 8 3            S             ♣ A 9 6 2
              ♠ 9 8 7 5 2
              ♡ K J 10 4
              ◇ 3
              ♣ K Q 5
```

Open Room

West	North	East	South
Versace	Rodwell	Lauria	Meckstroth
			pass
1◇	pass	3♣[1]	pass
3◇	pass	pass	dbl
pass	3♡	dbl[2]	pass
4◇	all pass		

1. Limit raise in diamonds.
2. Maximum, cooperative, usually balanced.

Versace's hand is too concentrated to comfortably defend 3♡ doubled, which probably would go down because, with only eight combined trumps, there is too much for declarer to do. In 4◇, Versace wins the spade lead in dummy and plays the ◇K followed by the ◇J. Rodwell covers, but declarer was intending to pass the jack once Meckstroth protected at the three-level, so it doesn't matter. Versace makes five, +150.

Closed Room

West	North	East	South
Nickell	Bocchi	Freeman	Duboin
			pass
1◇	pass	3♣[1]	pass
3◇	pass	3♠	pass
4◇	pass	5◇	all pass

1. Game-forcing raise in diamonds.

Freeman, who would have opened the five-control East hand, elects to drive to game. Here the auction points Bocchi to the heart lead, and after two rounds are cashed, there is no longer any play for 5◇. As there has been no opposition bidding, Nickell does not find the trump queen and loses a club in addition for two down, -100. That is 6 IMPs to Italy.

The Americans started the session with a 16-IMP lead following their huge turnaround in Segment Four. They built their lead to 48 IMPs after the first six boards with the wind at their back, but Italy had the best of the later deals, recouping 23 IMPs.

USA wins the set 40-31, and with one more segment that evening and two more to follow on the morrow, the Americans lead by 25 IMPs, 196-171.

Segment Six (Boards 81-96)

The Italian lineup again features the two most experienced partnerships; Hamman and Soloway return for USA, replacing Nickell and Freeman.

Board 81. Neither Vul.

```
              ♠ Q
              ♡ Q J 6 5 2
              ◇ 5
              ♣ A K J 9 4 3
  ♠ 9 4                        ♠ 10 8 3 2
  ♡ K 10 9 8        N          ♡ 7 4
  ◇ K 9 8 3 2   W     E        ◇ A Q J 10 7
  ♣ 10 6           S           ♣ 8 2
              ♠ A K J 7 6 5
              ♡ A 3
              ◇ 6 4
              ♣ Q 7 5
```

Open Room

West	North	East	South
Versace	Rodwell	Lauria	Meckstroth
	2♣*	2◇	3♠
5◇	dbl	all pass	

To the brave and remarkably carefree (that would be Lauria) go the spoils on this one. Although Meckstroth-Rodwell are already playing PDI (pass-double inversion) in certain strong club auctions and in strong auctions after 1♠, 1♡, and 1◇ openings, their convention card does not mention using this excellent treatment in strong auctions after their natural (6+ clubs) limited 2♣ opening. Meckstroth's forcing 3♠ describes a strong suit, and over 5◇,

PDI would avail Rodwell of a 'fit or takeout' double, a nice description of his hand, either way. However, with PDI apparently unavailable, Rodwell must choose between a forcing pass ('no clear opinion so far'), 5♡, 5♠, a commitment to slam (5NT perhaps), or a regressive double ('not the hand you're hoping for if you think we should be bidding on'), and his choice works badly on this occasion when Meckstroth passes the double. Lauria loses the five obvious tricks for three down, -500.

Closed Room

	West	North	East	South
	Hamman	Bocchi	Soloway	Duboin
		1♣[1]	1♢	2♡[2]
	4♢	4♡	pass	6♣
	all pass			

1. Natural, or balanced 15-17.
2. 6+ spades, invitational, or 5+ spades, game-forcing.

The scenario is different here, where Soloway's overcall is at the one-level and Duboin's transfer can be merely invitational. With no singleton, Hamman's 4♢ is perfectly normal, but it leaves room for Bocchi to slip in a 4♡ bid. That is enough encouragement for Duboin to jump to 6♣, giving up on seven. Soloway leads the ♢A to hold Bocchi to twelve tricks, +920, 9 IMPs to Italy, 180-196. Credit most of those IMPs to Lauria, who really sticks out his neck to get involved.

Lorenzo Lauria

Board 84. Both Vul.

```
              ♠ J 8 7 4 2
              ♡ 2
              ◇ A 8 4
              ♣ K J 7 2
♠ K 10                        ♠ A 6 3
♡ K 10 5 3       N            ♡ Q J 4
◇ K Q J 6 2   W     E         ◇ 10 9 7 3
♣ A Q            S            ♣ 10 8 4
              ♠ Q 9 5
              ♡ A 9 8 7 6
              ◇ 5
              ♣ 9 6 5 3
```

Open Room

West	North	East	South
Versace	Rodwell	Lauria	Meckstroth
1◇	1♠	2◇	2♠
dbl[1]	pass	2NT	pass
3NT	all pass		

1. Strong, relatively balanced.

Rodwell's 1♠ overcall is a telling blow, as Meckstroth duly leads the suit against Lauria's 3NT, choosing the unambiguous five rather than the nine, which caters to some unblocking positions, as here. If declarer finds the prescient play of dummy's ten and takes the jack with the ace to knock out the ◇A, he can exploit the spade blockage by forcing out the ♡A, but he calls for dummy's ♠K; Rodwell discourages with the eight, in theory denying the 'touching' nine. Lauria plays on diamonds first, Rodwell winning the second round as South discards the ♡6 (reverse attitude, in context). Rodwell continues spades, leading the jack, a play that seems to cater only to queen-third in *declarer's* hand, a holding with which he would surely have played dummy's ten at Trick 1.

On a lower spade return, Lauria would be without resource, but on this layout Lauria can block the suit if he takes the ace. Is it possible for Lauria to divine that his only chance is to do just that, hoping the ♠J is a serious error? If I had to pick one declarer with the table feel to make that play, it would be Lauria, but he ducks. Meckstroth overtakes with the queen and switches to the ♣6. Lauria rises with the ace (cursing himself, I am sure) and runs his diamonds, but Rodwell keeps all his clubs, so when declarer plays on hearts, Meckstroth wins and returns a club for two down, -200.

Closed Room

West	North	East	South
Hamman	*Bocchi*	*Soloway*	*Duboin*
1♣[1]	pass	1◇[2]	pass
1♡[3]	pass	2◇[4]	pass
3NT	all pass		

1. Strong, artificial.
2. Negative.
3. Possible canapé.
4. Artificial near-maximum, three-card heart support.

Bocchi leads the ♠4 (attitude) against Hamman, who takes the queen with the king and plays on diamonds, Bocchi ducking twice to see Duboin discard the ♣6 (discouraging) and the ♡7 (encouraging). As the bidding and early play have marked Hamman with 2=4=5=2, Bocchi continues with the ♠J to pin the ten, ducked by Hamman, and a third spade. Now declarer can play on hearts and reject the club finesse, claiming ten tricks, +630.

Bocchi's ♠J might be a good play at Board-a-Match Teams, but it is a clear error at IMPs. If Duboin held the ♠10 (a two-to-one shot, given the distribution), Hamman would have to duck a *lower* spade continuation to have a chance, and Duboin would win with the ten and switch to clubs. It seems that Bocchi simply doesn't realize that the defense is still alive, which might give you some idea about how fatigue and pressure can affect the players late in such an important event. That's 13 IMPs to USA, who lead 214-180.

Board 85. N-S Vul.

```
                    ♠ Q J 9
                    ♡ Q 9 7 4 3
                    ◇ A J 3
                    ♣ 5 2
  ♠ 10 7 4 2              ┌──────────┐      ♠ 3
  ♡ J 10 8 5             │    N     │      ♡ A K 6 2
  ◇ K                    │  W   E   │      ◇ 10 7 6 5 2
  ♣ A Q 9 6              │    S     │      ♣ K 10 8
                         └──────────┘
                    ♠ A K 8 6 5
                    ♡ —
                    ◇ Q 9 8 4
                    ♣ J 7 4 3
```

Open Room

West	North	East	South
Versace	Rodwell	Lauria	Meckstroth
	pass	pass	1♠
pass	2♣[1]	pass	2◇[2]
pass	3♠	pass	4♠
all pass			

1. Drury.
2. Some interest.

Meckstroth-Rodwell have paid their dues to earn their reputation as aggressive bidders, and this deal provides us with a graphic illustration. As Rodwell could have had a bit less for his Drury 2♣, he jumps to 3♠ to give away as little information as possible; he expects game to be a marginal proposition and the lead might be the critical factor. With no way to tell how well the hands will fit, Meckstroth is not about to hang a trick short of a vulnerable game. So here we are!

Versace leads the ♡J and Meckstroth plays low from dummy and ruffs in hand to lead the ◇Q, which Versace sagaciously covers. Meckstroth takes the ace and calls for a club, Lauria going in with the king (the textbook card to add an element of doubt on the *next* round of the suit for a declarer with an AJ9 holding) to lead the ♡A. Meckstroth ruffs and exits with the ♣J to West's queen, wins the trump switch with dummy's nine, ruffs a heart with the ♠A, and advances the ◇9. Versace ruffs in and leads a second trump, which declarer wins in hand with his last trump (the king) to lead yet another diamond. Versace ruffs and plays the ♣A to force dummy's last trump. Three down, -300.

Closed Room

West	North	East	South
Hamman	*Bocchi*	*Soloway*	*Duboin*
	pass	pass	1♠
pass	2♣[1]	pass	2◇[2]
pass	2♠	dbl[3]	pass
3♡	pass	pass	3♠
all pass			

1. Drury.
2. Not enough to insist on game, possibly very weak.
3. Takeout of spades.

Bocchi-Duboin are prepared to stop at 2♠, but Soloway has a full-value pre-balancing double and nudges them up a notch to 3♠. Indeed, it's likely that Lauria would have done the same had Meckstroth-Rodwell been willing to quit at 2♠. Bocchi can double 3♡ for penalty, but is reluctant to do so facing a third-seat opening.

Duboin ruffs the heart lead and starts clubs, Soloway winning the eight to switch to the ♠3. Dummy's nine wins, and on the second club trick, Hamman overtakes Soloway's ♣10 with the queen to continue trumps. Duboin overtakes dummy's jack to lead the ◇4 to the king and ace, then continues with the ◇J. Hamman ruffs and exits with a trump: Duboin can finesse against the ◇10, but must lose his remaining clubs for one down, -100. That makes it 5 IMPs to Italy, 185-214. If declarer plays a diamond earlier, he can follow by drawing trumps and taking all his diamond tricks for +140.

After the fact, Duboin reveals that he considers his 3♠ bid an error. The main advantage to using 2◇ as (at least temporarily) the 'no-interest' reply to 2♣ is that it leaves responder room to introduce hearts as an alternative strain. This caters to opener's having only four spades and (at least) three hearts. Those who prefer to rebid in their major with a sub-minimum opening gain an extra measure of obstruction in doing so, and can use the extra space more efficiently when they rebid 2◇ with better hands.

Although the match is close and the deals in this set have produced some swings, the VuGraph audience has grown restless. When Board 86 appears on the big screen, everything changes:

Board 86. E-W Vul.

```
              ♠ A J 2
              ♡ 10 6
              ◇ A Q J 3 2
              ♣ Q 10 3
  ♠ 10 7 6 4              ♠ —
  ♡ K J 2        N        ♡ 8 3
  ◇ 10 6      W   E       ◇ K 8 7 5 4
  ♣ K 9 6 5      S        ♣ A J 8 7 4 2
              ♠ K Q 9 8 5 3
              ♡ A Q 9 7 5 4
              ◇ 9
              ♣ —
```

Open Room

West	North	East	South
Versace	Rodwell	Lauria	Meckstroth
		pass	1♠
pass	2◇	pass	2♡
pass	4♠[1]	all pass	

1. Fast arrival.

As the final session of the Venice Cup is being played at the same time and with the same deals as Session Six of the Bermuda Bowl final, our match is deemed the undercard and can be followed in the VuGraph theater only on a side screen. Both matches are broadcast live on both Bridge Base Online and e-Bridge, however, so thousands of bridge fans around the world see Meckwell grind to a halt in 4♠. Although they are consistently very aggressive, and generally exchange as little information as possible when reaching *game* is the issue, their slam-bidding approach is much more scientific and closer to down-the-middle philosophically, with judgment and partnership trust critical components. Meckstroth is expecting to find a poor hand for slam in dummy, and is surprised to find two aces and relatively strong trumps.

Against 4♠, Versace leads the ♣6 and Meckstroth ruffs Lauria's ace to play ace and another heart from hand, claiming when they divide 3-2. Versace demurs, explaining that if he were to continue with the ♡K, Meckstroth would surely ruff high, and continue with the other high trump in dummy to make only five. Meckstroth can only agree, and the board is scored as North-South +450.

Closed Room

West	North	East	South
Hamman	Bocchi	Soloway	Duboin
		pass	1♠
pass	2♣[1]	pass	2♡
pass	2♠[2]	pass	3◇[3]
pass	3♡[4]	pass	3♠[5]
pass	4◇[6]	pass	4♡[7]
pass	4♠	pass	5♣[8]
pass	5◇[9]	dbl	pass[10]
pass	rdbl[11]	pass	5♡[12]
pass	6♠	dbl	rdbl
all pass			

1. Natural, 11+, or three-card limit raise or balanced game force, perhaps with fit.
2-4. Relay.
3. 6+ spades and 4+ hearts, 11-15.
5. 6+ spades and 5+ hearts.
6. Artificial slam try agreeing spades.
7-8-9. Control-showing.
10. Denies first-round diamond control.
11-12. Confirms first-round control.

As the spectators in Monte Carlo are strongly pro-Italy, the noise level increases when the Open Room result is posted first. It rises again when Bocchi-Duboin thread their way to slam, Soloway doubling both 5◇ and the ensuing 6♠. Duboin does not expect to go two down and fancies his chances once Bocchi jumps to slam, so feels the odds favor a business redouble.

Soloway has doubled 5◇ for the lead, but when it becomes clear that diamonds are not a concern for the Italians, he doubles the slam to cancel the message sent by the first double (which is more-or-less standard expert practice), hoping to convince Hamman to lead a club. This situation has never been formally discussed, however, and Hamman does not lead a club, which could defeat the contract legitimately: declarer's trumps are shortened, and he will need to ruff himself back to his hand, fatally, even after setting up his hearts without establishing a natural trump winner for West. Instead, Hamman leads the ◇10, giving Duboin a chance. Declarer wins the ace and tries to determine why he's been doubled.

He expects bad breaks, but considers 4-1 hearts to be the most likely danger. Accordingly, he plays ace and another heart, intending to ruff two hearts high if necessary, and in that scenario, rely on his assessment of the distribution to determine whether to take a first-round finesse against a putative ten-third of trumps in the East hand. When both follow to the second heart, Duboin begins to wonder whether he should have cashed a high trump in dummy before leading the second heart. Hamman makes him pay for his eminently reasonable line of play (given Soloway's double) by testing him with the ♡K. Duboin ruffs high (as who would not?), and cashes dummy's remaining high spade. Hamman has a trump trick now, so Duboin is one down, redoubled, -200. That is 12 IMPs to USA where it might have been 15 to Italy. The American lead is 41 IMPs now, 226-185.

Giorgio Duboin

Board 87. Both Vul.

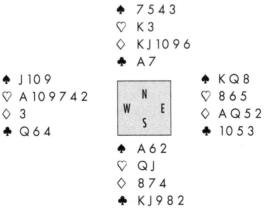

```
              ♠ 7 5 4 3
              ♡ K 3
              ♢ K J 10 9 6
              ♣ A 7
  ♠ J 10 9                      ♠ K Q 8
  ♡ A 10 9 7 4 2       N        ♡ 8 6 5
  ♢ 3            W         E     ♢ A Q 5 2
  ♣ Q 6 4                S       ♣ 10 5 3
              ♠ A 6 2
              ♡ Q J
              ♢ 8 7 4
              ♣ K J 9 8 2
```

Open Room

West	North	East	South
Versace	Rodwell	Lauria	Meckstroth
			1◊[1]
1♡	dbl[2]	2◊[3]	pass
2♡	dbl[4]	pass	3♣
3♡	all pass		

1. 2+ diamonds, 10-15.
2. Negative, promising exactly 4♠.
3. Heart fit, values.
4. Extra values.

The vulnerability does not dissuade Meckstroth from opening the bidding in first seat. While Rodwell has enough for two negative doubles and has the best hand at the table, he gives up over 3♡, but if treated to a preview of how well the defense to 3♡ would go, he would surely double. He leads the ♣A, and takes a third round ruff, Meckstroth returning his lowest remaining club, reverse suit-preference for the higher-ranking side suit. After the 'weak holding' switch to the ♠7 goes to the king and ace, Meckstroth returns a fourth round of clubs, so Rodwell scores the ♡K, and the queen-jack of trumps provide a second undertrick, -200.

Closed Room

West	North	East	South
Hamman	Bocchi	Soloway	Duboin
			pass
2♡	pass	3♡	all pass

Hamman, in the same contract uncontested after opening a weak 2♡, does two tricks better than Versace on the lead of the ♠4 (queen, ace, nine). Duboin switches to the ♣J to surround dummy's ten, but when Hamman follows low, so does Bocchi, who doesn't want to throw away a possible trump winner by overtaking with the ace to arrange a third-round ruff. That proves fatal this time, as after he wins the second club with the ace he is obliged to play a different suit. He tries spades, but Hamman wins and plays the ace of trumps (low, low, jack). Divining that Bocchi did not overtake the ♣J because he has king and one heart, Hamman plays a second round of trumps, and has time eventually to take the diamond finesse and discard his remaining club loser: +140. That's 8 IMPs more to USA, ahead now by 49, 234-185.

Board 89. E-W Vul.

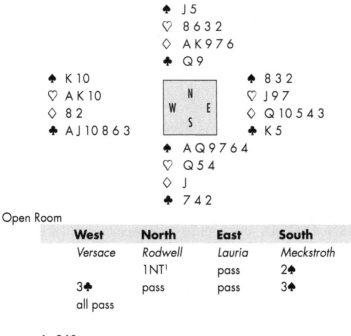

```
                    ♠ J 5
                    ♡ 8 6 3 2
                    ◇ A K 9 7 6
                    ♣ Q 9
   ♠ K 10                          ♠ 8 3 2
   ♡ A K 10            N           ♡ J 9 7
   ◇ 8 2          W        E       ◇ Q 10 5 4 3
   ♣ A J 10 8 6 3        S         ♣ K 5
                    ♠ A Q 9 7 6 4
                    ♡ Q 5 4
                    ◇ J
                    ♣ 7 4 2
```

Open Room

West	North	East	South
Versace	Rodwell	Lauria	Meckstroth
	1NT[1]	pass	2♠
3♣	pass	pass	3♠
all pass			

1. 9-12.

Although Versace has a natural 2NT overcall available over 2♠, he prefers to overcall 3♣, as he would need both a club fit and some useful bits and pieces to make 3NT. It's not clear whether Lauria would have raised 2NT to three, but it is straightforward for him to pass 3♣. When Meckstroth competes to 3♠, it proves difficult for anyone to take further action.

The defense is accurate, Lauria following to the lead of the ♡A with the jack, the clearest card to deny both the queen and a doubleton; if declarer holds queen-ten-low the damage has already been done. Versace switches to ace and another club for a second heart through the queen. Versace takes his hearts and leads a third club, but Meckstroth ruffs with dummy's jack and leads a spade to his ace, losing only to the ♠K for two down, -100.

Closed Room

West	North	East	South
Hamman	Bocchi	Soloway	Duboin
	pass	pass	2♠
2NT	pass	3NT	all pass

In a slightly different scenario, the Americans adopt a more aggressive approach, Soloway raising Hamman's somewhat wide-ranging 2NT to three.

Although Duboin has named his long suit, Bocchi leads a low diamond, reasoning that it requires the least from partner to defeat the contract. Hamman sensibly calls for dummy's queen and is rewarded when the jack drops.

Hamman, a true student of the game and a seeker of wisdom and truth, has seen this position many times in his illustrious career. A low club to the ten would see him home whenever the contract could be made, as the ♣K would afford him a delayed entry to dummy to lead a spade towards his king. But Hamman plays the ♣K and then a club to the jack, revealing just how tired he is on the twelfth day of play. Bocchi wins the ♣Q and cashes his high diamonds, the second of which squeezes declarer in three suits. Hamman parts with the ♡10, so Bocchi exits in that suit, and Hamman loses the last two tricks, leading away from the ♣K10. One down, -100; Italy gains 5 IMPs when it could have been 11 for USA. The margin is 44 IMPs, 190-234.

Board 91. Neither Vul.

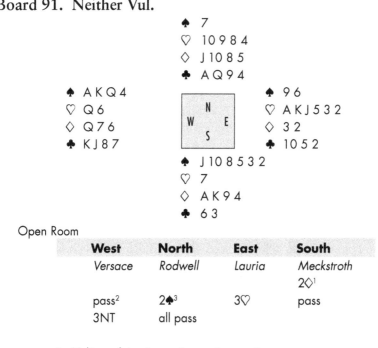

Open Room

West	North	East	South
Versace	Rodwell	Lauria	Meckstroth
			2◊[1]
pass[2]	2♠[3]	3♡	pass
3NT	all pass		

1. Multi: weak two in a major, no strong option.
2. Includes certain strong hand types.
3. Pass with spades, or correct to 2NT with hearts (which permits responder to sign off in his own clubs).

The Lauria-Versace defense to the Multi 2◊ builds some good hands into the direct-position pass, including a takeout double of hearts that includes four spades. As a direct 2NT would normally include certain stoppers in both majors, and his spades are so good, Versace decides to pass first, hoping to double later. Although most Multi users define responder's 2♠ as a hand willing to play in at least 3♡ opposite a weak 2♡ bid, the Meckwell version is different: 2♠ acts as a puppet to 2NT when opener has hearts, catering not only to invitational heart-support hands (3♡ next) but also to hands that would like to play in 3♣. Perhaps the nature of 2♠ convinces Lauria to risk a fearless, unsound 3♡ overcall. That works beautifully on the lie of the cards when Versace converts to 3NT and receives a spade lead from Rodwell. Lauria fools around for a while but settles for his nine top tricks in the majors, +400.

Closed Room

West	North	East	South
Hamman	Bocchi	Soloway	Duboin
			2♠
2NT	pass	4♢[1]	dbl
4♡	all pass		

1. Hearts.

Would you rather be in 3NT or 4♡ at single dummy if you knew that South had a weak two-bid in spades? With diamonds posing a real threat, and 4♡ requiring only a spade lead or a winning guess in clubs for one trick, you would surely choose 4♡, and if you could arrange for West to be declarer without tipping off the diamond lead, you'd make it.

Hamman-Soloway are not so lucky, because Duboin, the weak two-bidder, is able to double East's Texas transfer for a diamond lead. It no longer matters whether East or West declares 4♡, because both North and South will lead diamonds and South will soon switch to clubs to obtain a third-round ruff. Hamman is two down before catching his breath, -100, 11 IMPs to Italy, 201-234.

While it's certainly reasonable for East to transfer to hearts at the three-level and offer 3NT as a choice of games, it's fair to say that there will be many West hands with only two-card heart support that will play better in 4♡.

Board 92. N-S Vul.

```
                    ♠ Q 10 4 2
                    ♡ 7 5
                    ◇ 10 5 4 3
                    ♣ A 10 4
  ♠ K J 8 7 6                        ♠ 9 5 3
  ♡ Q 8 6 2          N               ♡ J 9
  ◇ K            W        E          ◇ Q J 9 6 2
  ♣ 6 5 3            S               ♣ K J 2
                    ♠ A
                    ♡ A K 10 4 3
                    ◇ A 8 7
                    ♣ Q 9 8 7
```

Open Room

West	North	East	South
Versace	Rodwell	Lauria	Meckstroth
pass	pass	1◇	1♡
dbl[1]	pass	1♠[2]	dbl
2♡[3]	pass	2♠	all pass

1. Four or five spades.
2. Three cards possible if balanced.
3. Game try.

Although Meckstroth shows a good overcall with club length and spade shortness, Versace's strong bidding makes it appear to Rodwell that it would be too risky to double 2♠, Lauria's potentially light third-seat opening notwithstanding. The defense is immaculate: ♡K, low club switch to the ace, ♣10 to the jack and queen, ♡A, third club, diamond taken by the ace, third heart; Rodwell has to score the ♣10 and the ♠Q and Meckstroth wins his ace, so Versace is three down, -150.

Closed Room

West	North	East	South
Hamman	Bocchi	Soloway	Duboin
pass	pass	pass	1♡
1♠	pass	2♠	dbl
pass	2NT[1]	pass	3♣
pass	3NT	all pass	

1. Normally a scramble for best partial.

Here too, North has the chance to defend 2♠ doubled, this time by converting a takeout double, with the potential for a three-trick set if the defenders get around to clubs in time, as in the Open Room. However, Bocchi takes out to 2NT, mildly hopeful that it will be interpreted as natural. Duboin treats 2NT as artificial, of course, and converts to 3♣. Bocchi is not prepared to resign himself to a post-mortem discussion about the big one that got away and takes the plunge to 3NT, albeit without much conviction.

Pleased that no one doubles 3NT, Bocchi permits himself to think that he might have a play for it. Soloway does well to lead the ◊6, and Bocchi ducks to the king. Hamman returns the ♠7 (four, three, ace). Declarer has his work cut out for him, and starts unpromisingly with a club to the ten and jack. Soloway drives out the ◊A, Hamman discarding the ♣6, and Bocchi runs the ♣8 to the king. Soloway does not cash the ◊J, instead shifting to the ♡J, an effective move. Bocchi wins the ♡A, crosses to the ♣A, goes back to the ♡K, and cashes the ♣Q, both opponents discarding spades while he releases a diamond. He exits with a heart, and Hamman takes the eight and queen, cashes the ♠K, and concedes the last trick to the ♠Q. Bocchi is two down, -200. 8 IMPs to USA, 242-201.

Norberto Bocchi

Board 95. N-S Vul.

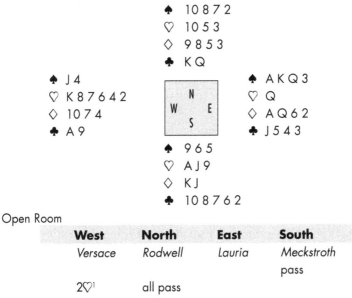

♠ 10 8 7 2
♡ 10 5 3
◇ 9 8 5 3
♣ K Q

♠ J 4
♡ K 8 7 6 4 2
◇ 10 7 4
♣ A 9

♠ A K Q 3
♡ Q
◇ A Q 6 2
♣ J 5 4 3

♠ 9 6 5
♡ A J 9
◇ K J
♣ 10 8 7 6 2

Open Room

West	North	East	South
Versace	Rodwell	Lauria	Meckstroth
			pass
2♡[1]	all pass		

1. Weak 2♡ or 2♠.

Versace happens to have a weak 2♡ this time, but he might have had a weak 2♠ instead. At this vulnerability, Versace doesn't need much for his two-way 2♡ opening, but Lauria is aware that he might be missing an easy game when he passes. He has a nice upside, of course, as the aggressive Meckstroth might reopen and create an opportunity for the Italians to collect a significant penalty. Not this time, however.

The lead against 2♡ is the ♣K (three, a reverse count eight, ace). Versace plays a club back and Rodwell wins the ♣Q as Meckstroth contributes the ten (reverse suit preference for diamonds). Rodwell switches to the ◇9 and Versace calls for dummy's ace, then discards a diamond on the ♣J as Rodwell scores the ♡3. A diamond to the king and a club ensure that the defenders score three more trumps, so Versace finishes one down in 2♡, -50.

Closed Room

West	North	East	South
Hamman	Bocchi	Soloway	Duboin
			pass
2♡	pass	4♡	all pass

Hamman, who would describe his hand as 'fair' if anyone were to ask, is soon in 4♡ on the lead of the ♣K. Duboin gives reverse count (as the king lead requests) with the eight, and Hamman wins with the ace. Unwilling to expose himself to a trump promotion or uppercut in spades, he decides not to try for an immediate discard. If he can lose a trump to the ace on his right, South would have to play a club or risk losing that trick. And then there might be time to discard one diamond on the ♣J and another on the third spade, ruff a diamond back to hand, and clear trumps. Hamman finds the heart position he is hoping for, but when Duboin returns the ♣2 (suit preference) to the queen, Bocchi switches to a diamond, and Hamman can no longer make his contract.

He goes up with the ace, and although Bocchi-Duboin use Rusinow leads and Bocchi's honor plays indicate king-queen doubleton, Hamman tries to cash the ♣J before playing on spades. Bocchi ruffs with the five and leads over to Duboin's ◊K, and another club allows Bocchi to overruff declarer's eight. Duboin still has a trump trick coming, so Hamman is three down, -150, and Italy gains 3 IMPs.

If Hamman plays three rounds of spades immediately, with the concomitant risks, to dispose of his losing club before starting trumps, he would most likely come to eleven tricks. Indeed, that is how China's Liping Wang plays 4♡ in the Venice Cup final! It's not often that the world's highest-ranked player takes four tricks fewer than a counterpart in the same suit contract on the same opening lead in a world championship, but this is one of those days. This might fall into the category of 'a lot of knowledge can be a dangerous thing'.

USA outscores Italy 46-34 in the session. With 32 boards to play, the Americans lead by 37 IMPs, 242-205. All too often, the bridge in the very late stages of the World Championship suffers from the players' exhaustion. Although the schedule in Monte Carlo is relatively kind to the players once past the 60 boards per day round robin, it is clear they are no longer at their best. Tonight, however, there will be enough time for a leisurely dinner and an early night to rest, so there is reason to hope that these two great teams will find a reserve of strength for the *denouement* of this momentous match.

Segment Seven (Boards 97-112)

It is a new day, the last of the 2003 Bermuda Bowl. Absolutely no one looks fresh and well-rested. Both captains field the same foursomes that had contested Segment Six. The Open Room is in the historic Sporting d'Hiver, on the same level as the VuGraph auditorium. It is a building once used to host glamorous parties and exhibitions for the world's high society. The Closed Room is at the Hotel Hermitage. Although it is 10:30 in the morning, good seats in the theater are at a premium. Many Italian supporters have made the short trip to Monte Carlo to see the final 32 deals and root for their heroes to come from behind to win the title that has eluded Italy's grasp since 1975.

Board 97. Neither Vul.

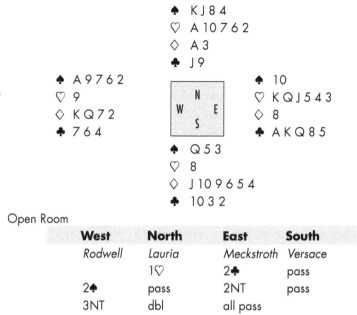

```
                    ♠ K J 8 4
                    ♡ A 10 7 6 2
                    ◇ A 3
                    ♣ J 9
  ♠ A 9 7 6 2                        ♠ 10
  ♡ 9                N               ♡ K Q J 5 4 3
  ◇ K Q 7 2       W     E            ◇ 8
  ♣ 7 6 4            S               ♣ A K Q 8 5
                    ♠ Q 5 3
                    ♡ 8
                    ◇ J 10 9 6 5 4
                    ♣ 10 3 2
```

Open Room

West	North	East	South
Rodwell	*Lauria*	*Meckstroth*	*Versace*
	1♡	2♣	pass
2♠	pass	2NT	pass
3NT	dbl	all pass	

With at least five hearts marked on his right, Meckstroth might have been forgiven for staying out of the auction at his first turn. He introduces clubs, however, because his opponents might be able to get together in spades and make it more dangerous for him to bid later. Rodwell treats the club overcall with respect, and moments later, Meckstroth finds himself in a very pushy 3NT. Perhaps Lauria senses that his opponents are stretching, for he doubles to ask for a spade lead, which might be the key to defeating the contract. However, Versace interprets the double as a request to lead a suit other than hearts (which is later revealed to be the actual partnership agreement), and while he does expect Lauria to have a strong spade holding, he thinks he has a better chance for a big set by starting with the ◇J. He hopes Lauria will play him for a spade honor because of his failure to lead that suit, which amounts to an interesting line of reasoning.

Lauria takes the ◇K with the ace and duly switches to a spade, but chooses the four (ten, queen, ace). If Meckstroth reads the spade position and is sufficiently inspired to cash the ◇Q (he needs clubs 3-2, and North seems to be 4-5 in the majors, so this is not an inconceivable play), he can knock out the ♡A, and take the ♠A, a diamond, two hearts and five clubs for nine tricks.

However, Lauria can prevent him from doing that by making his spade switch the king rather than the four (better than the jack as declarer could hold the singleton queen). If declarer ducks the ♠K and North envisions declarer with specifically 1=6=1=5, he can continue with the ♠J. If declarer wins and cashes the ◇Q, South has an entry with the ♠Q for his diamonds, and if declarer strands the ◇Q he never gets it; if declarer ducks the ♠J too, North exits with a club.

But Meckstroth does not cash the ◇Q; instead, he calls for the ♡9 at Trick 3. Lauria gives that a good look, but follows low. And so does Meckstroth. When the ♡9 holds, declarer crosses to a club and drives out the ♡A. He finishes with three hearts, the ♠A and five clubs for nine tricks and +550.

When Meckstroth asks Lauria about the nature of his double, Lorenzo tells him it asks for a spade lead. Meckstroth is willing to take his chances on spades after Rodwell has bid the suit, but had he been given the technically proper information ('don't lead a heart'), he might not have been so keen to stand his ground with a singleton in an unbid suit that might well be led. Had 3NT doubled gone down, there may well have been a Director call once all the information about the meaning of the double had come to light.

The winning move for North is to cover the ♡9 with the ten. If declarer wins and plays back a heart honor, North wins, cashes two spades and exits with a heart equal, scoring the setting trick with a second heart. All very complicated.

Closed Room

West	North	East	South
Duboin	Hamman	Bocchi	Soloway
	2◇¹	3♣	pass
3♡²	pass	3NT	all pass

1. Flannery: four spades and five or six hearts, less than a strong 16 HCP.
2. Asks for heart stopper.

After Hamman's Flannery 2◇ opening, Soloway needs no further urging to lead the ♠3, ducked to the king. Hamman returns the ♠4; Bocchi discards a heart and takes Soloway's queen with the ace. His next play is the ♡9, and here too North follows low. Bocchi duplicates Meckstroth's play by following low, and is soon recording +400 on his side of the scoresheet. He will be disappointed later to learn that he has lost 4 IMPs for this effort: USA, 246-205.

Would it be unkind to the North players to categorize 3NT as turning on the heart finesse?

Here too, covering the ♡9 would be the killer: North wins the heart continuation, cashes a spade, and exits with a club, eventually scoring a second heart and the ◇A.

Board 98. N-S Vul.

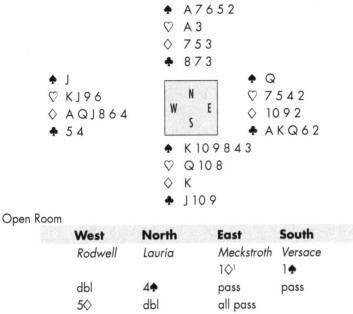

```
                    ♠ A 7 6 5 2
                    ♡ A 3
                    ◇ 7 5 3
                    ♣ 8 7 3
   ♠ J                              ♠ Q
   ♡ K J 9 6          N             ♡ 7 5 4 2
   ◇ A Q J 8 6 4   W     E          ◇ 10 9 2
   ♣ 5 4               S            ♣ A K Q 6 2
                    ♠ K 10 9 8 4 3
                    ♡ Q 10 8
                    ◇ K
                    ♣ J 10 9
```

Open Room

West	North	East	South
Rodwell	Lauria	Meckstroth	Versace
		1◇[1]	1♠
dbl	4♠	pass	pass
5◇	dbl	all pass	

1. 2+ diamonds, 10-15.

If North does not compete so vigorously, East-West will probably reach 4♡ and make it, but 4♠ is the normal pressure bid. Par at this point is to defend 4♠ doubled, which goes for 500 if the defenders get all their tricks, but Rodwell goes on to 5◇. It's easy to see why Lauria doubles; he has two aces for his preemptive game raise, and might be getting 300 after forcing his opponents to guess. Versace, expecting Lauria to have values outside spades, leads the ♣J. Meckstroth wins and starts on trumps, South's king providing added hope. He draws trumps and tests clubs, discarding a spade and two hearts when they break, then leads a heart to the jack, guided by Lauria's double. That produces an overtrick, +650.

Closed Room

West	North	East	South
Duboin	Hamman	Bocchi	Soloway
		1♣[1]	1♠
2♣[2]	4♠	pass	pass
dbl	pass	5◇	all pass

1. Natural, or balanced 15-17.
2. Diamonds, 8+ HCP.

Hamman hates to give away the extra 4 IMPs 'out of spite' in this type of situation, and is unwilling to count on the ♠A taking a trick. Had Soloway led the ♠K and switched to a heart, Bocchi might still be thinking. However, with his odds and ends in the rounded suits, Soloway has no clear sense of urgency and he starts with the ♠10 to Hamman's ace. Bocchi wins the club switch, picks up the trump king and runs clubs to discard three hearts, avoiding the guess in that suit: +400, USA gaining 6 IMPs, 252-205.

Board 102. E-W Vul.

```
              ♠ 8 6
              ♡ A 8
              ◇ A 10 8 4 2
              ♣ Q J 6 5
♠ K J 10 4              ♠ A Q 9
♡ Q J 5 4       N      ♡ K 10 9 7 2
◇ J 7 6      W   E     ◇ —
♣ 7 3           S      ♣ K 10 9 4 2
              ♠ 7 5 3 2
              ♡ 6 3
              ◇ K Q 9 5 3
              ♣ A 8
```

Open Room

West	North	East	South
Rodwell	Lauria	Meckstroth	Versace
		1♡	pass
3♡[1]	pass	4♡	all pass

1. 7+ to 9, 4+ hearts.

Meckstroth, delighted to be finding the trump length that would help him control the play, bids game with his five-loser hand over Rodwell's mixed raise. He makes five on the lead of the ◇K, ruffing to lead a trump to the queen and ace. Lauria, who knows that trumps are breaking well for declarer, switches to the ♣6. Meckstroth, who doesn't know about the trump break, puts in the ten, which proves the winning choice. Versace wins the ♣A and reverts to diamonds, but when both follow to the ♡K, declarer can claim: +650.

Closed Room

West	North	East	South
Duboin	Hamman	Bocchi	Soloway
		1♡	pass
2NT[1]	pass	3♣[2]	pass
3♡[3]	pass	3♠[4]	pass
3NT[5]	pass	4♣[6]	pass
4♡[7]	pass	5◇[8]	pass
5♠[9]	pass	6♡	all pass

1. 7-11, 4+ hearts, balanced.
2-4. Inquiry.
3. Neither super-minimum nor maximum.
5. 1, 2 or 3 controls.
6-9. Control-showing.

Bocchi, facing a higher potential maximum, has more room, and uses it to look for slam, which would require perfect cards, including no wastage in diamonds. When Duboin denies a diamond control, Bocchi thinks his luck is in, and goes past game. With no in-between action available over 5◇, Duboin commits to slam and keeps the ball rolling in case Bocchi has a 'real' hand, in the family of:

♠ A x   ♡ A K x x x x   ◇ —   ♣ A K x x x

(not everyone's 2♣ opening)

To his credit, Bocchi does not try for seven! Duboin, in a follow-up email, refers to everything after 3NT as 'a nightmare'. Soloway leads the ◇K, and Bocchi ruffs to lead a trump to the queen and ace. Hamman returns a trump and when they divide evenly, Bocchi asks who holds the ♣A and concedes two down when Soloway admits to its possession: -200. That is 13 IMPs from nowhere to USA, ahead now by 62, 267-205.

Halfway through the penultimate set, that lead is looking increasingly formidable, as the Italians are not playing well and have given no indication that they will be able to turn the match around with the deals remaining.

Board 106. Both Vul.

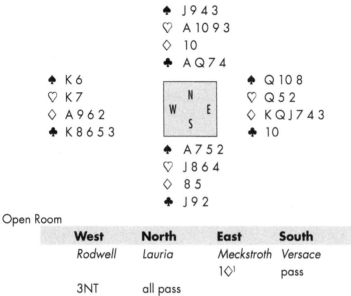

```
              ♠ J 9 4 3
              ♡ A 10 9 3
              ◇ 10
              ♣ A Q 7 4
  ♠ K 6                        ♠ Q 10 8
  ♡ K 7              N         ♡ Q 5 2
  ◇ A 9 6 2     W       E      ◇ K Q J 7 4 3
  ♣ K 8 6 5 3          S       ♣ 10
              ♠ A 7 5 2
              ♡ J 8 6 4
              ◇ 8 5
              ♣ J 9 2
```

Open Room

West	North	East	South
Rodwell	Lauria	Meckstroth	Versace
		1◇¹	pass
3NT	all pass		

1. 2+ diamonds, 10-15.

With three aces missing and the ♠10 and ♠8 the only promising intermediate cards, 3NT is an ambitious undertaking for East-West, but played by West it certainly has its chances. In typical fashion, Meckwell are there in two bids, leaving Lauria with a difficult lead problem. Although all three long suits *can* defeat the contract, all require accurate follow-up defense, which may involve South switching to the ♣J when and if he gains the lead before it's too late.

Unwilling to relinquish what might be a crucial tempo were he to lead the wrong suit, Lauria tries to preserve his options by leading the ♣A. In addition to retaining the lead, this might catch a modest club holding in partner's hand that would combine to produce three or four tricks in the suit. Sweden's Tjolpe Flodqvist contributed a wonderful Bols Bridge Tip on just this subject, one of my all-time favorites. Lauria strikes gold when Versace follows to the first trick with the jack over dummy's ten. Lauria places him with the nine and continues with the ♣4. Rodwell discards a heart from dummy, takes the nine with the king, and plays six rounds of diamonds. Lauria shows the ♡A and Versace the ♠A with their first discards while Rodwell discards a club and a heart before leaving dummy with a heart to the king and ace. Lauria leads a spade over to the ace, and Versace returns the ♣2 through declarer's eight-five to Lauria's queen-seven for one down, -100. That effort qualifies for my archive of professional defense.

There's something eerie about this set-up: the precise club spots, the defenders' entries being aces, and declarer being unable to come to more than eight tricks. The last time I encountered a deal that felt like it had been precooked to order was in Iceland circa 1993, in a team event with duplicated boards. I was declarer in 7♣, which was cold unless a trump was led. The opponents' trumps were the two, three, four and five, and I would have had a high crossruff. A trump was led, of course. There were many different possibilities, and the idea was to exhaust all other options in precisely the right order (which included a well-timed second round of trumps) before resorting to a finesse, a classic 'technique' deal. Our table was on VuGraph, and I remarked to my opponents that the deal was from someone's textbook and seemed to be prepared for the commentators to amuse the audience. Everyone nodded sagely. Those opponents? Lauria and Versace. I believe that the Great Shuffler has designated Lorenzo as the Chosen One, and that there are many more unusual chapters remaining in the story of his life in Bridge.

Closed Room

West	North	East	South
Duboin	Hamman	Bocchi	Soloway
		pass	pass
1♣[1]	pass	1♠[2]	pass
1NT	pass	2♣[3]	pass
2♢	dbl	2♡[4]	pass
3♢	all pass		

1. Natural or 11-14 balanced.
2. 4+ diamonds.
3. Inquiry, at best invitational.
4. Stopper.

Bocchi and Duboin conduct a controlled auction terminating in 3♢, a safe contract. Hamman, who finally doubled for the majors at his third turn to bid, leads the ♠3 (eight, ace, six). Soloway returns a spade to the king, and Duboin tests Hamman with the ♡7 before the position is clear. When Hamman follows low, the queen wins, and Duboin discards the ♡K on the ♠Q. He loses only to the ♣A, and so makes five, for +150. That's 6 IMPs to Italy, 213-271.

Board 109. Both Vul.

```
                    ♠ K 8
                    ♡ 10 6 2
                    ◇ K Q 8 6 4
                    ♣ K 10 2
      ♠ 5 4 3                         ♠ A 10 9
      ♡ K Q J 9 5 3      N            ♡ A 7
      ◇ J            W       E        ◇ 9 7 3
      ♣ 9 6 4            S            ♣ A J 8 7 3
                    ♠ Q J 7 6 2
                    ♡ 8 4
                    ◇ A 10 5 2
                    ♣ Q 5
```

Open Room

West	North	East	South
Rodwell	Lauria	Meckstroth	Versace
	pass	1NT[1]	pass
4◇[2]	dbl	pass[3]	pass
rdbl[4]	pass	4♡	all pass

1. 14-16.
2. Hearts.
3-4. Preference to be dummy.

Although the East-West hands fit quite well (the red-suit mesh is ideal) and the club suit accommodates declarer's percentage approach, 4♡ can still be defeated. It should come as no surprise that Meckwell reach game. As Lauria doubles the Texas 4◇ response for the lead, Versace thinks there might be some advantage to underleading the ◇A. Since he has something of value in both black suits, he leads the ◇5, a true count card that he intends as neutral. Unfortunately, when Lauria wins with the ◇Q, what he really needs is a suit preference signal, as there is really nothing conclusive to point him to the right black suit. Furthermore, it could be right to lead either the king or a lower card in either suit (the ♣10 would be essential to surround dummy's nine if South held ♣Q87x, while the ♠8 would be best if South held ♠Q10xxx and North couldn't regain the lead).

After a great deal of thought, Lauria switches to the ♠K, bringing the Italian supporters to their feet. Rodwell takes the ace, hoping that the spades are blocked, draws trumps, and leads the ♣9. Lauria plays the king, the best technical move, but Rodwell wins the ace, ruffs a diamond, and leads a second club to the eight. That holds his loss to one down, as Versace has two spade winners to take when he wins the ♣Q, -100.

Closed Room

	West	North	East	South
	Duboin	Hamman	Bocchi	Soloway
		pass	1♣[1]	pass
	1♢[2]	pass	1NT	pass
	2♡	pass	pass	2♠
	all pass			

1. Natural or 11-14 balanced.
2. Hearts.

It is mildly surprising that Duboin sells out to 2♠, but that proves an acceptable strategy when perfect defense sets the contract. Duboin leads his singleton diamond, and Soloway wins the king in dummy (nine from Bocchi) to lead the ♠8. Bocchi rises with the ace, returns the ♢3 for Duboin to ruff, regains the lead with the ♣A (six, ten, ace), cashes the ♡A (queen from West to discourage), and gives Duboin another diamond ruff. The ♡K is the setting trick; one down, -100, 5 IMPs to Italy, 218-271.

Board 110. Neither Vul.

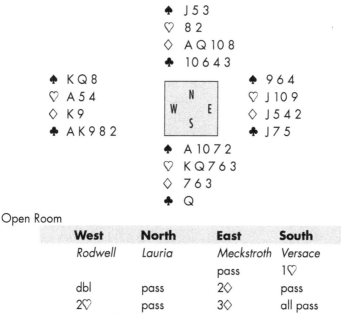

Open Room

	West	North	East	South
	Rodwell	Lauria	Meckstroth	Versace
			pass	1♡
	dbl	pass	2♢	pass
	2♡	pass	3♢	all pass

With primarily defensive cards, Lauria is content to pass over West's double, and that works very well for him when his opponents struggle their way to a terrible contract. It's easy to see what Rodwell has in mind when he cuebids at his second turn rather than bid 2NT or 3♣, but angling to reach 3NT from the East side comes with a price. When Meckstroth retreats to 3◇ for want of anything better to do, Rodwell has to give up.

Versace leads the ♣Q and Meckstroth wins with the ace to lead a second club to his seven. Versace ruffs with the three and switches to the ♡K, which Meckstroth takes with dummy's ace to return the suit. Versace wins, gives Lauria a heart ruff, and takes another club ruff before leading a low spade. Meckstroth wins with dummy's king and plays the ♦K to discard a spade, allowing Versace to score his remaining trump. The ♠A stands up and declarer, down to only trumps, must ruff the spade return. When Versace shows out on the next trick, Meckstroth claims one more trick for four down, -200. Good to be non-vulnerable.

Closed Room

West	**North**	**East**	**South**
Duboin	Hamman	Bocchi	Soloway
		pass	pass
2NT[1]	pass	3NT	all pass

1. 20-22.

When Soloway doesn't open in second position (he would have to start with 2◇, Flannery), Bocchi and Duboin steam into 3NT, Bocchi taking a rather optimistic view, even non-vulnerable.

Hamman leads the ♣6, second-best from a weak suit: five, queen, ace. Duboin returns the ♣2 and Hamman could deprive him of an entry to dummy by inserting the ten, but that is far from obvious. Duboin wins with dummy's seven and calls for the ♡9, Soloway covering with the queen. Duboin wins the ace, crosses to the ♣J and leads the ♠4 to his king before cashing the ♣K, Soloway discarding a spade, a heart and a diamond on the clubs. Without cashing the last club (which would bring some pressure to bear on dummy; a diamond had been discarded so far), Duboin plays a second heart, which Soloway ducks. Now, when Duboin plays a second spade, Soloway wins and cashes two hearts, then leads a diamond to Hamman's two winners. Dummy's ◇J takes the last trick, but Duboin is one down, -50. The Italians gain 4 IMPs in unusual fashion to bring their deficit below 50, 222-271.

Board 111. N-S Vul.

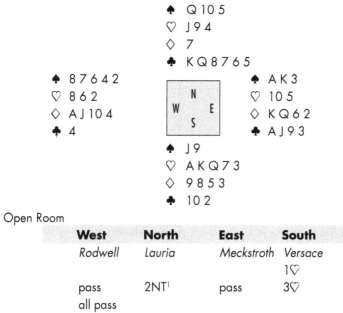

```
                    ♠ Q 10 5
                    ♡ J 9 4
                    ◇ 7
                    ♣ K Q 8 7 6 5
  ♠ 8 7 6 4 2                        ♠ A K 3
  ♡ 8 6 2          N                 ♡ 10 5
  ◇ A J 10 4     W   E               ◇ K Q 6 2
  ♣ 4              S                 ♣ A J 9 3
                    ♠ J 9
                    ♡ A K Q 7 3
                    ◇ 9 8 5 3
                    ♣ 10 2
```

Open Room

West	North	East	South
Rodwell	Lauria	Meckstroth	Versace
			1♡
pass	2NT[1]	pass	3♡
all pass			

1. Three-card limit raise.

Versace's light opening bid coupled with Lauria's 2NT and Rodwell's failure to overcall 1♠ serve to convince Meckstroth that he might do best by defending without revealing his strength.

Against 3♡, Rodwell leads his singleton club. Meckstroth wins and returns the three for West to ruff, requesting a spade return in the process (reverse suit-preference signals). If Rodwell knew that his partner held two cashing spade tricks and that declarer was also out of clubs, he would cash the ◇A before returning a spade. He switches to the ♠8, however, and follows with the six when Meckstroth wins the king and cashes the ace. As Rodwell might have played the deuce (reverse suit-preference) to direct a diamond switch, Meckstroth returns a club, hoping to promote a trump trick for West's original queen-third. Versace ruffs high, draws trumps ending in dummy, and claims, discarding three diamonds on club winners and his last diamond on the ♠Q, +140. As Meckstroth-Rodwell could make 3♠, this result is doubly painful for them.

Closed Room

West	North	East	South
Duboin	Hamman	Bocchi	Soloway
			pass
pass	pass	1♣[1]	1♡
dbl[2]	2♡	dbl[3]	pass
2♠	pass	3♠	all pass

1. Natural or 15-17 balanced.
2. Four or five spades.
3. Good hand, usually without four spades.

When Soloway passes the South hand and Hamman the North hand, showing some respect for the vulnerability, Bocchi is left to open 1♣ in fourth position. The East-West spade fit comes to light and the Italians reach 3♠ of their own volition, trying for game. Hamman leads the ♡4 and Soloway wins the ace, cashes the queen and switches to the ♠J. Duboin wins the ♠A, cashes the ♠K and claims, conceding a trump after taking his heart ruff: +170.

Although both a diamond lead and a trump lead (South ducking the second heart lead from dummy) would seem to defeat 4♠, that is not so. Declarer can play dummy's high trumps and ruff three clubs in hand, using the ◇K and the ◇Q as entries. Italy gains 7 IMPs and trails now by 42, 229-271, going into the final deal of the session.

Board 112. E-W Vul.

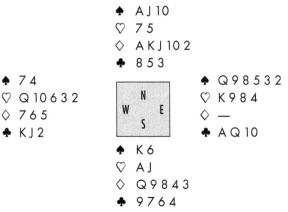

♠ A J 10
♡ 7 5
◇ A K J 10 2
♣ 8 5 3

♠ 7 4
♡ Q 10 6 3 2
◇ 7 6 5
♣ K J 2

♠ Q 9 8 5 3 2
♡ K 9 8 4
◇ —
♣ A Q 10

♠ K 6
♡ A J
◇ Q 9 8 4 3
♣ 9 7 6 4

Closed Room

	West	North	East	South
	Duboin	Hamman	Bocchi	Soloway
	pass	1◇[1]	1♠	3◇[2]
	pass	pass	dbl	pass
	4♡	all pass		

1. 3+ diamonds.
2. Limit raise

With all his values concentrated in two suits, Hamman elects to start with 1◇ rather than upgrade to a 14-16 notrump, which his hand is otherwise worth. He might well take a shot at 3NT over 3◇, but takes a conservative position, not vulnerable. Missing this perfect-fit game wouldn't be the end of the world, but by passing 3◇, Hamman gives Bocchi a second opportunity to bid with only moderate risk. His reopening takeout double suits Duboin very well, and suddenly it is East-West who are in game! Hamman leads the ◇K and Duboin ruffs in dummy to lead a low spade, the ten winning. A second diamond forces dummy to ruff and Duboin crosses to a club to ruff his last diamond and lead the ♡K. Soloway wins the ace, cashes the ♠K, and plays another diamond, but Duboin ruffs, cashes the ♡Q, and claims, +620. So 3NT would have been an advance 'save' for North-South against 4♡, perhaps a more subtle reason to bid it.

Open Room

	West	North	East	South
	Rodwell	Lauria	Meckstroth	Versace
	pass	1◇	1♠	3♣[1]
	pass	3NT	all pass	

1. Limit raise in diamonds.

Although desperation tactics are hardly in order for the Italians, Lauria isn't about to settle for 3◇ when there might be a decent play for 3NT. That effectively silences Meckstroth, and Italy is due to gain significantly. Although Meckstroth finds the best lead (the ♡4), 3NT is flat out on finding the ♠Q, and there is every reason for Lauria to play Meckstroth for it. After winning the ♡A and cashing four rounds of diamonds ending in his hand, Lauria leads the ♠J, intending to pass it. Meckstroth covers, +400.

Italy makes game at both tables for a gain of 14 IMPs, scoring 30 IMPs without reply over the last four deals of the set, winning the seventh segment 38-29 to reduce the American lead to just 28 IMPs with 16 boards remaining.

Those who felt that the match was over when the USA had built their lead to 64 IMPs just seven deals earlier were sorely mistaken. It had promised to be a nail-biting finish before the match began, and with the momentum now favoring the trailing team, it looks as if it might well go down to the wire.

After a short break, the players will have to go back to war. There is really no time to dwell on the previous session.

Segment Eight (Boards 113-128)

It is clear to anyone following the Bermuda Bowl final that it is still anyone's match. Neither NPC has any intention of changing their lineup for the final 16 deals, so it will be a fight to the finish between two teams that know each other well, featuring four pairs who all know how to win and are used to doing so.

Meckstroth and Rodwell have played every board in the final, but are holding up well. Fatigue will surely continue to be a factor, but sometimes the adrenaline rush trumps exhaustion when it matters most. The Italians are much more demonstrative with their emotions than the stoic American foursome, and that too might be a factor, albeit one that could work either way. While everyone is hoping that the quality of the bridge will be decisive, it is likely that the intangibles also will play a role.

The VuGraph theatre is jammed with spectators, many of them standing, few of them non-partisan. Both e-bridge and Bridge Base Online are reporting tremendous interest in their real-time webcasts; indeed, this is the first time that BBO records at least 10,000 logins for a single match. Bridge is becoming much more accessible, and a match of this magnitude is certainly a magnet for the curious. I am at the commentators' table, as I have been throughout, and it's been an emotional roller-coaster experience for me as coach of the American team. That does not figure to change as the match draws to a close. The players are in their seats and ready to go...

Board 113. Neither Vul.

```
                    ♠ 9 5 3
                    ♡ A Q 9 4
                    ◇ 10 9 2
                    ♣ Q J 4
  ♠ A 8 7                          ♠ 10 4 2
  ♡ K J 5 2         N              ♡ 10 8 6 3
  ◇ Q 6 3       W       E          ◇ A 8 4
  ♣ A 8 3           S              ♣ 7 6 2
                    ♠ K Q J 6
                    ♡ 7
                    ◇ K J 7 5
                    ♣ K 10 9 5
```

Open Room

West	North	East	South
Hamman	Lauria	Soloway	Versace
	pass	pass	1♣[1]
dbl	rdbl	1♡	1♠
pass	1NT	pass	2◇
pass	3♣	all pass	

1. 2+ clubs.

Closed Room

West	North	East	South
Duboin	Rodwell	Bocchi	Meckstroth
	pass	pass	1◇[1]
dbl	rdbl[2]	pass	1♠
pass	1NT	all pass	

1. 2+ diamonds, 10-15.
2. Hearts.

Both Wests are willing to double for takeout with less than ideal distribution, inspired to a degree by the tendency of both North-South pairs to open and respond light. Although North might not have four cards in either minor, it's interesting that Meckstroth, who can bid 2♣ and play at the two-level, passes 1NT, while Versace, who risks playing at the three-level by introducing the other minor, makes that commitment.

Rodwell's 1NT proves to be an adventure. Bocchi leads the ♣6: five, eight, queen. Rodwell runs the ◇10 to the queen, and puts in the nine when Duboin switches to the ♡2. Bocchi wins with the ten and returns the ♡3 to the king and ace, dummy parting with a spade. Declarer leads the ♣4 to the nine and ace, and takes the ♡J with the queen, dummy discarding a diamond. Rodwell cashes his clubs, discarding a heart, then plays the ♠Q, which holds, and the ♠K, which does not. Duboin plays a heart over to the eight as Rodwell discards the ♠9 and dummy the ◇J. Bocchi cashes the ◇A, but as his last card is the ◇8, he has to concede the last trick to Rodwell's ◇9 for +90. Whew!

If your system gets you to 3♣ with the North-South cards on your own steam, there's a hole in the system, but when Hamman leads a heart and dummy's queen holds, Versace is in good shape, thanks to the 3-3 breaks in all the key suits. He starts on spades, elects to believe Soloway's count card, and continues the suit although Hamman ducks twice. Versace takes the continuation of the ♡K with dummy's ace, discards a diamond, and passes the ◇10 to the queen. Hamman switches to a low trump and Versace wins in hand to play the ◇K. Soloway wins and can do no better than play a heart, but Versace ruffs, cashes his diamond winner, and ruffs his spade winner in dummy, losing only to the ace of trumps for +110. That is yet another strange IMP to Italy, 244-271.

Board 114. N-S Vul.

```
              ♠ K 9 4
              ♡ K 9 4
              ◇ J 9 8
              ♣ J 9 4 3
  ♠ Q                        ♠ A J 10 8 7 6
  ♡ A 3           N          ♡ 10 8 7
  ◇ K 10 7 5   W   E         ◇ A Q 6
  ♣ A 10 8 7 6 5   S         ♣ K
              ♠ 5 3 2
              ♡ Q J 6 5 2
              ◇ 4 3 2
              ♣ Q 2
```

	West	North	East	South
	Hamman	*Lauria*	*Soloway*	*Versace*
			1♠	pass
	2♣[1]	pass	2♠[2]	pass
	2NT[3]	pass	3♣[4]	pass
	3◇	pass	3NT[5]	pass
	4♣[6]	pass	4◇[7]	pass
	4NT[8]	pass	5♡[9]	dbl
	6♣[10]	all pass		

1. Clubs, or a three-card limit raise.
2. Five-plus spades, non-minimum, could conceal 4-5 diamonds
   (2◇ = artificial, minimum with fewer than four hearts).
3. Natural, forcing to game.
4. Puppet to 3◇, extra values.
5. Six spades, balanced (treating the ♣K as a 'balanced' value).
6-7. Control-showing, for spades.
8. RKCB for spades.
9. 2 keycards, no ♠Q.
10. He who bids Blackwood places the contract.

Hamman, an inveterate scientist who has developed some wonderful special-ized treatments, had come up with that idea for 3♣ just the week before the Bermuda Bowl, and passed it on to Soloway in a telephone conversation. While Soloway committed it to memory, Hamman forgets where they had left their discussion. At the table, he treats 3♣ as support, intends 3◇ as con-trol-showing for clubs, believes 3NT is natural, and goes past 3NT to try for 6♣. He treats Soloway's 4◇ as RKCB for *clubs*, shows two keycards without the ♣Q, and interprets 5♡ as control-showing, a grand slam try with all the keycards and the trump queen accounted for. The fact that Soloway would not have bid 3NT with *that* prime 16-count (♠A, ◇A, ♣KQ, ♡K) is sufficiently disturbing to cause Hamman to reconsider his analysis of the bidding, but there is really no practical way for him to extricate himself from the auction below 6♣. There can be no denying that a little knowledge is a dangerous thing, a lot of knowledge even more so.

Lauria leads the ♡4 against Hamman's 6♣. Hamman takes Versace's queen (is that a congratulatory card to let Lauria know as early as possible that he made a good lead?) with the ace. He passes the ♠Q, crosses to the ♣K, discards his losing heart on the ♠A, ruffs a heart, and plays ace and another trump, learning that he has two trump losers a moment later: one down, -50. In addition to parking the heart loser, 6♣ needs trumps either 3-3, honor-nine doubleton or queen-jack doubleton, a 45.21% chance. Not that it deserves to make, but it is not a slam without hope.

Closed Room

West	North	East	South
Duboin	Rodwell	Bocchi	Meckstroth
		1♠	pass
2♣[1]	pass	2◇[2]	pass
2♡[3]	pass	2NT[4]	pass
3♣[5]	pass	4♣[6]	pass
4◇[7]	pass	4♠[8]	all pass

1. Artificial one-round force: many hand types.
2. Any minimum hand without 4♡.
3-5. Game-forcing relay.
4. One-suiter.
6. Six-plus spades, singleton club, maximum (for a minimum).
7. Diamond control.
8. Denies both heart control or a special hand like seven or eight spades.

Duboin, with a difficult hand to develop naturally in his methods, tries the relay route and discovers enough to believe that 4♠ will usually be a respectable contract. Bocchi ducks Meckstroth's lead of the ♡Q and Rodwell overtakes to return the ♡9, hoping to find his partner with the ♠10 if declarer needs to ruff a heart in dummy. Bocchi crosses to the ♣K, goes back to the ◇K, discards a heart on the ♣A, and passes the ♠Q. He returns to hand with the ◇A and plays ace-jack of spades, losing a trump and a heart for +450: 11 IMPs to Italy, within 16 now at 255-271.

Board 117. N-S Vul.

```
                    ♠  J 10 8 7
                    ♡  5 4
                    ◇  5 3
                    ♣  J 8 4 3 2
   ♠  9 6                              ♠  A K 5 2
   ♡  K Q 10 9 6        N              ♡  A J 8 7 3
   ◇  K Q 9 7      W          E        ◇  A J 6
   ♣  10 6              S              ♣  K
                    ♠  Q 4 3
                    ♡  2
                    ◇  10 8 4 2
                    ♣  A Q 9 7 5
```

Open Room

West	North	East	South
Hamman	Lauria	Soloway	Versace
	pass	1♣*	pass
1♡[1]	pass	2♡	pass
3♡	pass	3♠	pass
4◇	pass	4♡	all pass

1. Artificial: 8-11, any distribution.

Hamman gets his strength across early, but his heart raise could have been based on honor-third. Soloway's 3♠ is a slam try and Hamman shows his diamond control while denying a club control. Soloway, with weak trumps and a certain club loser, signs off. Hamman really owes his partner a raise to 5♡, but fears two fast club losers and passes. He could have stalled with 3NT over 3♠, a clear slam try denying a club control, but even then, after 4♣ - 4◇ - 4♡, he would be worth 5♡ on the strength of his spectacular trumps, marriage in diamonds, and potentially useful doubletons. Lauria leads the ♣2 to hold Hamman to twelve tricks, +480.

Closed Room

West	North	East	South
Duboin	Rodwell	Bocchi	Meckstroth
	pass	1♡	pass
2NT[1]	pass	3♣[2]	pass
3NT[3]	pass	4♣[4]	pass
4◇[5]	pass	4NT[6]	pass
5♣[7]	pass	5◇[8]	pass
6◇[9]	pass	6♡	all pass

1. 7-11, 4+ hearts, balanced.
2. Inquiry.
3. Maximum: fewer than four controls, no spade control.
4-5. Control-showing.
6. RKCB for hearts.
7. One keycard.
8. Asks for the trump queen.
9. Trump queen plus extra values in diamonds.

Bocchi and Duboin seem to have a good grip on the auction and coast into 6♡ after Duboin reveals quite a bit about his hand, but the doubleton spade, the key to slam, is a bonus. Meckstroth leads the ◇4 and there is nothing to the play; Bocchi discards his club on dummy's fourth diamond for +1010. That is 11 IMPs to Italy, suddenly just 6 IMPs behind, 266-272.

The Italian supporters are very loud now and there is some valid concern that the noise might be heard in the Open Room (perhaps through the card-caller's earphone), inadvertently conveying unauthorized information about the state of the match.

Board 118. E-W Vul.

```
                    ♠ J 3 2
                    ♡ Q 4 3
                    ◇ A 4
                    ♣ A K J 9 6
   ♠ Q 9                          ♠ A 10 8 7 6
   ♡ J 6 5 2          N           ♡ K 7
   ◇ J 7 2        W     E         ◇ K Q 10 8 6
   ♣ 7 5 4 2          S           ♣ 10
                    ♠ K 5 4
                    ♡ A 10 9 8
                    ◇ 9 5 3
                    ♣ Q 8 3
```

West	North	East	South
Hamman	*Lauria*	*Soloway*	*Versace*
		1♠	pass
pass	dbl	2◇	pass
pass	3♣	pass	3♠
dbl	3NT	all pass	

For Lauria-Versace, 1NT in the reopening position suggests 11+ to 14 HCP, balanced or quasi-balanced; a takeout double indicates either a little less (about 7-11) or at least a little more (15+); overcalls are somewhat limited. Thus, Lauria feels he can double and bid clubs voluntarily without seriously overstating his values. With Soloway bidding two suits, Versace, who has enough for game, bids the suit he has stopped. Hamman doubles to show one of the top honors and Lauria, with help in spades and a certain diamond stopper, is not unhappy to bid 3NT.

If Soloway leads a spade, Lauria can make his contract by playing the ♠K from dummy and playing hearts appropriately, basing his play in the suit on whether Hamman unblocks the ♠Q at Trick 1. But Soloway, despite Hamman's double of 3♠, does not lead a spade; he leads the ◇K, asking for an attitude signal. Although everyone follows low, Soloway (whose lead might have been from either the ace-king or king-queen) has seen Hamman pass 2◇, so he continues with the ◇10. Soloway has no trouble discarding on the run of the clubs, parting with four spades, so Lauria can't avoid defeat. He tries a spade, and Soloway cashes out for one down, -50.

West	North	East	South
Duboin	*Rodwell*	*Bocchi*	*Meckstroth*
		1♠	pass
pass	2♣	2◇	3♣
all pass			

Rodwell could have protected with an in-range 1NT, but lacking a true spade stopper, prefers to bid his good five-card suit. He is surely tempted to bid over Meckstroth's competitive raise, and certainly would do so with a sixth club, but not vulnerable, he takes the conservative course.

Against 3♣, Bocchi leads the ◇Q, Rusinow, Duboin encouraging with the seven (odd cards encourage). Rodwell wins and plays ace-jack of trumps, East discarding a spade. He continues with the ♡Q, covered, wins the ace and draws the remaining trumps, Bocchi discarding two diamonds, which is not the best defense. When Rodwell continues with a second heart, Duboin takes his jack and plays a diamond. Rodwell ruffs the third diamond and leads a spade, and as Bocchi is out of diamonds, loses only to the ♠A for +130.

If Bocchi were to keep all his diamonds, discarding a heart and two spades, Rodwell would have to play a spade immediately to get home. Bocchi could not take the ace with profit and, after winning with the ♠K in dummy (Duboin unblocking), Rodwell would knock out the ♡J for nine tricks. It would be much easier for Rodwell if he had led a *low* heart first, rather than the queen.

The Americans, who have been outscored 1-53 since the late stages of Segment 7, record a modest but welcome 5-IMP gain, taking some of the steam (well, not *much*) out of the VuGraph crowd. USA by 11, 277-266.

Board 119. Both Vul.

```
              ♠ 5 4 2
              ♡ A Q 8 7 4
              ◇ 5 2
              ♣ 9 7 4
♠ A 6 3                      ♠ Q J 10 8
♡ J 6 5          N           ♡ K 9 3 2
◇ K Q J 3    W     E         ◇ A 10 6 4
♣ K 5 2          S           ♣ 8
              ♠ K 9 7
              ♡ 10
              ◇ 9 8 7
              ♣ A Q J 10 6 3
```

Closed Room

West	North	East	South
Duboin	Rodwell	Bocchi	Meckstroth
			2♣[1]
pass	2♡[2]	pass	3♣
pass	pass	dbl	pass
3NT	all pass		

1. 6+ clubs, limited.
2. Nonforcing.

It takes Bocchi-Duboin a while to get into the auction, but when they do, they reach game, Duboin gambling that there will be nine fast tricks after the opponents knock out his club stopper. And right he is. Rodwell leads the ♣4, which goes to the eight, ten and king. Duboin plays three rounds of diamonds ending in dummy, Rodwell discarding the ♡4, and passes the ♠Q, both following low. Meckstroth does not cover the ♠J and when his nine comes up, with the king to follow, Duboin claims nine tricks: +600. If Meckstroth covers the second spade, Duboin could conceivably go wrong by finessing the eight on the way back, as Rodwell has given false count in spades to suggest an even number, surely with this position in mind. As Duboin has not yet seen the ♣3, it is possible that Rodwell has four-three doubleton and Meckstroth has been dealt 2=1=3=7. However, Meckstroth must consider the possibility that the closed hand is 2=3=4=4 in keeping with Rodwell's count card, in which case declarer needs to have him cover the second spade as his only chance to make his contract. A fascinating position!

Open Room

West	North	East	South
Hamman	Lauria	Soloway	Versace
			1♣[1]
dbl	1♡[2]	2♣*	dbl
2◊	3♣	3♠	pass
4♠	all pass		

1. 2+ clubs.
2. 5+ hearts, non-forcing.

That is a superb result for Italy, but Soloway saves the board for USA by introducing his chunky spades over 3♣. As that is forcing (3◊ would not have been), Hamman has to choose between 4♠ and 3NT. Believing that his 2◊ denied four spades and concerned that one club stopper might not be enough, Hamman raises to 4♠. Versace leads the ♡10: jack, ace, deuce. Lauria continues with the ♡Q and Versace ruffs away the king to switch to the ◊9. Soloway wins in hand, draws trumps without difficulty, and has time to lead his club towards the king to build a discard for his fourth heart, +620. 1 IMP to USA, ahead by 12, 278-266.

Board 120. Neither Vul.

```
                      ♠ K 7 4
                      ♡ J 8 7 4
                      ◇ A J 9 6 5
                      ♣ Q
        ♠ 10 5                        ♠ A 6
        ♡ A 9 6         N             ♡ K Q 3 2
        ◇ 10 7       W     E          ◇ Q 3 2
        ♣ A J 9 7 3 2     S           ♣ K 10 6 5
                      ♠ Q J 9 8 3 2
                      ♡ 10 5
                      ◇ K 8 4
                      ♣ 8 4
```

Closed Room

West	North	East	South
Duboin	Rodwell	Bocchi	Meckstroth
pass	1◇[1]	pass	1♠
2♣	dbl[2]	rdbl	2♠
dbl[3]	pass	3NT	all pass

1. 2+ diamonds, 10-15.
2. Three-card spade support.
3. Maximum values for a passed-hand overcall.

After a thin opening bid by Rodwell, Meckstroth would love to bid 3♠ to jam the auction once he learns he is facing three-card support, but that would be invitational. Duboin's 'extras' (in the context of his initial pass) double of 2♠ is just what Bocchi needs to see to bid 3NT with some confidence. Meckstroth leads the ♠J (Rusinow) and Bocchi takes the ace immediately to lead a low club, catering to South showing out on the first round, but if anyone is void in clubs, can it be Meckstroth, who is known to hold queen-jack sixth of spades, yet settled for a gentle 2♠? All is well for Bocchi, however, and Rodwell holds on to his hearts to limit declarer to his ten top tricks, +430.

	West	North	East	South
	Hamman	*Lauria*	*Soloway*	*Versace*
	pass	pass	1NT	2◊¹
	3NT	4♡²	dbl	4♠
	pass	pass	dbl	all pass

1. 6+ hearts or 6+ spades.
2. Pass or correct.

Lauria has no idea whether 3NT is cold or going three down, but it seems to him that the safe action is to bid game and worry about it later. As Soloway has a minimum with no known source of tricks and the auction is forcing for his side, he doubles both 4♡ and 4♠, albeit with different degrees of confidence.

Hamman leads the ♠5, which looks like a good idea when dummy appears as long as Soloway has diamonds locked up. Soloway wins the ♠A and must decide whether to try to cash out or to cut down potential club ruffs, the latter strategy requiring that Hamman hold a balanced hand with four decent diamonds. When Soloway decides to play a second trump, Versace has a chance for a make if he can pick up diamonds without loss. Lacking the ◊Q, Soloway would surely try to take his tricks before they disappeared on the threatening diamond suit, and at the commentators' table we are speculating on how long (in small units of 30 seconds) it would take Versace to call for the ◊J. In practice it takes him about five minutes, but when he finishes his deliberations, he does not disappoint the audience. Soloway does not cover the jack, of course, and a moment later, Versace is claiming an overtrick for +690.

That is 15 IMPs to Italy for the double game swing, and the match has a new leader; Italy by 3, 281-278.

Had Soloway switched to hearts at Trick 2 to defeat the contract, he would have saved 7 IMPs and the Americans would have retained a fragile 4-IMP lead with eight deals remaining in the match. Italy has outscored USA 38-7 over the first eight boards of the session to reclaim the long-lost lead.

Of course, it is pure pandemonium now in the VuGraph auditorium.

Board 121. E-W Vul.

```
                ♠ Q 8
                ♡ A K 8 7
                ◇ Q 9 6
                ♣ Q J 7 5
   ♠ A K 6 5 4 3 2              ♠ 10 9 7
   ♡ Q 9 5          N           ♡ 10 6 4 3
   ◇ 4          W     E         ◇ A 10 2
   ♣ A 8            S           ♣ 10 6 4
                ♠ J
                ♡ J 2
                ◇ K J 8 7 5 3
                ♣ K 9 3 2
```

Open Room

West	North	East	South
Hamman	Lauria	Soloway	Versace
	1♣¹	pass	1◇
2♠²	pass	pass	3♣
pass	pass	3♠	dbl
pass	5♣	all pass	

1. 2+ clubs.
2. Intermediate.

Although East-West can make 4♠ whether the defense leads a club or takes a heart ruff, they can't logically get there unless West takes a hopeful stab at it.

Soloway isn't worth more than a competitive raise of Hamman's intermediate jump overcall. When Versace shows a maximum for his previous bidding by doubling 3♠, Lauria plays him for a slightly better hand and takes a somewhat undisciplined shot at game. Although the inconsistency of the auction suggests that someone should double 5♣, neither Hamman nor Soloway can really do so based on their own cards or a reasonable estimate of their combined defensive strength.

Soloway leads the ♠10 to the jack and king and Hamman switches to the ♡5 rather than his singleton diamond, hoping he'll have time to negotiate his diamond ruff later. Lauria, playing with the house's money, as 5♣ has no play while East-West seem likely to make at least 3♠, wins the ♡A and leads the ◇6 himself, a technical play (get the side suit going in a fragile eight-card fit) that happens to have a subtle tactical angle, as well. This is not an easy position for Soloway, but he gets it right, going in with the ◇A and continuing diamonds when Hamman follows with the four. The diamond ruff is the defenders' third trick and the trump ace the fourth, -100.

West	North	East	South
Duboin	Rodwell	Bocchi	Meckstroth
	1◊[1]	pass	3◊[2]
3♠	all pass		

1. 2+ diamonds, 10-15.
2. Preemptive.

It is straightforward for the Americans to sell out to 3♠ here. After three rounds of hearts, Meckstroth ruffing the third, Duboin shows his cards, his club loser going on the ♡10, +170. Italy gains 2 IMPs and leads by 5, 283-278.

Board 123. Neither Vul.

```
              ♠ A97
              ♡ 98
              ◊ K743
              ♣ K1097
♠ 63                          ♠ KQJ842
♡ J1054          N            ♡ 76
◊ A62        W       E        ◊ J8
♣ QJ86           S            ♣ A52
              ♠ 105
              ♡ AKQ32
              ◊ Q1095
              ♣ 43
```

	West	North	East	South
Open Room	Hamman	Lauria	Soloway	Versace
Closed Room	Duboin	Rodwell	Bocchi	Meckstroth
				1♡
	pass	1NT	2♠	pass
	pass	dbl[1]	pass	3◊
	all pass			

1. Cooperative takeout.

Identical auctions lead to South declaring the touch-and-go 3◊ at both tables.

Versace ducks the lead of the ♠6 to the jack and takes East's continuation of the ♠Q with dummy's ace to start trumps. Versace leads low to his queen, reasonably enough. When Hamman follows low the trump position is not clear to Versace, who elects to start hearts from the top, discarding dummy's last spade on the third round. Soloway ruffs the ♡Q with the ◊J and leads a spade. As Soloway would cash the ◊A if he had it, and both the auction and his suit-preference ♠Q at Trick 2 suggest something useful in clubs, Versace's best chance seems to be to discard a club, take the ruff in dummy, and lead the ♣K. East will win and continue clubs — better than offering a ruff-and-discard — but declarer ruffs, ruffs a heart, ruffs a club, and leads the good heart, restricting West to one trump trick with the ace-six. Instead, however, Versace ruffs in hand, ruffs a heart with the ◊K and leads a trump to the nine and ace. Hamman exits with his remaining trump and Versace wins, cashes the long heart, and leads a club, losing the last two tricks for one down: -50. It does not help for Hamman to switch to the ♣Q when he wins the ◊A because both declarer and dummy have a high trump to handle another ruff and discard.

Meckstroth also ducks the lead of the ♠6 to the jack and takes East's continuation of the ♠Q with dummy's ace to start trumps, but when he puts in the ten, he is in very good shape. Duboin ducks, but wins the trump continuation with the ace to play a third round. Meckstroth ruffs the hearts good, ruffs a spade, cashes the long heart, and leads a club, losing the last two tricks, but making his contract: +110. USA gains 4 IMPs and now trails by just a single IMP, 282-283. There are five deals left to play.

Board 124. N-S Vul.

```
              ♠ J 10 9 4 2
              ♡ 6 5 3
              ◊ A Q J 8
              ♣ 5
    ♠ A 7 3              ♠ K 8 5
    ♡ 2          N       ♡ Q 10 9 8 7
    ◊ 7 4 2   W     E    ◊ K 10 9
    ♣ A K Q J 10 7  S    ♣ 8 2
              ♠ Q 6
              ♡ A K J 4
              ◊ 6 5 3
              ♣ 9 6 4 3
```

Open Room

West	North	East	South
Hamman	Lauria	Soloway	Versace
2♣[1]	2♠	3♣	dbl[2]
3♠	pass	3NT	dbl
4♣	all pass		

1. 6+ clubs, limited.
2. Cards.

The West hand is a slightly awkward one for most strong club systems, as it's technically not quite strong enough for 1♣, yet strong enough to fear that East might pass a 2♣ opening with no support and the right bits and pieces to make 3NT. Hamman settles for 2♣, which would keep most mere mortals out of the bidding, but Lauria, sensing that he has the wind at his back and expecting his team to be in the lead or at least close behind now, is not to be deterred from introducing the highest-ranking suit. Soloway, hoping to push his opponents a level higher, settles for a gentle raise rather than compete with an under-strength negative double. It comes as no surprise to him that Versace has enough to compete, but Hamman's 3♠ (solid clubs and extras) is an unexpected piece of good news. Although 3NT is an easy continuation for Soloway, he expects to be doubled much of the time. As Soloway seems to have a spade card but has not made a negative double, Hamman fears that hearts are the basis for Versace's penalty double, so after some soul-searching, he elects to remove himself to 4♣, which ends the unusual auction.

Lauria leads the ♠J (five, six, ace). Hamman draws four rounds of trumps, discarding a heart and a spade from dummy (♠2, ♠4, ♡3 from Lauria), and leads a heart to the ten and jack. Versace knocks out the ♠K, and Hamman calls for the ♡Q. Versace follows low in tempo, playing Hamman for 2=1=4=6 (Lauria's spade discards have indicated an even number of cards in that suit) with queen-fourth of diamonds, in which case one discard will do him no good, while placing the high cards might help him. But that is not the position, and Hamman discards his spade loser. With the ◇A onside, he loses two diamonds for +130.

Although both Hamman and Versace surely have reason to regret their actions on this deal, the closed-circuit TV cameras do a great job of catching their reactions, and both of them look completely deadpan, maintaining their composure and doing their best to fight through the pressure and fatigue.

Closed Room

West	North	East	South
Duboin	Rodwell	Bocchi	Meckstroth
1♣[1]	1♠	dbl*	rdbl[2]
3♣	pass	3NT	all pass

1. Natural, or 15-17 balanced.
2. Two-card spade support, cards.

Bocchi-Duboin conduct a standard sequence to their best money contract, North-South offering roughly as much interference as you might expect. Meckstroth leads the ♡A, looking for a standard attitude signal, notes Rodwell's three, and stays off spades again as Bocchi figures to have the king for his bidding and might have the jack too. The ◇6 finds Rodwell's best suit, but establishes Bocchi's ninth trick, shortening the play, +400. Italy gains 7 IMPs, and with four deals remaining, leads by 8, 290-282.

Board 125. Both Vul.

```
                    ♠ 7
                    ♡ Q J 9 6
                    ◇ A 4 3
                    ♣ Q 9 8 6 2
        ♠ K 9 8 3 2                 ♠ A J 6 5
        ♡ 8 7            N          ♡ A 10 4
        ◇ Q 8 5      W     E        ◇ J 7 6 2
        ♣ K 7 5          S          ♣ J 4
                    ♠ Q 10 4
                    ♡ K 5 3 2
                    ◇ K 10 9
                    ♣ A 10 3
```

Open Room

West	North	East	South
Hamman	Lauria	Soloway	Versace
	pass	pass	1♣[1]
pass	1♡	pass	2♡
pass	3♣	pass	3♡
all pass			

1. 2+ clubs.

Closed Room

West	North	East	South
Duboin	Rodwell	Bocchi	Meckstroth
	pass	pass	1◇[1]
pass	1♡	pass	2♡
pass	3♣	pass	3♡
all pass			

1. 2+ diamonds, 10-15.

When both Easts decline the opportunity to open in second position, perhaps only because they are vulnerable, North-South have the auction to themselves. Both North players choose the same 3♣ trial bid, but South, who would normally have four-card support for his raise, can't find a sound reason to bid game.

Soloway leads a low diamond to the nine, queen and ace. Lauria plays the ♡J, which holds, and tries a club to the ten and king. Hamman returns a diamond, so Lauria can revert to trumps and loses only the ♡A and a spade for +170.

After the same low-diamond opening lead, Rodwell leads a spade at Trick 2, Bocchi going in with the ace to continue diamonds. Rodwell puts in the ten and leads the ♠10, ruffing when Duboin follows low. He continues with the ♡J, which holds, crosses to the ◊K, ruffs the ♠Q with the ♡9, and leads the ♡Q to Bocchi's ace. As declarer is out of trumps, Bocchi can force dummy with a diamond or a spade, leaving Duboin with a winner to cash when he comes in with the ♣K after the last trump is drawn (or allowing Bocchi to take a trick with his remaining trump if declarer leaves it at large). Apparently losing his concentration for a moment, Bocchi exits instead with his remaining trump. Rodwell wins the ♡K, and with a trump still in dummy, has time to build a second club trick. He plays ace and another, and although Duboin plays low, Rodwell plays the queen; he knows where the king is, as Bocchi has not opened the bidding and has shown two aces and the ◊J already. That is +170 and no swing, but Bocchi has missed one of those 1-IMP 'slopped trick' opportunities to which I alluded earlier. How often would that trick matter?

It is still Italy by 8 IMPs, 290-282, still anyone's match. It is difficult to breathe in the jammed VuGraph theater, and with everyone talking at once there is a steady hum for the commentators to overcome.

To those watching on the Internet, the auctions on the next deal must seem like a series of mis-clicks by the data-entry technicians.

Norberto Bocchi

Board 126. Neither Vul.

```
                        ♠ Q J 10 7 5 4
                        ♡ K J 9 4
                        ◇ A K 6
                        ♣ —
   ♠ A K 9 8 3                           ♠ —
   ♡ —                  ┌─────────┐      ♡ 10 7 5 3 2
   ◇ Q 8 4             │    N    │      ◇ 9 7 3
   ♣ A K Q 10 3        │  W   E  │      ♣ 9 6 5 4 2
                        │    S    │
                        └─────────┘
                        ♠ 6 2
                        ♡ A Q 8 6
                        ◇ J 10 5 2
                        ♣ J 8 7
```

Open Room

West	North	East	South
Hamman	Lauria	Soloway	Versace
		pass	pass
1♣[1]	1♠	pass[2]	pass
2♣	dbl	5♣	dbl[3]
pass	5♡	pass	pass
6♣	dbl	all pass	

1. Strong, artificial.
2. 0-4 HCP, or spades.
3. Cooperative takeout.

The bidding through 5♣ makes perfect sense, North showing a good hand with primary spades and secondary length in the red suits. Versace doesn't have much, but what he has looks good, and he competes with an aggressive high-level responsive-style double. The manual on overcaller's five-level continuations in this family of auctions has not yet been written, and here Lauria offers his opinion on the subject by taking out to 5♡.

Hamman and Soloway's agreement is that forcing passes do not apply unless there is a clear balance of power *and* the opponents are not bidding to make, so when Soloway passes 5♡ he does not expect Hamman to bid again unless he has a compelling reason to do so; he does not expect 5♡ to be hurt badly, if at all. As it happens, 5♡ doubled would go two down on either of Soloway's normal leads — a club or a trump - so doubling would increase the penalty from 100 to 300. Hamman's unexpected 6♣ is an 'insurance' wager that one or both sides can take eleven or twelve tricks, perhaps with an unfortunate opening lead. His upside play — buying a diamond honor and strong intermediate trump spots — is a long shot, as with such a hand Soloway would have redoubled 2♣ or cuebid 2♠ before jumping to 5♣.

Lauria doubles 6♣ and leads the ◊A, getting a count card from Versace. He continues with king and another diamond, and with trumps 3-0, Hamman can't get the third spade ruff in dummy that he needs to take the rest. Versace gets his overruff, so Hamman is two down, -300.

Soloway would be widely criticized for not doubling 5♡ with five trumps headed by the ten, facing a strong club opener, but with no picture cards in hearts (where he might have had several trump tricks) or anywhere else, a non-forcing pass seemed to be more accurate. Those who feel that by not doubling he steered Hamman toward bidding 6♣ would do well to appreciate that this was surely a partnership matter.

This result brings great joy to the Italian fans, but there is even better news to come for them.

Closed Room

West	North	East	South
Duboin	Rodwell	Bocchi	Meckstroth
		pass	pass
1♠	pass	pass	dbl
rdbl	2♠*	pass	3◊
4♣	4♡	5♣	pass
pass	5◊	pass	pass
dbl	all pass		

Meckstroth would surely be forgiven for passing out 1♠, but he goes for the throat by reopening with a takeout double. If Duboin passes, Rodwell will have a choice of apparently-positive strategies, as 1♠ figures to be down several tricks while 4♡ rates to be a good contract; indeed, 6♡ is not out of the question, even facing a passed hand. When Duboin redoubles to show a strong hand, Rodwell considers two down in 1♠ redoubled very unlikely, so he decides to look for a higher-scoring contract of his own. Meckstroth doesn't know whether his side can beat 7♣, so is not about to double 5♣ out of spite. As Rodwell's 5◊ is an offer to play, Meckstroth expects at least four of those. Perhaps with the idea of discarding a spade from hand on North's putative fifth heart to make 5◊, Meckstroth passes, then passes again when doubled.

While 5◊ doubled is no picnic, it isn't so terrible either. Meckstroth ruffs the lead of the ♣K in dummy, cashes the ace-king of trumps, and leads a heart to the ace. Duboin ruffs with the ◊Q, and cashes two clubs and two spades, but that is all for the defense as Meckstroth can draw the last trump when he gains the lead. Three down, -500, and 13 IMPs to Italy, ahead now by 21, 303-282.

I find it interesting to read later that Paul Marston, a very aggressive bidder himself, writing in *Australian Bridge*, summarizes the events at this table by saying that 'Rodwell plainly bid too much'. It's his perception that Meckstroth had nothing to do with any of this. Who knows? Maybe he's right. Again, that too is a partnership matter, and much depends on whether doubling 1♠ is an acceptable action for South.

There is dancing in the streets of several Italian cities, at least figuratively, and it is impossible to ignore the outbreak of Italian song shaking the Vu-Graph theater. While it is mathematically possible for the Americans to pull out the match, anyone in the room would have given you 300 to 1 if you were inclined to wager a meaningful unit.

Well, sure. But there are still two boards to play...

Board 127. N-S Vul.

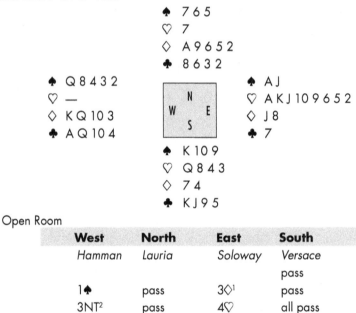

Open Room

West	North	East	South
Hamman	Lauria	Soloway	Versace
			pass
1♠	pass	3◇¹	pass
3NT²	pass	4♡	all pass

1. Strong jump shift in hearts.
2. No heart fit, negative opinion about slam.

East has a huge hand opposite an opening bid, even a light, non-vulnerable opening bid, but can he underwrite security at the five-level to convey his power? Soloway does not think so, and indeed here, where Hamman has a full opening bid with a couple of kicking tens, 4♡ is high enough.

Versace leads the ◇7. Lauria wins the ace (eight from declarer) and switches immaculately to the ♠6. Soloway, trying to play as safely as possible, wins the ace, cashes ace-king of trumps, and faces another decision. If he drives out the ♡Q, he will go down only if Versace can cross to Lauria's onside ♠K to get a diamond ruff. If, instead, he plays a second diamond, he will go down if Versace can ruff, regardless of who holds the ♠K. Although Soloway, like Hamman, is very good at 'parking' his bad results to focus on the board he's playing, he knows just how bad their session has been, and realistically can't be thinking that the match might be decided by the potential lost overtrick if he were to drive out the trump queen. He decides to lead a second diamond. When Versace follows, Soloway overtakes the jack to play another diamond to discard the ♠J. Versace ruffs with the ♡8, and the ♡Q is the third trick for the defense. Soloway's judgment to stop at 4♡ is vindicated and the Americans finally have something positive to show for the session.

Closed Room

West	North	East	South
Duboin	Rodwell	Bocchi	Meckstroth
			pass
1♠	pass	2◇[1]	pass
2♡[2]	pass	2♠[3]	pass
3♣[4]	pass	3◇[5]	pass
3NT[6]	pass	5♡[7]	all pass

1. 5+ hearts, game force unless responder's rebid is 3♡.
2. 4+ clubs.
3-5. Artificial game force, relay.
4. Specifically five spades and four clubs.
6. 5=1=3=4 or 5=0=4=4.
7. Too strong to settle for 4♡.

Bocchi has at least as much information as Soloway, but can't bring himself to sign off in 4♡ with a hand worth nearly nine tricks. As the distributional information is not crucial, Bocchi would probably do better to describe a strong hand with hearts and start a dialogue.

Duboin, declaring 5♡ from the short side, receives the lead of the ◇A from Rodwell: eight, seven, three. A second diamond goes to dummy's jack, and Duboin plays three rounds of trumps. Meckstroth wins the queen and must play a club now to give Duboin a problem, and he duly switches to the ♣5. The only winning play for Duboin on the lie of the cards is to finesse the ♣Q. However, with two other options in the spade finesse or a third diamond, he elects to play the ♣A and take the spade finesse for the contract, losing to Meckstroth's king for one down: -50. Certainly, it is unlucky to fail in 5♡, but if slam figures to be marginal at best based on the early auction, the odds favor stopping at the four-level.

When the 10-IMP gain to USA appears on the VuGraph screen, the boisterous crowd settles down a bit. The atmosphere, which had been celebratory ten minutes earlier, is suddenly extremely tense. The margin is down to 11 IMPs, Italy leading 303-292.

After all the long runs, significant leads, and dramatic changes of fortune, some brilliant moments and too many of the other kind, the 2003 Bermuda Bowl has come down to the last deal, with the match still in doubt. With Italy 11 IMPs ahead and only East-West vulnerable, the Americans require a miracle of sorts. They need to make a non-vulnerable game in one room and collect a non-vulnerable two-trick set or a doubled one-trick set in the other to tie, or gain a full vulnerable game swing to win. Or perhaps some unlikely combination of pluses in both rooms...

Board 128. E-W Vul.

```
                  ♠ 2
                  ♡ A J 9 3
                  ◇ K Q 10 9 8 6 5
                  ♣ 5
  ♠ J 10                           ♠ A 6 5 4 3
  ♡ 5 4 2              N           ♡ K Q 10 8 6
  ◇ A 7          W         E       ◇ 4 2
  ♣ K 10 7 6 4 2      S           ♣ A
                  ♠ K Q 9 8 7
                  ♡ 7
                  ◇ J 3
                  ♣ Q J 9 8 3
```

Closed Room

West	North	East	South
Duboin	Rodwell	Bocchi	Meckstroth
pass	1◇[1]	2◇[2]	pass
2♡	3◇	pass	pass
3♡	pass	4♡	all pass

1. 2+ diamonds, 10-15.

2. Hearts and spades.

The Closed Room result flashes up on the side screen first. It is a poor one for Italy, and the groan from the partisan audience speaks volumes. Duboin, with a fair hand opposite a two-suited overcall at unfavorable vulnerability, does not think he can be hurt by competing to the three-level, but Bocchi, not a negative thinker, is not going to hang a trick short of a vulnerable game on the last deal of the World Championship if it is going to have any practical chance of success. That this in effect meant his partnership can virtually never stop in 3♡ after stopping in 2♡ does not concern Bocchi unduly, and he is lucky that Meckstroth doesn't double on the strength of his black-suit holdings and the sound of the auction. We can imagine Bocchi thinking, 'How terrible can 4♡ be, after all?' The short answer to that hypothetical question is, 'Very'.

Rodwell leads the ◇Q, knocking out Duboin's ace while the clubs are blocked. Duboin leads a trump to the king, cashes the ♣A, and tries a low spade from dummy. Meckstroth wins the queen and leads over to the ◇K. Rodwell returns the ♡9 and Duboin rises with the queen, gets the disappointing news, and tries to cash the ♣A. Rodwell ruffs with the jack, cashes the trump ace, and exits with a diamond. Duboin can take only dummy's remaining trumps, and loses all those low spades to Meckstroth for four down, -400.

Open Room

West	North	East	South
Hamman	Lauria	Soloway	Versace
pass	1◇	2◇[1]	dbl[2]
2♡	3◇	pass	pass
3♡	5◇	dbl	all pass

1. Hearts and spades.
2. Cards.

Now everything has changed. All the Americans need to tie is +100 from Hamman and Soloway, +200 or more to win. But how can they achieve *any* plus score with the East-West cards? North-South are not vulnerable and are unlikely to get higher than 3◇, and if East-West compete to 3♡, the terrible breaks will be very difficult to overcome.

Sure enough, Lauria-Versace come to rest at 3◇, which no one can double, and only two early rounds of trumps would beat it (East will get endplayed to allow declarer a second heart trick for just one down). So the Americans cannot win, and are unlikely to tie by passing out 3◇. Hamman, like Duboin, protects with 3♡, which is what he needs to do to give his team a chance to survive. As it happens, even a refreshed Bob Hamman at his best could not make 3♡, so to ensure that Italy wins its first Bermuda Bowl in 28 years, all that is required from Lauria is to pass.

But he doesn't know that, of course, although his heart holding and Versace's double of 2◇ (which suggests defensive values) point to passing as the easiest way to go plus. If Lauria were thinking only about passing 3♡ or competing to 4◇, perhaps the evidence would have been enough to convince him to defend, but Lauria has bigger things in mind. As he knows Versace is short in hearts, he thinks there is an excellent chance to buy a dummy with three trumps and a black ace, and perhaps even something else of value. As Lauria expects to have a good chance to make 5◇ facing that sort of hand, he backs his judgment and bids it. This would be a remarkable action at any time, but it is quite astounding on the last deal of a match that he has every reason to think his team is winning. It's ironic, bordering on the incredible, that *both* Lauria and Bocchi decide to bid game after their side had stopped in a partscore.

When Soloway doubles 5◇, all the cavalier bettors, who had given hundreds to one to all takers a quarter of an hour earlier, begin to slink towards the exits. Soloway leads the ♣A and Hamman contributes the seven, hoping Soloway will read this as a neutral card and stay away from a costly switch to either major. Two rounds of trumps now would lead to -300 or -500 and an 'easy' American victory, but Soloway is giving his next play plenty of thought.

Versace gets up and leaves the table. Then he leaves the room, apparently anxious to find his teammates to compare scores. That leaves Lauria to play both his own cards and dummy's, which pleases none of the remaining players at the table.

Eventually, Soloway switches to the ♡Q: seven, deuce (attitude), ace. Lauria continues with the ♡J, ruffing Soloway's king in dummy (four from West), hoping another ruff will bring down the tripleton ten from Hamman's hand. He ruffs a club with the ◇8, ruffs the ♡3 with the ◇J, showing his disappointment on camera and to his screenmate (Soloway) when Hamman follows with the five. At this point Lauria is 'sure' to go two down, and the Italian supporters have been reduced to a near-catatonic state of disbelief. Lauria reaches over to dummy and extracts the ♠K: jack, deuce, ace.

Everyone 'knows' that Soloway will cash the ♡10 now, and that the ace of trumps will provide the second undertrick for -300... but Soloway has not made the apparently-obvious play yet. He has been watching the cards carefully, of course, and Hamman's innocuous four-five of hearts, according to the partnership's remainder-count agreements, indicated an original holding of four cards. If Hamman's carding is to be believed (and we've seen throughout the match a tendency towards accurate count by both partners), Lauria is out of hearts, and it can't hurt to play a spade; Hamman might be ruffing it, and if he can't, declarer would be 1=3=8=1. But would Lauria have bid this way with the same high cards and 2=3=7=1? And would Hamman have bid this way *and* played the ♣7 at Trick 1 with 1=4=2=6? That doesn't add up, but Soloway is tired and perhaps put off by Lauria reaching across the table to play dummy's cards, and so he goes with Hamman's carding in hearts and plays a spade. Suddenly, the Italian supporters who had not given up have something totally unexpected to cheer about. Lauria can discard his heart loser on the ♠Q and get out for -100. The match will be tied, and the teams will have to play another eight boards!

But that is not what happens.

Lauria, either because he is expecting Soloway to cash the ♡10, or because he simply doesn't see what Soloway has played, reaches out and detaches the seven of spades as his *discard* from dummy. We know this to be true because we see it on the Bridge Vision screen and because Babette Piganeau, the card caller in the Open Room, names that card on the microphone for everyone to hear. Hamman follows suit, and only then does Lauria realize what has happened. He tries to replace the ♠7 with the king, but this is clearly a situation that requires the Tournament Director.

Lorenzo Lauria

After satisfying herself that the facts are not at issue, she rules that the ♠7 is a played card, as declarer had detached it with the intent of playing it. It is an unfortunate mental error, but an error nonetheless, and the ruling is a clear decision on a point of law. That means Lauria loses the ♡3 after all, and so is down 300.

USA, 28 IMPs ahead to start the final session, but 21 behind with two boards to play, gains 12 IMPs on this final deal to win the Bermuda Bowl by a single IMP, 304-303. It is a miracle finish to a magical match. Italy has gallantly come back to win the final segment by 27 IMPs, 60-33, only to fall cruelly inches short of victory.

But it is not over. Italy appeals. The Appeals Committee has been standing by and convenes immediately. Its deliberations do not drag on. After about twenty minutes, the decision is announced: the table result would stand. That makes it official.

The unlikely parlay on the last deal should not detract from the American victory, but it is impossible not to have sympathy for Lauria, whose loss of focus was not caused by fatigue or bridge error, but by the distraction created by having to reach across the table to play dummy's cards. He had played particularly well in the final stanza when his team needed an inspired performance. At the same time, although Lauria could have insisted that his partner remain at the table or asked the Director to handle dummy's cards, Versace really should not have left the table at such a crucial moment, with the match very possibly on the line.

It is sad that such a fiercely contested match had to end on such a bizarre note and inevitable that there would be accusations of unsportsmanlike conduct. The Americans had no choice but to call the director; it would have been an infraction for them not to do so. It was out of the players' hands entirely, as indeed it should have been. The Director could not have allowed a played card to be changed in this situation, and it was impossible to avoid involving the Director, as the entire episode was plainly visible on Bridge Vision. On the other side of the coin, Versace did not have to leave the table, Lauria did not have to attempt to amend his play, and Italy did not have to appeal a Director's ruling that was a matter of Law. The bottom line is that it was simply a terribly unfortunate incident, and that the consequences could not be avoided.

Perhaps we should not end this account with another 'what might have been' scenario. However, it would be remiss to overlook the matter of Board 55, where Versace's revoke cost Italy only 1 IMP instead of the 2 IMPs that would have been awarded to USA had the Director apprised himself of all the facts over the Americans' attempt to have *any* penalty waived. Had the match ended in a tie, that incident would undoubtedly have surfaced again. We can be thankful that it didn't come to that.

As Jean-Paul Meyer would remark in *Le Bridgeur*, 'I have been a witness over too many years to the most important international and European matches, but I will never forget the three hours of the final session in Monte Carlo.'

Epilogue

Italy won the 128-board final by 12 IMPs, but lost the match by 1 IMP, thanks to the 'carryunder' of 13 IMPs from their last-round encounter with USA in the round robin. If my reading of *Bridge d'Italia* and some articles posted on Italian web sites is not completely out to lunch, the general feeling emanating from those sources is that the world would be better off if there were no carryover. Italy had already clinched first place and USA 1 second when that round robin match was contested, and perhaps the Italian intensity was not at its highest level at the time. However, the Conditions of Contest were no surprise, and the importance of head-on matches against potential qualifiers for the Knockout phase was evident *a priori* to everyone concerned. As it's ideal to have the Conditions underscore that it's in each team's interest to play its best bridge until the end, there is a strong case to maintain the status quo.

SWINGS

The Americans won fifteen swings of at least 10 IMPs; the Italians had only thirteen, but theirs included the three biggest swings of the match (16, 14 and 15 IMPs).

When a single IMP decides a match, it's natural to look at those tiny swings with added respect. The Americans gained 1 IMP on nine different deals, Italy on only three. There were several 1-IMP opportunities that didn't show up on the scoresheet, however, like the slopped overtrick on Board 125 that appears as a push. There was one *visible* IMP given up on a revoke on Board 55 and another that did not officially appear due to an uncorrected Director's error. Many, if not most, of these very small swings were induced by fatigue, pressure, or both. That's the nature of the final, and this trend is likely to continue while the major events require two weeks of play, although the playing schedule was not as taxing in 2003 (with many 48-board days) as it had been in the past.

Each team gained at least 1 IMP on 46 deals, leaving 36 pushes.

Although superior methods, outstanding play and fine judgment accounted for some of those 92 swings, far more were a function of error, breach of discipline or a variety of random factors. That too, is typical of long matches late in a long event.

2. 2004 Dead Men Walking

In the annals of bridge there is nothing more thrilling than a comeback where the trailing team overturns a huge deficit. It doesn't happen very often, since many teams, faced with a mountain of IMPs to climb, adopt a very aggressive strategy that includes psychic bids, undisciplined preempts, speculative penalty doubles and so-called 'tactical' openings and overcalls. While these wild actions often generate swings, at least some of those go to the team enjoying the big lead. Of course no one ever won a match by conceding, but big comebacks require a lively set of deals that offer some opportunities — for sensible swing actions, for the momentum to turn, and for the trailing team to outplay its opponent.

In the semifinal of the 2004 Spingold in New York, NICKELL (Nick Nickell-Dick Freeman, Jeff Meckstroth-Eric Rodwell, Bob Hamman-Paul Soloway) found themselves trailing by 71 IMPs against JACOBS (George Jacobs-Ralph Katz, Steve Garner-Howard Weinstein, Lorenzo Lauria-Alfredo Versace) with one 16-deal segment left to play. If that weren't bad enough for NICKELL, there was also a pending JACOBS appeal that might substantially increase that deficit.

George Jacobs, who made his fortune in the limousine business in Chicago, was the first American sponsor to build his teams for the North American Championships around the strongest Italian pairs, and his teams had won three majors since 1999. In this Spingold semifinal, NICKELL waived its seeding rights, so JACOBS chose to sit their pairs second in the first quarter. When NICKELL took quarters two and three, JACOBS was left with the fourth. Wanting to avoid having to face Meckwell — a growing objective of many pairs in that era — Jacobs and Katz seemed to have done the right thing by opting to play in the sets where they had the right to be seated after their opponents announced their positions; they could play the final set with a huge lead, and under very little pressure. Meanwhile, Lauria and Versace, who had played the first three quarters, were pleased to get some rest before the next day's final.

It's surprising to note that it's become much more common in recent years for teams with significant but theoretically not insurmountable deficits to concede defeat. Whether that is because players simply have less stamina than they used to and prefer to conserve their energy for the next event on the tournament schedule, or because they believe they are not playing well enough to muster a late challenge to opponents in good form, the effect is that a concession gives the winners an unexpected opportunity to relax and get a good night's sleep.

Not that the team with the best-ever record in the Spingold was going to wave the white flag when trailing by fewer than 100 IMPs: NICKELL's front-line pairs took their seats to deal with the grim situation. As the other semifinal was closer and there were few experienced VuGraph operators on site, this set would not be covered on BBO, although both these teams would normally attract large online audiences.

In my early days[†] as coach of the NICKELL team, most of my time was devoted to Bob and Paul, with whom I shared a week in 1998 developing and organizing an initial set of system notes for their new partnership. Since then it had been my normal *modus operandi* to take a seat on Soloway's side of the screen in the second half of matches when we were not on BBO, and this was no exception, the lopsided score notwithstanding.

Sitting on a 141-70 lead, JACOBS was hoping for a run of dull boards, and Board 49, an open-and-shut 3NT+1, filled that prescription.

The next board offered a subtle opportunity to create a swing. It's the sort of deal that is often overlooked in a comeback strategy, but rejecting a seemingly attractive 'normal' opening lead is a gambit far more likely to work than a wildly undisciplined or random bid.

Board 50. N-S Vul.

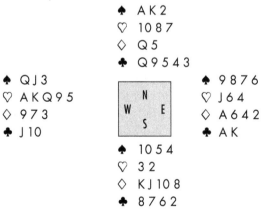

```
              ♠ A K 2
              ♡ 10 8 7
              ◇ Q 5
              ♣ Q 9 5 4 3
♠ Q J 3                        ♠ 9 8 7 6
♡ A K Q 9 5        N           ♡ J 6 4
◇ 9 7 3        W       E       ◇ A 6 4 2
♣ J 10             S           ♣ A K
              ♠ 10 5 4
              ♡ 3 2
              ◇ K J 10 8
              ♣ 8 7 6 2
```

---

† Primary author Eric Kokish.

Open Room

West	North	East	South
Rodwell	Garner	Meckstroth	Weinstein
		1◇[1]	pass
1♡	pass	1♠	pass
2♣[2]	pass	2♡	pass
4♡	all pass		

1. Precision, 2+ diamonds.
2. Fourth suit forcing.

Garner led the 'textbook' ♠K and switched accurately to the ◇Q. Rodwell ducked, won the diamond continuation, drew trumps ending in dummy, and reverted to spades, eventually discarding his losing diamond on dummy's long spade for +420.

Closed Room

West	North	East	South
Jacobs	Hamman	Katz	Soloway
		1◇	pass
1♡	pass	1♠	pass
2♣[1]	pass	2♡	pass
4♡	all pass		

1. Fourth suit forcing.

Same auction, but here East was known to have at least four diamonds. With spades bid on his left, Hamman did not want to help declarer develop tricks in dummy's suit when there was no chance of giving Soloway a third-round spade ruff, and so he led the ♣4. Jacobs won with the king, drew trumps ending in dummy (a bit hastily, as dummy was running out of entries) and led a spade to the jack and king. Hamman exited with a club, and declarer played a second spade, realizing now that he needed to find someone with a doubleton ten to make the contract legitimately. When Jacobs' ♠Q lost to the ace, Hamman switched to the ◇Q, and the contract was two down, -100; 11 IMPs to NICKELL, 81-141.

If Jacobs plays low on the second spade, finessing against the ten, he saves a spade trick but can't make the contract, as Hamman will win and shift to diamonds, removing the final (and vital) entry to dummy while spades are still blocked. If Soloway started with ace-third of spades he could defeat the contract simply by rising with the ace and leading a diamond with the same effect — the long spade cannot be cashed.

In theory, declarer's best line of play is to lead spades at Trick 2, playing for 3-3 spades and no diamond shift, or for one defender to hold the ace-king-third and a doubleton diamond (as here). We can imagine that Hamman's not leading a spade from this holding was a strong influence in dissuading declarer from adopting this line.

As the defense does not have a clear read on declarer's shape or diamond holding, perhaps there is more to gain than to lose by starting spades at Trick 2, retaining enough entries in dummy to handle 3-3 spades and enjoy the long card. It may not be clear to shift to diamonds: imagine declarer with 2=5=3=3 and jack-ten-third of diamonds, when a diamond shift from honor-third is disastrous.

Board 51. E-W Vul.

```
            ♠ Q 6
            ♡ 10 3
            ◇ A 10 7 5 4
            ♣ K 10 9 2
♠ 7                          ♠ A J 10 9 5
♡ A Q 7 5 2      N           ♡ K J 8 6 4
◇ Q J 9 2     W     E        ◇ 3
♣ 6 5 3          S           ♣ A 8
            ♠ K 8 4 3 2
            ♡ 9
            ◇ K 8 6
            ♣ Q J 7 4
```

Closed Room

West	North	East	South
Jacobs	Hamman	Katz	Soloway
			pass
pass	1◇	2◇[1]	pass
4♡	all pass		

1. Majors.

Hamman was not willing to pass in third seat at favorable vulnerability though he would be awkwardly placed over a major-suit response. East and West took normal actions and reached the par contract. North's club lead held declarer to eleven tricks, +650.

	West	North	East	South
	Rodwell	*Garner*	*Meckstroth*	*Weinstein*
				pass
	pass	pass	1♠	pass
	2♡	pass	6♡	all pass

After Garner passed, preferring to take no needless risks, the auction was of a completely different species. Rodwell stretched to respond 2♡, and Meckstroth, seeing an opportunity to perhaps steal a slam, bounced to 6♡, giving away no information. As it's so often best to lead an ace on this type of unscientific auction rather than try to build a trick, Garner duly led the ◇A, then switched to a trump (boldly choosing the potentially-valuable ten, trying to create the impression that he did not have a second trump in case declarer were to consider a ruffing finesse in spades without drawing a second trump).

Declarer, with two possible ways to avoid a club loser (one additional diamond trick or two additional spade tricks), won in hand and played a spade. Garner played the queen, a lovely card as he knew Rodwell would not play him for the king-queen if he followed low and a second-round ruff brought the queen (he'd have split his honors on the first round). Rodwell took the ace and ruffed a spade safely with the five, ruffed a diamond and had reached the critical point, with the three of trumps still at large.

Rodwell was not planning a ruffing finesse in diamonds, so to build a second trick in that suit he needed to ruff out the king on the third round, after which he could establish spades without a guess, provided North did not start with king-queen-fifth. In that scenario he could draw the second round of trumps in dummy and ruff another spade to clarify the position, then ruff a diamond to build his winner there and finish establishing spades, with his communications intact.

However, if the ◇K was *not* going to ruff out tripleton, he would require *two* more spade tricks to discard clubs from hand, and that would require his guessing whether Garner had been dealt queen doubleton or king-queen third. In the first case he could not afford to take a second ruff as he would be able to establish only one more spade winner with a late ruffing finesse.

By drawing the last trump in hand, Rodwell could delay his choice of plays in spades until he knew what was going on in diamonds, although he could not cater to both winning layouts.

When Rodwell led the ♡K from dummy, Weinstein teased him with a spade discard, trying to look like a man who had started with four low spades resigned to having declarer ruff out North's king-queen third. It was still open to Rodwell to overtake the ♡K with the ace to take his diamond ruff before deciding what to do on the third round of spades, but he elected to remain in dummy and ruffed another spade, now reduced to his diamond play. The appearance of South's king was a great relief. Now the ♠K ruffed out, and he discarded dummy's ♣8 on his high diamond for +1430. That was 13 IMPs to NICKELL, 94-141, reducing the deficit to 47.

Rodwell revealed later that he was more confident of the spade position than the diamond layout, but his line of play suggests that he had not formed that picture of the distribution until he saw the spade discard from Weinstein, who ironically had been trying to paint a rather different picture of the spade suit for declarer.

Meckstroth's gambit was more typical of the popular swing strategy, and it should go without saying that it could have lost 13 IMPs on a normal game deal. However, 6♡ might be a normal contract, in which case a more careful auction might tip off the best opening lead; now we must consider the possibility of gaining 17 when bashing the slam gains. That type of opportunity is difficult to resist when you're miles behind.

Steve Garner and Howard Weinstein

Board 52. Both Vul.

```
              ♠ 4 3
              ♡ Q 8 6 5 3
              ◇ 7 6 2
              ♣ A J 8
♠ 10 9 6 2                      ♠ J 8
♡ J 10 7 2          N           ♡ K 9
◇ Q 8 5         W       E       ◇ A K J 10 9 3
♣ Q 9               S           ♣ K 7 5
              ♠ A K Q 7 5
              ♡ A 4
              ◇ 4
              ♣ 10 6 4 3 2
```

Closed Room

West	North	East	South
Jacobs	Hamman	Katz	Soloway
pass	pass	1NT	2♣[1]
pass	2◇[2]	dbl	2♠
all pass			

1. Spades and a minor.
2. Prefers diamonds to spades if South has diamonds.

Opening 1NT in third seat with the East hand, apart from tactical obstruction, has the more subtle appeal of precluding a second-round rebid decision between two and three diamonds; indeed, 1NT would probably be a majority expert choice today. However, one of the downsides, at least in theory, is not being able to compete cooperatively in diamonds. That is what happened to Katz, despite enjoying a serendipitous opportunity to show some diamonds by doubling North's pass-or-correct 2◇. As Soloway's 2♠ did not guarantee a fifth club, Hamman passed, settling for the known 5-2 fit and expecting his strong clubs to facilitate the play. Soloway ruffed the second diamond, and led a club to the nine, jack and king. On a third round of diamonds, Soloway discarded his heart loser, maintaining control. He lost a spade, two diamonds and a club for +140.

	West	North	East	South
	Rodwell	*Garner*	*Meckstroth*	*Weinstein*
	pass	pass	1♣[1]	2♠[2]
	pass	3♣	3◇	all pass

1. Strong.
2. 5+ spades and 5+ clubs.

At this table, Meckstroth adopted a different tactical approach by opening a mildly shaded strong 1♣. North-South had the right method to locate their eight-card fit, but when Meckstroth volunteered 3◇, Weinstein, whose initial action was not defined as particularly constructive, was unwilling to bid again with only modest extra values and fair defense. Rodwell gave his partner plenty of leeway by passing 3◇, and tabled a rather spectacular dummy. When Mecktroth led a heart to the nine he held his losers to four, for +110 and a 6-IMP pickup for NICKELL, 100-141. In just four boards, 30 IMPs of the 71-IMP JACOBS lead had disappeared.

Board 53 brought a bidding challenge for North-South, whose mission was to reach an excellent 28-point 6◇ with two balanced hands:

Board 53. N-S Vul.

```
                  ♠ K Q 4
                  ♡ A 9 6
                  ◇ J 7 6 3 2
                  ♣ 10 8
     ♠ 9 5 3                    ♠ 10 8 7 6 2
     ♡ Q 10 7 3     N           ♡ K J 5 4
     ◇ 9 8      W       E       ◇ 5 4
     ♣ K J 4 2      S           ♣ Q 3
                  ♠ A J
                  ♡ 8 2
                  ◇ A K Q 10
                  ♣ A 9 7 6 5
```

Closed Room

	West	North	East	South
	Jacobs	Hamman	Katz	Soloway
		pass	pass	1♣[1]
	pass	1♠[2]	pass	2♣
	pass	2◇	pass	3◇
	pass	4◇	pass	4♠[3]
	pass	4NT[4]	pass	5◇[5]
	pass	6◇	all pass	

1. 17+.
2. 8-11 balanced.
3. Control bid denying a heart control.
4. RKCB for diamonds.
5. 1 or 4.

The 5◇ reply to Blackwood left no room to check for the ◇Q without committing to slam, but as long as South had four diamonds slam would still be worth bidding, especially for the trailing team.

Open Room

	West	North	East	South
	Rodwell	Garner	Meckstroth	Weinstein
		pass	pass	1♣[1]
	pass	1♠[2]	pass	2◇
	pass	4◇	pass	4♠[3]
	pass	5♡[4]	pass	5♠[5]
	pass	6◇	all pass	

1. Natural or 2+ clubs balanced (11-13 or 17-19).
2. Artificial, no four-card major unless game-forcing with 5+ diamonds.
3. Control bid denying a heart control.
4-5. Ace, grand slam possible.

Garner's 4◇ was a crucial bid. Although the deal proved to be an honorable push at +1370, both North-South pairs could realistically hope they had gained 12 or 13 IMPs.

Board 54. E-W Vul.

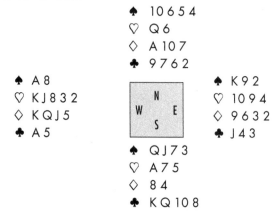

<pre>
            ♠ 10 6 5 4
            ♡ Q 6
            ◇ A 10 7
            ♣ 9 7 6 2
♠ A 8   ♠ K 9 2
♡ K J 8 3 2   ♡ 10 9 4
◇ K Q J 5   ◇ 9 6 3 2
♣ A 5   ♣ J 4 3
            ♠ Q J 7 3
            ♡ A 7 5
            ◇ 8 4
            ♣ K Q 10 8
</pre>

On these cards, 4♡ is no bargain for East-West, given that East has only one entry and there is danger of a diamond ruff, but given the state of the match it would not have been surprising for one or both pairs to push to game. However, East was dealer and South had a normal opening bid in second chair, which slowed down the East-West steam engine.

Competing against a 1♣ opening promising 2+ clubs, Meckstroth and Rodwell reached an awkward 2NT, which was due to fail against straightforward defense. Mercifully for NICKELL, that was not forthcoming: +120.

Competing against a 1♠ opening that promised only four spades, Jacobs and Katz understandably reached 3♡, which succeeded against normal defense: +140. That was the first gain (1 IMP) to JACOBS, ahead by 42, 142-100. Of greater importance to JACOBS was that there was one fewer board available to NICKELL to eat into the lead.

Board 55. Both Vul.

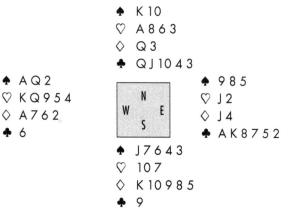

<pre>
            ♠ K 10
            ♡ A 8 6 3
            ◇ Q 3
            ♣ Q J 10 4 3
♠ A Q 2   ♠ 9 8 5
♡ K Q 9 5 4   ♡ J 2
◇ A 7 6 2   ◇ J 4
♣ 6   ♣ A K 8 7 5 2
            ♠ J 7 6 4 3
            ♡ 10 7
            ◇ K 10 9 8 5
            ♣ 9
</pre>

West	North	East	South
Jacobs	Hamman	Katz	Soloway
			pass
1♡	pass	1NT	pass
2◇	pass	2♡	all pass

In 2♡, Jacobs took the ♣Q with the ace and tried to cash the ♣K. Soloway ruffed with the ♡10, killing one of declarer's eight 'sure' winners. Declarer overruffed with the ♡Q and played the ◇A and another diamond. Soloway overtook the ◇Q to lead the ♡7 through, ducked to the jack. Jacobs ruffed a club and led a diamond loser, but Hamman ruffed with the six in front of dummy, cashed the ♡A, and exited with a club to force declarer's last trump. Jacobs could take only the ♠A for one down, -100.

Open Room

West	North	East	South
Rodwell	Garner	Meckstroth	Weinstein
			pass
1♡	pass	1NT	pass
2◇	pass	2♡	pass
2♠	pass	2NT	all pass

Where Jacobs disliked his intermediates enough to stop at 2♡, Rodwell, with a maximum for a non-1♣ opening, tried for the vulnerable game bonus with a shape-showing 2♠. When Meckstroth, whose maximum for 2♡ facing a limited opening bid was a bit higher than Katz's, could not jump to 3NT, Rodwell had reason to believe he had done the wrong thing by moving forward.

With the hearts coming in, 2NT could not be defeated: four hearts, two clubs and two aces, +120, 6 IMPs to NICKELL, 106-142.

JACOBS was pleased to learn that Board 56 was a dull 3NT; another board gone and another IMP scored for a more successful queen guess. JACOBS led by 37, 143-106, halfway through the set.

Board 57. E-W Vul.

```
              ♠ J 8 7 6 5 3
              ♡ 10 8 7
              ◇ A 2
              ♣ J 3
  ♠ K Q 2                      ♠ A 10 9
  ♡ K J 6 4        N           ♡ A 2
  ◇ 5 4         W     E        ◇ K Q 10 9 8
  ♣ A K Q 2        S           ♣ 10 7 6
              ♠ 4
              ♡ Q 9 5 3
              ◇ J 7 6 3
              ♣ 9 8 5 4
```

Board 57 had significant swing potential. 6NT is a respectable contract for East-West, normally turning on North holding the ◇J (first-round finesse) less than five-long, and there are extra chances if diamonds are 5-1.

Closed Room

West	North	East	South
Jacobs	Hamman	Katz	Soloway
	pass	1◇	pass
1♡	pass	1NT	pass
3NT	all pass		

Without opposition, Katz and Jacobs stopped safely in 3NT without sniffing at slam. Katz, making sure of his contract after a heart lead through dummy's king-jack, made five by leading the first diamond to his king, +660.

Open Room

West	North	East	South
Rodwell	Garner	Meckstroth	Weinstein
	2♠	3◇	pass
3NT	all pass		

Garner picked a good moment for an atypical (for the times) weak two-bid on a poor suit, which gave his opponents a less-than-smooth ride. A 3◇ overcall on a five-card suit, even a chunky one, with a high-card near-minimum may seem straightforward, but I consider it closer to a necessary battlefield choice. Rodwell, who later confessed that he felt the match could not be won if he went minus on this deal, settled for a gentle 3NT. Although Meckstroth would have passed a natural 4NT invitation, it was quietly courageous of

Rodwell to back his judgment and 'swing low' by giving up on what might have been an easy slam at a crucial stage of the match. He made six on a spade lead by playing diamonds to best advantage, scoring +690, so 1 IMP to NICKELL, 107-143.

Board 58 slipped by for JACOBS without incident, NICKELL gaining a further overtrick IMP to make it 108-143, now a 35-IMP difference.

Then, on Board 59, some early good news for JACOBS. Weinstein got to open a weak 2◇ with:

♠ 6 3　♡ A 6 2　◇ K 10 9 8 7 2　♣ 4 3

Although he caught Garner with a decent 4=4=0=5 15-count, he managed to stop safely right there. On a normal line of play, Weinstein finished +90 in 2◇, a good-looking result that looked even better when Soloway opened 3◇, which appeared due to fail as the play developed. The defense missed its chance, however, and Soloway scrambled home with +110, so that was another IMP to NICKELL where it might well have been 4 IMPs to JACOBS. With five deals remaining, JACOBS' lead was 34 IMPs, 143-109.

Paul Soloway

If the four-board run of 1-IMP swings continued a bit longer JACOBS would be able to exhale, home and dry in the bar, with nothing worse than a good scare to carry into the final the next morning.

But Board 60 was not the sort of deal JACOBS was hoping for.

Board 60. N-S Vul.

```
                    ♠ 2
                    ♡ K Q J 9 6 5 2
                    ◇ 8
                    ♣ Q 10 9 6
    ♠ K J 8 5 4 3              ♠ A Q 9
    ♡ 8 4 3          N         ♡ —
    ◇ 10 9 5 2     W   E       ◇ A Q 3
    ♣ —              S         ♣ A K J 7 5 4 3
                    ♠ 10 7 6
                    ♡ A 10 7
                    ◇ K J 7 6 4
                    ♣ 8 2
```

Open Room

West	North	East	South
Rodwell	Garner	Meckstroth	Weinstein
3♠	4♡	4NT[1]	dbl
pass[2]	pass	7♠	all pass

1. RKCB for spades.
2. One keycard.

Meckstroth could have taken a practical shot at 7♠ over Garner's hopeful 4♡, but thought he could afford to check on the ♠K (he would assume that a one-keycard response would deliver the ♠K rather than the ♡A). Weinstein, concerned that at the prevailing vulnerability Meckstroth might be taking liberties with a weak hand and a fit, thought it best to show values by doubling 4NT, a seemingly innocent action whose disastrous consequences could not easily be foreseen. As his partner had advertised high-card values, Garner understandably placed dummy with a long *diamond* suit that might need a ruff or two to establish. Trying to kill dummy's side entry, he made the well-reasoned lead of a club. Rodwell could establish that suit painlessly now, and use the ◇A as the late entry, for +1510.

With trumps 3-1, a diamond lead would have removed the vital timely entry to East's hand and left declarer a trick short, as he could not use dummy's trumps to ruff even one heart. We can see that a 5◇ bid by Weinstein would have worked brilliantly, but as he was an unpassed hand and this was a jammed auction there was no reason to think that 5◇ would not have been interpreted as natural, or that a diamond lead had to be best. And besides, Garner might have had an attractive diamond lead without being prompted.

Closed Room

West	North	East	South
Jacobs	Hamman	Katz	Soloway
2♠	3♡	4NT[1]	dbl
pass[2]	pass	5♡	dbl
pass	pass	6♠	all pass

1. RKCB for spades.
2. Intended as 1 keycard; interpreted as 0.

Katz, not keen to tip off the heart void when the opening lead might matter, also launched into Blackwood at his earliest opportunity. Here too, South preferred to double 4NT rather than bid 5◇ or 5♡.

After Soloway doubled 4NT, he excused himself, found the Director, and left the table. When he had not returned after about ten minutes, Hamman summoned the Director, and they left to check on Soloway, whose health had been an issue for the past five years. Five minutes later, everyone returned, and the bidding resumed, but the interruption and concern for Soloway's well-being may have affected the players' concentration.

It was soon evident that East-West were not in sync about West's pass over the double of 4NT: although undiscussed and not on their convention card, Jacobs assumed that ROPI (redouble = 0; pass = 1) applied as the standard treatment, but Katz, who 'knew' there was no such agreement in place, thought pass — the cheapest bid — was the weakest response.

Although it was certainly possible that Jacobs had opened a weak two-bid at favorable vulnerability with a topless suit, Katz was aware that there might have been a misunderstanding in an auction (Blackwood doubled) that had never occurred before for their partnership. Indeed, Katz knew it was even possible that Jacobs had interpreted 4NT as simple Blackwood rather than Keycard. In a last-ditch effort to resolve the critical spade-king issue, Katz continued with a 5♡ cuebid, an imaginative 'safety play' of sorts in the auction.

When Soloway doubled 5♡ and Jacobs neither redoubled nor took any other positive action, Katz decided he could not hold the ♠K, and so settled for six. North led the ♡K, so declarer ruffed in dummy, and played to establish the clubs for a less-than-gratifying overtrick, +1010. Had Katz bid seven, there would have been no obvious reason for Hamman to find the killing diamond lead after Soloway had doubled 5♡. NICKELL gained 11 IMPs, and with four deals to play, now trailed by only 23, 120-143.

If you were North-South, would you consider your -1010 a plus position, given that the more likely 7♠ could be defeated? As the number of boards left to play counts down in a one-sided 'comeback' session, it's human nature to estimate the score and what might be needed to win, but this is where one of Hamman's great strengths comes into play — the ability to focus only on the deal at hand. Regardless of how well they had done so far in this set, there was almost certainly still plenty of work to be done, and this was no time to waste energy on earlier deals.

Board 61. Both Vul.

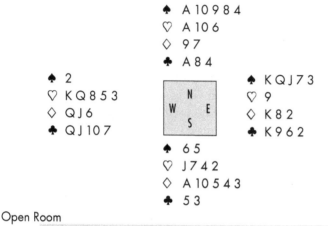

Open Room

West	North	East	South
Rodwell	Garner	Meckstroth	Weinstein
	1♠	pass	1NT
dbl	pass	pass	rdbl[1]
pass	2♣	dbl	2◇[2]
pass	2♡	dbl	all pass

1. Scrambling.
2. Four hearts, five diamonds (else redouble).

Knowing that partner is 4-5 in the red suits, which contract would you choose on the auction as North — 2◇ or 2♡?

On this layout, 2◇ would have been the safer option, as declarer should be able to piece together at least seven tricks — for example, on a spade lead declarer wins with dummy's ace and ducks a diamond to West. He wins the club switch with dummy's ace and plays two more rounds of trumps, and can develop at least one additional trick in hearts.

Despite the bad trump break, 2♡ would have been relatively inexpensive had East failed to find a trump lead, but Meckstroth had doubled with a singleton trump with the intention of protecting his side's wealth of high cards, so he followed through on his plan by leading the ♡9. Declarer took West's queen with the ace and ducked a diamond to Rodwell, who played two more rounds of hearts. Deprived of a diamond ruff in hand, Garner could amass only six tricks for two down, -500.

Closed Room

West	North	East	South
Jacobs	Hamman	Katz	Soloway
	1♠	pass	1NT
dbl	pass	pass	2◇
pass	pass	dbl	all pass

As Soloway did not expect Hamman to have six spades or a second four-card suit when he passed over the double of 1NT, he ran to 2◇, and was mildly disappointed not to buy a third trump in dummy's expected balanced hand. Jacobs led the ♣Q rather than a trump, and when it was allowed to hold, switched to his singleton spade. Declarer won with dummy's ace and ran the ◇9 to the jack. West switched to the ♡K. Soloway won with dummy's ace and played two rounds of trumps, craftily discarding a spade from dummy. Katz won, cashed a spade (heart from West) and led a third round of the suit, West parting with another heart as declarer ruffed the third spade. Now Soloway could play a heart to establish two more winners in that suit for +180.

By escaping directly to his long suit, Soloway had left Jacobs in the dark about his fourth heart; but even if West had discarded a club to keep a third heart, declarer would surely have finessed the ♡6 after ruffing the third spade, West following low to the second heart. The winning defense is for East to switch back to clubs after taking his spade trick. Declarer wins with dummy's ace, and needing to play hearts towards dummy's ten, ruffs a club and plays a heart; now West can rise with the queen, blocking the suit, and exit with a club. One way or another, the defenders will come to a sixth trick.

NICKELL had gained another 12 IMPs. The JACOBS lead had been reduced to 11 IMPs, 143-132, and there were still three deals remaining. Would anyone bet against NICKELL at that point?

Board 62. Neither Vul.

```
                      ♠ A J 8 4
                      ♡ K Q 10
                      ◇ A 10 2
                      ♣ K 8 2
      ♠ Q 9 7 5 3 2               ♠ —
      ♡ 9 6             N          ♡ A 8 5 3 2
      ◇ Q 6 5        W     E       ◇ 8 3
      ♣ A 7             S          ♣ Q J 10 9 5 3
                      ♠ K 10 6
                      ♡ J 7 4
                      ◇ K J 9 7 4
                      ♣ 6 4
```

Open Room

West	North	East	South
Rodwell	Garner	Meckstroth	Weinstein
		2♣[1]	pass
2♠[2]	2NT	all pass	

1. 6+ clubs, 10-15.
2. Nonforcing.

Meckstroth was not willing to pass as dealer with so much playing strength, and borrowed a point or two from a kibitzer to introduce his chunky club suit, known to be at least six cards long. It's difficult to imagine passing the somewhat wide-ranging natural 2NT with the South hand unless desperate to try for a 'swing low' result while trying to wipe out a big deficit, but that is the action Weinstein chose! 'I probably should have raised to 3NT,' said Weinstein after the match, 'but I was not vulnerable and had some bad vibes about the hand, with the ♠K possibly not pulling its full weight, and presuming things weren't splitting too well.'

The defenders cleared clubs. Garner won the third round, cashed the ◇A and ran the ◇10 (the technical play to cater to queen-fourth in the East hand as the extra chance), losing a diamond, a heart and five clubs for two down, -100.

Closed Room

West	North	East	South
Jacobs	Hamman	Katz	Soloway
		pass	pass
2♠	2NT	pass	3NT
all pass			

Although Katz, who did not have the luxury of a natural, limited 2♣ available, did not open, Jacobs' third-seat weak 2♠ led to a scenario not unlike the one in the Open Room. Soloway, who earlier in the session might have been able to justify passing 2NT to create a swing position, was looking for normal upside actions at this stage, and so raised to 3NT.

Here too, the defenders started clubs, declarer winning the third round with the king. Although there had been only one bid by East-West, Hamman had a fair amount of information. The club position had been revealed and he could expect the spade layout to be as it was. As West might well have opened 1♠ if he owned the ♡A, Hamman was inclined to play East for the ♡A; and if that were so, might not East have opened if he also held the ◇Q? While neither of these inferences could be taken to the bank, there were certainly some bridge reasons to go against the percentages in diamonds by playing West for the ◇Q.

Tactically, it was not obvious whether most of the huge deficit had been wiped out, especially when that -1010 on Board 60 could be an 11-IMP gain, a push or a 17-IMP loss. If NICKELL was still behind in the match, there was another reason for Hamman to make a different play than his counterpart next door in what seemed to him the normal contract; he crossed to the ◇K and led the ◇J, passing it successfully when it was not covered. He could not arrange a fourth spade trick now but he had five diamonds, three spades and a club for +400, and 11 IMPs to NICKELL.

If you've been keeping track of the score, you will know that both teams were sitting on 143 IMPs now, with two deals remaining.

Board 63. N-S Vul.

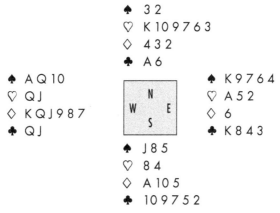

```
              ♠ 3 2
              ♡ K 10 9 7 6 3
              ◇ 4 3 2
              ♣ A 6
♠ A Q 10                      ♠ K 9 7 6 4
♡ Q J              N          ♡ A 5 2
◇ K Q J 9 8 7   W     E       ◇ 6
♣ Q J              S          ♣ K 8 4 3
              ♠ J 8 5
              ♡ 8 4
              ◇ A 10 5
              ♣ 10 9 7 5 2
```

With nothing bad happening, East-West can take eleven tricks in spades. What a peculiar hand West was dealt in this tense situation. If you open 1◇, what can you rebid after a 1♠ response? A 2NT call is misdirected with those red suits, but 3♠ is a trump short, so you're left with 3◊, heavy on high cards but not on playing strength if the quacks are not working, and with the opportunity to show spade support looming elusive.

Fortunately for Jacobs and Katz in the Closed Room, Hamman overcalled 1◊ with 1♡, so East's spade bid showed at least five, and West had a comfortable target to aim for. Still, they climbed to 5♠ on their own power and were mildly lucky to chalk up +450.

Meanwhile, after a strong club by Rodwell, and natural positive response by Meckstroth, East-West had no difficulty reaching 4♠ in the Open Room for +450 and a push. Not quite a routine flat game, but there we were, still tied at 143.

This was the last board:

Board 64. E-W Vul.

```
              ♠ 10 8
              ♡ A Q J 7 2
              ◊ K 10 7 3
              ♣ 9 8
♠ A K J 9                      ♠ 7 6 5 4 3
♡ 10 6            N            ♡ K 9 5 4
◊ J 9 4 2     W     E          ◊ 6 5
♣ 10 7 5          S            ♣ Q 4
              ♠ Q 2
              ♡ 8 3
              ◊ A Q 8
              ♣ A K J 6 3 2
```

Open Room

West	North	East	South
Rodwell	Garner	Meckstroth	Weinstein
pass	1♡	pass	2♣
pass	2◊	pass	3♣[1]
pass	3♡	pass	4♡
all pass			

1. Forcing.

With 26 combined high-card points it was inevitable that North-South would bid game, left to themselves. With no spade guard in a 2-2 fit, 3NT is best avoided; meanwhile 5♣ needs the ♣Q onside with a 3-2 break, and, even with all that, if West cashes two spades and switches to a heart, declarer is forced to guess which red suit is coming in.

Garner and Weinstein did very well to reach 4♡, which needed considerably less than the other games to succeed, but Meckstroth had an easy spade lead and declarer lost two spades and two trumps, -50.

Closed Room

West	North	East	South
Jacobs	Hamman	Katz	Soloway
pass	1♡	pass	2♣[1]
pass	2♢[2]	pass	2NT[3]
pass	3♢	pass	3♠[4]
pass	3NT	all pass	

1. Natural, or an artificial three-card limit raise in hearts.
2. Artificial, minimum.
3. Natural game force with clubs.
4. Uncertainty about strain.

Despite declarer's 2NT bid that suggested a spade guard, 3NT was not much of a contract, not nearly as good as the 4♡ reached at the other table. However, the relative quality of the two contracts was not the yardstick for measuring success, and a close look at the blocked spade suit will reveal that the Great Shuffler had decided that 3NT *could* be made on this momentous day.

Jacobs cashed the ♠K, looking for an attitude signal, and when Katz discouraged, switched to a heart. The heart finesse was not relevant to the success of 3NT if declarer was going to play on clubs, so Soloway called for the ♡A, played a club to the jack, and soon claimed eleven tricks (Jacobs eventually revealing himself in the pointed suits), +460. Those 11 IMPs were the difference in the match. NICKELL had won the fourth quarter 84-2, and won the match, 154-143.

"I'm sorry, Ralph, I couldn't beat that disgusting 3NT"

When we emerged to compare I thought we had a legitimate chance to win, and Meckwell said they were good too. It was simply amazing. Meck was keeping a running score, and as we wrote +11 on the last deal he screamed, 'Win by 11' — he and Rodwell were extremely excited, as if it was their first big win. It was truly great drama.

As nearly always, the secret to erasing a large deficit is to avoid going crazy while playing an enterprising and thoughtful game, avoiding unforced errors, and looking for opportunities to do something reasonable that would probably not be duplicated at the other table. It is remarkable that of the 16 deals, eight were pushes or one-IMP swings, and two of Hamway's strong results were duplicated by Garner and Weinstein. NICKELL won anyway!

George Jacobs: 'All we ever wanted was a flat board.'

Paul Soloway: 'Luck best describes what happened.'

Team NICKELL
(l-r) Eric Rodwell, Jeff Meckstroth, Nick Nickell, Eric Kokish,
Bob Hamman, Dick Freeman, Paul Soloway

However, that's not quite the end of the story.

Writing in *The Bridge World*, David Berkowitz reported on a JACOBS appeal from an earlier session that had to be resolved before the result could be confirmed:

N-S Vul.

```
              ♠ A 5 2
              ♡ A Q 6 4
              ◇ 8 6 4 3 2
              ♣ 7
♠ Q 3                        ♠ J 10 7 6
♡ K 9 8 7 5       N          ♡ J 3 2
◇ 10          W       E      ◇ K 9 5
♣ A J 10 9 3      S          ♣ K 6 2
              ♠ K 9 8 4
              ♡ 10
              ◇ A Q J 7
              ♣ Q 8 5 4
```

West	North	East	South
Lauria	Meckstroth	Versace	Rodwell
	pass	pass	1◇[1]
2NT[2]	3♣[3]	3♡	3♠
pass	3NT	pass	4◇
pass	5◇	all pass	

1. 2+ diamonds, 10-15.
2. Hearts and clubs.
3. Strong diamond raise.

With considerable luck and skillful play by declarer (aided substantially by clues from the bidding), the contract made: heart lead to dummy's queen, diamond to the jack, club lost, heart to the ace (club discard), two more rounds of trumps, then (counting West for 2=5=1=5) the ♠8 passed to East. In the fullness of time, declarer picked up the rest of the spade suit with a late finesse of the nine for +600.

But there had been some irregular table action. West and South were screenmates. The director was called after the 4◇ bid; East-West claimed that the 3NT bid had taken between one and five minutes (the BBO operator estimated it at three minutes), and the hesitation might have stimulated the 4◇ takeout.

The director let the result stand. East-West appealed; they contended there were many North hands where 3NT would be the best North-South contract — indeed, they provided quite a few such hands. North-South argued that passing was not an alternative, as North, a passed hand, could have at most 10 HCP and would normally open with that strength and a six-card suit.

The excitement of the match was subdued, as the Appeals Committee took several hours to determine which team had won. The committee concluded that there had been a temporary break, not an exceptionally long one. With this premise, and the possibility that either hidden player had done all or most of the lengthy thinking, it was deemed that there had been no unauthorized information, so no adjustment would be applied. (Whether the committee would have decided that passing 3NT was a reasonable alternative, and what the result at that contract might have been, remains cloudy).

At about 3:30 AM, the comeback was officially complete.

Although it's unlikely that the NICKELL team members got much sleep after the emotional experience of that remarkable set and the long wait for a decision on the appeal, there would be no anticlimax. NICKELL went on to record yet another Spingold victory later that day by defeating the SPECTOR team (Warren Spector-Mark Feldman, Billy Cohen-Ron Smith, Gavin Wolpert-Vincent Demuy), 150-106. It was Bob Hamman's twelfth Spingold win, his first having come twenty-five years earlier, in 1979.

3. 2014 Gunfight at the O.K. Corral

The original Gunfight at the O.K. Corral, immortalized many times on screen, was in reality nothing more than a thirty-second shoot-out between lawmen led by Wyatt Earp and a number of outlaws called the Cowboys. It took place on the afternoon of 26 October 1881, in Tombstone, Arizona and is arguably the best known shoot-out in the history of the American West.

We[‡] are not in Tombstone, but rather in Scottsdale, in Arizona's Sonora desert, between Phoenix and the McDowell Mountains. Known as 'The West's Most Western town', Scottsdale is annually rated among the nation's most desirable communities in which to live, visit and do business. It is hot and dry nearly always. How hot is it? Well, in 1994, by mayoral proclamation, chili was declared Scottsdale's official food. Everyone seems to like it hot. We're here for a bridge match, which promises to be a different sort of gunfight, spanning two full days of play, a bit longer than the thirty-second battle in 1881.

There are two teams remaining in the Trials to select USA 1 for the 2015 Bermuda Bowl in Chennai, India. Having last qualified for the Bermuda Bowl in 2009, team NICKELL (Nick Nickell-Ralph Katz, Jeff Meckstroth-Eric Rodwell, with Bobby Levin-Steve Weinstein, who were on board for the 2013 Trials) is hoping to end that drought in the 120-board USA 1 final. NICKELL defeated BRAMLEY (Bart Bramley-Lew Stansby, Howie Weinstein-Ross Grabel, Bob Hamman-Roger Lee), 254-147, in their semifinal.

Blocking NICKELL's path is DIAMOND (John Diamond-Brian Platnick, Geoff Hampson-Eric Greco, Kevin Bathurst-Brad Moss). As team DIAMOND, with Fred Gitelman playing with Moss, had beaten NICKELL in the final of the 2010 Rosenblum in Philadelphia, there is an element of revenge lurking between the lines. DIAMOND reached the final by beating FLEISHER (Marty Fleisher-Chip Martel-Gary Cohler, Michael Rosenberg-Chris Willenken), 237-180.

All the players are well-acquainted with the style and approach of their opponents, but it will be interesting to see whether either team enjoys an edge accruing from system choice. All three DIAMOND pairs are playing a slightly simpler version of Meckwell's R-M Precision (the high-frequency

---

‡ Primary author Eric Kokish.

difference being an artificial 1♡ response to 1♣ showing 8-11 HCP without five or more spades), while the other two NICKELL pairs are 2/1 guys with lots of accoutrements. There will be no system issues in choosing opponents when NICKELL has the seed, for better (no extra preparation needed) or for worse (three active pairs who rarely pass when they could open, respond or interfere) but DIAMOND perhaps can do more with the seed, notably deciding which pair should be holding Meckstroth and Rodwell's cards.

Set 1 (Boards 1-15)

NICKELL scores on seven of the first fifteen deals — this is their biggest gain:

Board 5. N-S Vul.

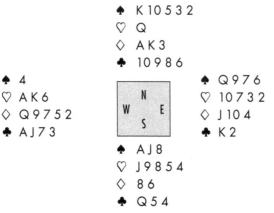

```
                    ♠ K 10 5 3 2
                    ♡ Q
                    ◇ A K 3
                    ♣ 10 9 8 6
    ♠ 4                              ♠ Q 9 7 6
    ♡ A K 6          N               ♡ 10 7 3 2
    ◇ Q 9 7 5 2    W   E             ◇ J 10 4
    ♣ A J 7 3        S               ♣ K 2
                    ♠ A J 8
                    ♡ J 9 8 5 4
                    ◇ 8 6
                    ♣ Q 5 4
```

Open Room

West	North	East	South
Diamond	Levin	Platnick	Weinstein
	1♠	pass	2♠
dbl	pass	2NT*	pass
3◇	pass	3♡	dbl
all pass			

East's 2NT is described by West as 'better-minor Lebensohl', but East, under the impression that 2NT is simple Lebensohl, is trying to show a weak 3♡ bid. Weinstein, after inquiring to West about East's sequence, doubles for penalty and finds the best lead of a low heart. Platnick wins with dummy's ace and calls for the ◇2. Levin goes in with the king, and accurately switches to the ♠2. South wins cheaply and returns the ♡9. Declarer wins with dummy's king, plays a club to the king, ruffs a spade, cashes the ♣A and plays a second diamond. North ducks, wins the next diamond, and when South discards the ♣Q, gives him a club ruff. South has wisely unblocked the ♠A on the second round of the suit, so can now put North in with the king, and is left with ♡J8 over declarer's ♡107 — three down, -500.

At this point the Director comes into the room and says, 'Only five boards in an hour'. Levin chuckles and replies, 'We'll slow down for you'.

Bobby Levin

West	North	East	South
Katz	Greco	Nickell	Hampson
	1♠	pass	2♠
dbl	pass	3♡*	all pass

Again at the other table we have East-West confusion. West alerts 3♡, East does not, so here too there is some uncertainty about how much East is showing. Hampson does not double, and leads the ◇8. Greco wins with the king, and switches to the ♠3. South wins with the eight and returns the jack. When declarer discards a club from dummy, North wins with the king, cashes the ◇A, and gives South a ruff. Declarer is booked for three down, but here that's only -150, 8 IMPs to NICKELL.

DIAMOND scores on only three deals, but unlike Board-a-Match scoring, it is not a question of how often, but how much.

Board 7. Both Vul.

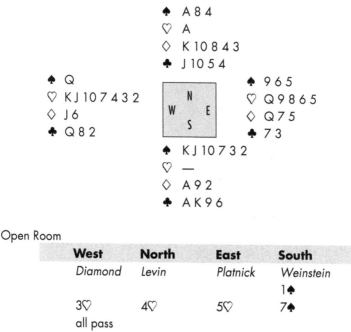

♠ A 8 4
♡ A
♢ K 10 8 4 3
♣ J 10 5 4

♠ Q
♡ K J 10 7 4 3 2
♢ J 6
♣ Q 8 2

♠ 9 6 5
♡ Q 9 8 6 5
♢ Q 7 5
♣ 7 3

♠ K J 10 7 3 2
♡ —
♢ A 9 2
♣ A K 9 6

Open Room

West	North	East	South
Diamond	Levin	Platnick	Weinstein
			1♠
3♡	4♡	5♡	7♠
all pass			

West leads the ♡J, and declarer wins with the ace, pitching the ♢2. He cashes the ♠A, playing East for spade length. West's queen is bittersweet news, however, as dummy will have no late entry to cash diamonds after ruffing out the suit. Weinstein draws trumps and needs to take the club finesse, going one down when it loses, -100.

Closed Room

West	North	East	South
Katz	Greco	Nickell	Hampson
			1♣[1]
2♡	3♢[2]	4♡	pass[3]
pass	dbl	pass	4♠[4]
pass	5NT[5]	pass	6♡[6]
pass	6♠	pass	7♢
pass	7♠	pass	pass
dbl	all pass		

1. 16+ unbalanced or 17+ balanced.   5. Pick a slam.

2. Natural, game forcing.   6. Interest in a grand slam.

3. Requests a double.

4. Flexible hand, playable in other strain.

West's double is speculative, based on his assessment that North-South seem uncertain about both strain and level, and the possibility that his double might lead declarer to misjudge the layout. North-South stand their ground, and Katz leads the ♡K. Hampson pitches a diamond and, crucially (as it happens), plays a spade to the king. When the queen appears, he cashes the ♠J, plays three rounds of diamonds, ruffing safely, returns to dummy with the ♠A to draw the last trump, and claims, +2470, and a cool 21 IMPs to DIAMOND, ahead now 23-19.

Geoff Hampson

Inevitably, this board generates a great deal (pun not really intended) of discussion about the best line of play, given the information from the bidding. We're inclined to trust the math used by Bart Bramley for his analysis in *The Bridge World*, which leads him to the surprising conclusion that the most promising approach by roughly 3.5% (over the second-best line of leading a low trump to the jack at Trick 2) involves starting trumps with the king, intending to play the ace next if the queen has not appeared. If West follows with the queen to the first round of trumps, cash the jack, then try for 3-2 diamonds, with the club finesse as the fallback option. Singleton queen in the East hand points to West being more likely to be short in diamonds, so it's slightly better to draw all the trumps, try for the unlikely doubleton quack of diamonds, and resort to the club finesse. The most interesting part of Bramley's analysis might be that there are twenty-one layouts where West has exactly two spades, but only twenty where he has zero or one spade.

Board 15. N-S Vul.

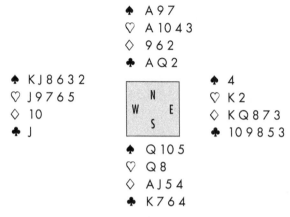

```
                 ♠ A 9 7
                 ♡ A 10 4 3
                 ◇ 9 6 2
                 ♣ A Q 2
  ♠ K J 8 6 3 2              ♠ 4
  ♡ J 9 7 6 5       N        ♡ K 2
  ◇ 10          W       E    ◇ K Q 8 7 3
  ♣ J               S        ♣ 10 9 8 5 3
                 ♠ Q 10 5
                 ♡ Q 8
                 ◇ A J 5 4
                 ♣ K 7 6 4
```

There is no perfect action with the West hand, but it's unimaginable to pass South's 1◇ opening at this vulnerability, so the three choices are 1♠, a Michaels-style cuebid, and a weak 2♠.

Open Room

West	North	East	South
Diamond	Levin	Platnick	Weinstein
			1◇
2◇*	dbl*	2♡	pass
pass	dbl	pass	pass
2♠	pass*	pass	dbl
all pass			

After Diamond's two-suited cuebid, Platnick is obliged to offer a preference with unequal lengths in the majors when the doubling starts (the first double is card-showing), and 2♡ doubled has the potential to be very messy. Diamond, hoping for 2-3 in the majors opposite rather than 1-2 (or worse), escapes to 2♠, where he is doubled by South after a forcing pass by North. After a diamond lead to the king and ace, followed by two rounds of clubs, declarer leads a heart to the king, cashes the ◇Q, and ruffs away South's ♣K, exiting in hearts. There is no stopping six tricks now, and -300 feels like a triumph for both Diamond and DIAMOND!

Brian Platnick and John Diamond

Closed Room

	West	North	East	South
	Katz	Greco	Nickell	Hampson
				1◇
	2♠	dbl*	pass	2NT
	pass	3NT	all pass	

Katz prefers to focus on his long suit, which spawns an entirely different auction. Against 3NT, he leads the ♠6, and dummy's seven holds. Hampson tries a low heart from dummy, and when Nickell follows low without a tell, puts in the eight. Katz wins the nine and switches to his club, won in dummy for a second low heart lead, the king winning. When Nickell switches to the ◇7, Hampson does the right thing by putting in the jack. Although he can't know the actual layout in hearts, he believes that East would usually try to surround dummy's ◇9 by leading the ten from an honor-ten-eight holding. Hampson still needs a ninth trick, and after crossing to dummy in clubs to cash the ♡A, the distribution is revealed, so he simply cashes the ♡A and exits in hearts to give West the defense's third and fourth heart tricks before conceding a third spade trick and +600. DIAMOND gains 7 IMPs.

At the end of the set DIAMOND leads 30-28.

Set 2 (Boards 16-30)

Traditional wisdom suggests you won't go far wrong at favorable vulnerability by competing to the five-level over four of a major with a solid ten-card fit, but on Board 19, when Hampson, after 2♣ - (2♠) - 4♣ - (4♠), takes the plunge with:

♠ 9 3   ♡ Q 4   ◇ Q 7 3   ♣ A K J 10 4 2

he buys a dummy with no shortness and is four down off the top, -800. As 4♠ is cold and yields a lucky +680 at the other table, the damage to DIAMOND is only 3 IMPs, still ahead 38-31.

Board 20. Both Vul.

```
                    ♠ J 10 5 2
                    ♡ J 9 4 3 2
                    ◇ A Q J
                    ♣ 3
    ♠ A Q 9                        ♠ K 8 3
    ♡ 10 7 5            N          ♡ Q
    ◇ K 8 6 4      W       E       ◇ 9 7 5 3 2
    ♣ A 7 2            S           ♣ K J 8 6
                    ♠ 7 6 4
                    ♡ A K 8 6
                    ◇ 10
                    ♣ Q 10 9 5 4
```

Open Room

West	North	East	South
Bathurst	Katz	Moss	Nickell
1◇[1]	pass	1♠	pass
1NT	pass	2♣[2]	pass
2◇	all pass		

1. 2+ diamonds, 10-15.
2. Forces 2◇.

When Katz does not deem his honor location appropriate for a light vulnerable overcall, Moss invents a 1♠ response before wriggling into 2◇, where he was headed all along. Nickell has length in both unbid suits, but as 2◇ might be a poor contract for the opposition when West has only two diamonds, he goes quietly. North leads the ♡2 and South wins with the king and returns his trump to the king and ace. The contract is in no danger despite the poor lie in the minors, +90.

Closed Room

West	**North**	**East**	**South**
Meckstroth	Greco	Rodwell	Hampson
1◇[1]	1♡	3♣[2]	4♡
all pass			

1. 2+ diamonds, 10-15.
2. Clubs and diamonds, less than invitational.

Greco, less concerned about his suit quality, prefers to act immediately with nine cards in the majors, which gets him to 4♡ in a hurry. There is no compelling reason for East to lead a black suit, and after the count lead of the ◇2 (the attitude ◇7 would have been better this time) to the king and ace, declarer can pitch two spades on the diamonds. He gives up a club (a spade first would work better as the long card can be established), and the defense has time for two rounds of trumps to hold 4♡ to ten tricks, but +620 is excellent and worth 12 IMPs to DIAMOND, now ahead by 19, 50-31.

Eric Greco

Board 23. Both Vul.

```
                    ♠ K
                    ♡ K J 10 5
                    ◇ A J 10 8 4
                    ♣ Q 9 5
    ♠ A J 9 8 3                      ♠ 10 7 5 2
    ♡ A 8 4 3          N             ♡ Q 6
    ◇ 9 7         W         E        ◇ 6 3
    ♣ K 3             S             ♣ A 10 8 4 2
                    ♠ Q 6 4
                    ♡ 9 7 2
                    ◇ K Q 5 2
                    ♣ J 7 6
```

	West	**North**	**East**	**South**
Open Room	Bathurst	Katz	Moss	Nickell
Closed Room	Meckstroth	Greco	Rodwell	Hampson
				pass
	1♠	dbl	3♠[1]	all pass

1. Preemptive.

North has a tough opening-lead decision with nothing to guide him. Katz leads the ♡J and when dummy's queen holds, Bathurst can ruff out the clubs, cash the major-suit aces, ruff a heart, and play a club, which is ruffed and overruffed. He ruffs a heart, and although South can overruff with the queen and cash two diamonds, declarer has the rest, +170.

Greco does much better when he hits upon the imaginative and ultimately devilish lead of the ♣Q. Meckstroth wins with the king and plays a club to the ten, as who would not? South wins with the jack that North was supposed to hold and switches to the ◇K, North following with the descriptive jack. Hampson switches to the ♡9 and declarer can't avoid losing the ♡K, the ◇A, and a trump trick for a rather spectacular down one, -100; 7 IMPs to Diamond, 57-35.

The concept of leading an unsupported honor is discussed in some detail in *The Rodwell Files*[§]. Perhaps dummy is sufficiently impressed to make a note to include this deal in the next edition; as Eddie Kantar told me too many years ago, 'If you want to write about bridge, never get caught without a pen and paper: interesting material is where you find it!'

---

§ *The Rodwell Files*, Eric Rodwell, Master Point Press, 2011.

Board 24. Neither Vul.

```
                    ♠  A J 10 8
                    ♡  Q J 8
                    ◇  9 6 5 3
                    ♣  A J
     ♠  Q 4                          ♠  K 5
     ♡  A 9 7 5 3        N           ♡  K 10 6 2
     ◇  K 2          W       E       ◇  J 8
     ♣  10 8 5 4         S           ♣  K Q 7 6 2
                    ♠  9 7 6 3 2
                    ♡  4
                    ◇  A Q 10 7 4
                    ♣  9 3
```

Open Room

West	North	East	South
Bathurst	*Katz*	*Moss*	*Nickell*
pass	1◇	pass	1♠
dbl	2♠	4♡	4♠
pass	pass	dbl	all pass

Bathurst's second-round double in a live auction, with more than half his points in the opponent's suits, gives us some idea of the value he places on holding nine combined cards in the unbid suits. He catches his partner with a huge hand in context, and Moss is feeling no pain when he jumps to 4♡, although his big club fit surely offers reason for concern about everyone's potential if the bidding were to continue. Indeed, it is clear for Nickell, with his own double fit (Katz has shown a fourth spade with his competitive raise), to bid 4♠. Moss, although his rounded-suit honors may not be worth many tricks on defense, doubles to protect his presumed equity in 4♡. At double dummy, Moss is exactly right, as a black-suit lead would set 4♠, while 5♡ or 5♣ would have no chance.

   Unfortunately for DIAMOND, Bathurst leads the ♡A, hoping to be able to judge what to do next. That kills the defenders' chance to set the contract, as dummy has two timely entries to establish and cash a heart winner for a club discard, but when Moss followed with the discouraging ♡10, Bathurst treats that card as suit-preference for diamonds rather than an instruction to make the 'obvious' switch (to clubs). His switch to the ◇K eliminates the defensive diamond trick, so Nickell has time for everything and posts an overtrick, +690.

West	North	East	South
Meckstroth	Greco	Rodwell	Hampson
pass	1◇[1]	1♡	1♠[2]
4♡	all pass		

1. 2+ diamonds, 10-15.
2. 5+ spades.

Rather than pass or overcall 2♣ on a mediocre five-card suit, Rodwell invents a 1♡ overcall on an even more mediocre suit and hits a home run (baseball often provides appropriate references). Greco has too much defense in a balanced hand to commit to 4♠ over 4♡, despite knowing of his side's nine-plus-card fit. South's lead of the ♣9 doesn't affect the outcome, and Rodwell loses a trick in each suit for one down, -50, but that is 12 IMPs to NICKELL, back within 10, 47-57.

Board 26. Both Vul.

```
                    ♠ —
                    ♡ J
                    ◇ A K Q 10 8 7 6 4 2
                    ♣ A Q 6
   ♠ 10 9 7 4 2            ♠ A K Q J 6 5
   ♡ K 8 7 6 5 3     N     ♡ Q 10 9 2
   ◇ 5            W     E   ◇ J
   ♣ 10              S     ♣ K 3
                    ♠ 8 3
                    ♡ A 4
                    ◇ 9 3
                    ♣ J 9 8 7 5 4 2
```

Open Room

West	North	East	South
Bathurst	Katz	Moss	Nickell
		1♣[1]	pass
1◇[2]	6◇	all pass	

1. Precision.
2. 0-7.

The textbooks won't tell you how to bid the North hand, especially after a strong-club opening and artificial negative response, but the approach taken by Katz gives him the upside of a possible make to go with the more likely outcomes of finding a profitable save or inducing a misjudgment by the opponents. It would be terribly unkind to call Moss's pass over 6◇ or Bathurst's conclusive pass as misjudgments, but the wisdom of Katz's big bounce is highlighted when he buys a sensational dummy and chalks up +1370, while it is the strong-club side that needs to take a vulnerable save this time.

Ralph Katz

Closed Room

West	North	East	South
Meckstroth	Greco	Rodwell	Hampson
		1♣[1]	pass
1◇[2]	5◇	pass[3]	pass
5♡	6◇	6♡	all pass

1. Precision.
2. 0-7
3. Non-forcing.

When Greco settles for the down-the-middle bid, he expects to have a good chance to buy the contract that figures to be his best destination, especially when 5◇ gets past the strong hand. But Meckstroth, though he can't show both suits wholesale, takes a chance and reopens in his six-card suit. Greco can't afford to give up without a fight, and banks on his long suit, rather than doubling to let Hampson know he bid 5◇ to make and has some defense. Rodwell, in turn, can't afford to pass, and it is less complex to bid one more for the road than try to guess everyone's potential in a different way. Now it is unclear which side owns the hand, and 6♡ quietly buys the exciting auction. Meckstroth has three unavoidable losers for -200, which translates into 15 IMPs for NICKELL, ahead now by 5, 62-57.

NICKELL goes on to win the set 40-32, and leads, 68-62.

Set 3 Boards 31-45

On Board 31, with neither vulnerable, West is dealt:

♠ 10 4   ♡ A 9 7 5   ◇ 10 8 5   ♣ K J 8 7

and sees partner open a 14-16 1NT. Diamond, with only the mildest of reservations because of his promising intermediates, passes. Meckstroth, in contrast, tries Stayman, catches a 2♡ reply, and raises to 3♡, reaching a 'perfecto' 4♡ opposite Rodwell's:

♠ A K 9   ♡ K Q 6 3 2   ◇ J 3   ♣ Q 10 9

Would it be easier if East opens 1♡? Only if West offers more than a single raise.

One brave BBO commentator observes that East-West can make game, but doubts anyone will bid it. That's 7 IMPs for NICKELL, 75-62.

Board 34. N-S Vul.

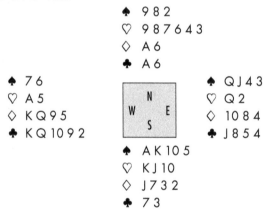

```
              ♠ 9 8 2
              ♡ 9 8 7 6 4 3
              ◇ A 6
              ♣ A 6
  ♠ 7 6                      ♠ Q J 4 3
  ♡ A 5           N          ♡ Q 2
  ◇ K Q 9 5    W     E       ◇ 10 8 4
  ♣ K Q 10 9 2    S          ♣ J 8 5 4
              ♠ A K 10 5
              ♡ K J 10
              ◇ J 7 3 2
              ♣ 7 3
```

Open Room

West	North	East	South
Diamond	Levin	Platnick	Weinstein
		pass	1◇[1]
2♣	2♡	4♣	4♡
all pass			

1. 2+ diamonds, 10-15.

Although North-South might barely reach 4♡ uncontested, here the East-West activity more-or-less jostles them into the thin game. Platnick, expecting to have only one opportunity to do something proactive, attacks with the ♠Q. Levin needs to assume that's a true card from a queen-jack holding. With communications fragile, he wins and plays the ♡K, which West takes to switch to the ♣K. Declarer wins and plays a second trump to East's queen. After cashing the ♣J, East returns the ♠3, but declarer plays low, and can claim by repeating the spade finesse, +620. The less attractive alternative line — use North's aces to finesse against the ♡Q — also would have worked on this layout.

Closed Room

West	North	East	South
Meckstroth	Greco	Rodwell	Hampson
		pass	1◇¹
1NT	2♡	dbl²	3♡
all pass			

1. 2+ diamonds, 10-15.
2. Takeout.

Meckstroth considers his hand closer to a 15-17 1NT than a 2♣ overcall, which turns the auction into a battle for the partscore. Greco gives some thought to bidding game, but here East-West have advertised some high-card values, so he eventually passes. Against 3♡, Rodwell, like Platnick, starts spades, leading the Rusinow (from known length) ♠J. Greco, playing as Levin does in the Open Room, soon records +170. So 10 more IMPs to NICKELL, ahead 85-62. Those who advocate for the strategy, 'When partner freely supports your six-card major, bid game', would add this deal to their 'plus' file.

Board 36. Both Vul.

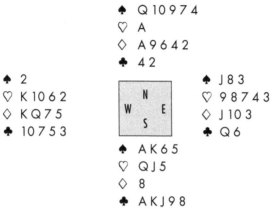

```
                    ♠ Q 10 9 7 4
                    ♡ A
                    ◇ A 9 6 4 2
                    ♣ 4 2
    ♠ 2                              ♠ J 8 3
    ♡ K 10 6 2          N           ♡ 9 8 7 4 3
    ◇ K Q 7 5       W       E       ◇ J 10 3
    ♣ 10 7 5 3          S           ♣ Q 6
                    ♠ A K 6 5
                    ♡ Q J 5
                    ◇ 8
                    ♣ A K J 9 8
```

Open Room

West	North	East	South
Diamond	Levin	Platnick	Weinstein
pass	1♠	pass	2♣[1]
pass	2◇	pass	4◇[2]
pass	4♡[3]	pass	4NT[4]
pass	5♠[5]	pass	5NT[6]
pass	6♠	all pass	

1. 2+ clubs, game forcing.
2. Splinter agreeing spades.
3. Control bid.
4. RKCB for spades.
5. 2 keycards + ♠Q.
6. Asking for side kings.

The jack of trumps or five-card support would make 7♠ a significantly better contract, but although Levin knows of the excellent mesh in diamonds, he envisions handling issues, and so did not accept Weinstein's grand slam invitation. He plays low from dummy on the lead of the ♡9, wins the ace, plays a club to the ace, and leads the ♡J, pitching a club when it is not covered. He throws a diamond on the ♠A, draws trumps, ending in dummy, and claims all the tricks, as he can ruff a club safely, +1460.

Closed Room

West	North	East	South
Meckstroth	Greco	Rodwell	Hampson
pass	1♠	pass	2NT[1]
pass	3♣[2]	pass	3◇[3]
dbl	4◇[4]	pass	4NT[5]
pass	5♠[6]	pass	7♠
all pass			

1. Game-forcing spade raise.
2. Artificial, minimum.
3. Relay.
4. Singleton heart, diamond control.
5. RKCB for spades.
6. 2 keycards + ♠Q.

Hampson can't be sure of North's minor-suit distribution and secondary honors, but elects to take the pressure off partner by just bidding the grand slam, knowing that at worst it will depend on bringing in the clubs. The lead of the ◇J runs to the ace, and Greco gives his line of play a good nine minutes thought before cashing dummy's top clubs. When the queen falls, he comes to hand with the ♡A, cashes the ♠Q, and plays a spade to the ace. When trumps split 3-1, he needs an extra trick, and so runs the ♡J, throwing a diamond. He can claim when it holds (ruff a heart, cross to dummy's high trump, ruff a club, ruff a diamond and cash two clubs): +2210 gives DIAMOND 13 IMPs, 75-86.

You are in third seat, at unfavorable colors; what would you open with:

♠4 ♡AKQ97543 ◇KJ ♣106

Board 37. N-S Vul.

```
                    ♠ A 10 8 7 2
                    ♡ 6
                    ◇ 10 9 5 2
                    ♣ 7 5 3
    ♠ Q 6 3                          ♠ K J 9 5
    ♡ 10 8              N            ♡ J 2
    ◇ A Q 3         W       E        ◇ 8 7 6 4
    ♣ A K 9 4 2          S           ♣ Q J 8
                    ♠ 4
                    ♡ A K Q 9 7 5 4 3
                    ◇ K J
                    ♣ 10 6
```

Open Room

West	North	East	South
Diamond	*Levin*	*Platnick*	*Weinstein*
	pass	pass	4♡
dbl	pass	4♠	dbl
all pass			

An opening 4♡, or perhaps a stronger version (3NT or 4♣) would have lots
of expert support, and Weinstein's bid seems to work well when it nudges
his opponents into a shaky 4♠ on a 4-3 fit. Those total tricksters who tell
you that East should pass the takeout double with his modest balanced hand
probably believe their hype, but I am quite certain the records of major events
will confirm that taking out to 4♠ would be the popular choice, right or
wrong. When Weinstein doubles 4♠ to show his 4♡ opening was on the
strong side, Levin is delighted to pass, but 4♠ doubled doesn't fare too badly.
On the second heart, Levin needs to find a discard, and thinks a diamond
switch might be more expensive than a more passive club switch, so he parts
with the ♣3, nominally encouraging, but really denying the ◇J or ◇K. When
Weinstein exits with the ♣10, Platnick has time to play on trumps, and then
revert to clubs to discard diamonds as North scores his long trump for down
one, -100. A diamond switch at Trick 3 gives the defense time to build a
diamond trick for a second undertrick.

Closed Room

West	North	East	South
Meckstroth	*Greco*	*Rodwell*	*Hampson*
	pass	pass	1♣*
2♣	pass	3♣	4♡
all pass			

It's interesting to note that, through the years, several expert strong-club pairs have tinkered with playing those methods only when not vulnerable, as it is much more dangerous for their opponents to compete aggressively. Hampson's short-on-defense 1♣ opening at unfavorable vulnerability seems to fly in the face of that idea, but sometimes a show of strength with this sort of hand catches the opponents with the preponderance of strength and no easy way into the auction. Indeed, 1♣ is almost a psyche in some ways! Here, it gets Meckstroth to risk an overcall at the two-level on an atypical hand (strongish, balanced, modest five-card suit), but that has no effect and Hampson's game bid over 3♣ shuts everyone out.

On the lead of the ♣K, Rodwell elects to give a true count with the eight rather than play the queen to show the jack. With spades locked up and a series of easy discards, the defenders can afford a third round of clubs and wait for West's diamond tricks, one down, -100, and 5 IMPs to NICKELL, 91-75.

Board 39. Both Vul.

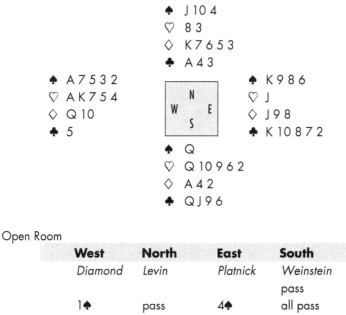

Open Room

	West	North	East	South
	Diamond	Levin	Platnick	Weinstein
				pass
	1♠	pass	4♠	all pass

With no opening bid from South, Levin leads the ◊3 (count): eight, ace, queen, and Weinstein switches to the 'safe' ♡Q. Declarer takes the ace, plays a spade to the king, and a second diamond, to the four, ten and king. Having seen his partner's ♠Q, Levin cashes the ♣A before the mice get at it, and his trump winner is the setting trick, -100.

Closed Room

	West	North	East	South
	Meckstroth	Greco	Rodwell	Hampson
				1♡
	1♠	pass	2NT[1]	pass
	4♠	all pass		

1. Limit raise plus with at least four spades.

Here, Hampson opens the South hand with 1♡, so Greco leads the ♡8: jack, queen, ace. When Meckstroth leads the ♣5 at Trick 2, North ducks, which would be a good idea if declarer's clubs were ♣J5, but that is the last chance for the defense on this lie, as declarer calls for dummy's king, and then delays playing on trumps until he has developed a diamond winner: +620, 12 IMPs for NICKELL, 103-75. Unless Hampson holds a seven-card heart suit, declarer is marked with at least four hearts, so there is significant danger in playing low on the club. If Greco took his ace, he would certainly switch to diamonds.

Board 40. Neither Vul.

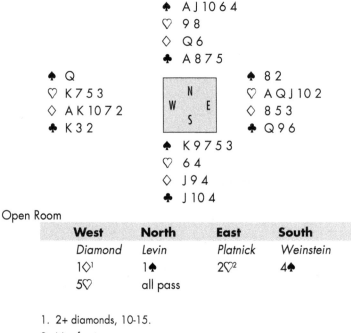

```
                    ♠ A J 10 6 4
                    ♡ 9 8
                    ◇ Q 6
                    ♣ A 8 7 5
   ♠ Q                              ♠ 8 2
   ♡ K 7 5 3              N         ♡ A Q J 10 2
   ◇ A K 10 7 2      W       E      ◇ 8 5 3
   ♣ K 3 2               S         ♣ Q 9 6
                    ♠ K 9 7 5 3
                    ♡ 6 4
                    ◇ J 9 4
                    ♣ J 10 4
```

Open Room

	West	North	East	South
	Diamond	Levin	Platnick	Weinstein
	1◇[1]	1♠	2♡[2]	4♠
	5♡	all pass		

1. 2+ diamonds, 10-15.
2. Non-forcing.

Weinstein's 4♠ exposes his side to a possible -500, but what he gets for his enterprise is +50. He leads the ♠K against 5♡ in case he needs to hold the lead for an important switch. When Levin follows with the six, 'suggesting' a club switch, Weinstein tries the ♣J, but Platnick can run that to his queen and lead a hopeful diamond to the ten after drawing trumps. Levin wins and has to cash the ♣A for one down, -50.

Closed Room

West	North	East	South
Meckstroth	Greco	Rodwell	Hampson
1NT[1]	2♠	3♢[2]	3♠
4♡	all pass		

1. 14-16.
2. Invitational-plus with hearts.

Bidding less, as Hampson does, precludes -500, but sacrifices the opportunity for +50 when his side sells out to 4♡, which is played from the short side thanks to Meckstroth's mildly off-center notrump opening. Greco leads the nine of trumps, and declarer draws a seemingly-gratuitous third round, which curiously gets Hampson to discard a diamond (not that it matters). Declarer ducks a diamond to North and so takes the ten tricks to which he is entitled, +420 and 10 more IMPs for NICKELL, ahead 113-75.

Playing a strong-club system in which a 1NT rebid (11-13 balanced) would be both an underbid and misbid, opening 1NT is a logical choice, often solving rebid problems with an awkward pattern (imagine 1=4=3=5 as an even worse case). It is interesting that Diamond and Meckstroth, playing the same methods, adopt different strategies with the West hand.

Over the years, the ACBL Board of Directors has at different times seriously considered implementing legislation against opening 1NT with a singleton, a remarkably draconian idea theoretically aimed at 'protecting' less-experienced players. Recently, however, some sanity has been restored in this domain with the announcement that 'A notrump opening bid or overcall is natural if, by agreement, it contains no void, at most one singleton which must be the A, K or Q, and no more than two doubletons. If the hand contains a singleton, it may have no doubleton.' As this decree places natural 1NT bids with appropriate 4-4-4-1, 5-4-3-1 and 6-3-3-1 hands on the side of the angels, a righteous protest march on League headquarters in Horn Lake, Mississippi, can be avoided.

I can't help thinking about a statement by Pierre Elliott Trudeau (current Canadian Prime Minister Justin's dad), when he was a heroic Justice Minister: 'There's no place for the state in the bedrooms of the nation.'

The defense has a tiny double-dummy chance to beat 4♡ by East: South must lead the ♣10 in the fashion of Zia, who has told me more than once, 'It might help, you see, and probably won't hurt if partner is alive and breathing'. That might well convince declarer to cover, as ducking to the queen won't work if North has ♣AJxxx and South has a spade entry.

Board 42. Both Vul.

```
                    ♠ A K 2
                    ♡ J 7 5
                    ◇ 4
                    ♣ Q 10 5 4 3 2
   ♠ 10 6 5                           ♠ 9 8 7
   ♡ K 10 8           N               ♡ 9 6 4 3 2
   ◇ K J 8 7 6 3    W   E             ◇ A 10 9 5
   ♣ 6                 S               ♣ 7
                    ♠ Q J 4 3
                    ♡ A Q
                    ◇ Q 2
                    ♣ A K J 9 8
```

Open Room

West	North	East	South
Diamond	*Levin*	*Platnick*	*Weinstein*
		pass	2NT
pass	3♣[1]	pass	3NT
pass	4◇[2]	pass	4♡[3]
pass	4♠[4]	pass	6♣
all pass			

1. Forces 3NT.
2. Clubs.
3. RKCB for clubs.
4. One keycard.

Diamond gives a lot of thought to his lead against the excellent 6♣ (at worst on the heart finesse if the defense takes its diamond trick on the go). To relieve the tension, he says, with a straight face: 'Brian, you could be coughing over there or something, to help me out!'[¶]

¶ At the time, only the German doctors, Entscho Wladow and Michael Elinescu, had been indicted and convicted for collusive cheating (coded coughing was their modus operandi); the deluge would come the following year before the 2015 Bermuda Bowl, when three more pairs (with higher profiles) were caught and a fourth was refused accreditation by the World Bridge Federation.

John Diamond

West leads a third-from-even red eight.

It is a... heart. Declarer claims, +1390.

Do you think East should double 4◇? There are reasons not to do so, which include solving a king-jack guess, establishing the strong hand's diamond honor(s) for discard(s), and the more remote possibility of North-South making 4◇ redoubled.

Closed Room

West	North	East	South
Meckstroth	Greco	Rodwell	Hampson
		pass	2NT
pass	3♣[1]	pass	3♠[2]
pass	4♣[3]	pass	4◇[4]
pass	4♠[5]	pass	5♣
all pass			

1. Stayman.
2. Four or five spades, fewer than four hearts.
3. Natural, no reference to hearts.
4. RKCB for clubs.
5. One keycard.

Just as well for North-South at this table that they do not bid 6♣, as East leads the ◇A, and the heart trick is not going away. That's +600, but another 13 IMPs to NICKELL, 126-75.

Board 44. N-S Vul.

```
              ♠ 10 8 5
              ♡ Q 10 9
              ◇ K J 4 2
              ♣ 7 3 2
  ♠ K J 4                      ♠ A Q 7 3
  ♡ 8 7 3          N           ♡ 6 5 4
  ◇ Q 9 3      W       E       ◇ 10 8 7 6
  ♣ J 10 6 4       S           ♣ K 5
              ♠ 9 6 2
              ♡ A K J 2
              ◇ A 5
              ♣ A Q 9 8
```

Open Room

West	North	East	South
Diamond	Levin	Platnick	Weinstein
pass	pass	pass	1♣
all pass			

On BBO, Chip Martel comments, 'I don't believe Levin really passed'. Bramley, in contrast, describes that pass as 'good judgment'. Indeed, 3NT is not much of a contract (needing no five-card spade threat as well as two finesses), even in pursuit of the vulnerable game bonus, and responding to 1♣ on this layout would normally lead to 3NT: 1♣-1◇; 2NT-3NT. What might not have been apparent to analysts was a recent agreement that a 1◇ response would normally be reserved for suits of at least *five* cards, so that Levin's main alternative would have been 1NT, testing the minimum expectation for that action. In 1♣, Weinstein comes to eight tricks, +90.

Closed Room

West	North	East	South
Meckstroth	Greco	Rodwell	Hampson
pass	pass	1◇[1]	dbl
pass	1NT	pass	3NT
all pass			

1. 2+ diamonds, 10-15.

Against Greco's 3NT, Rodwell leads the ◇6. Declarer takes West's queen with the king and plays a club to the queen for +600, and 11 badly-needed IMPs to DIAMOND, 90-126.

Rodwell later berates himself for not opening a tactical 1♠, which would have given North-South reason to be worried about the possibility of losing five spade tricks. Many (well, most) strong-club aficionados love their 1♢ openings, especially in third seat, where they can have even less than the garbage that is acceptable in first and second. I am surprised that 1♠ is not a much more popular choice facing a passed partner, especially when opening one of a minor on a weak, potentially short holding has so little to gain: 1♠, in addition to creating stopper concern for the opponents, has lead value, allows opener to comfortably pass any non-forcing response, and shuts out the one-level.

NICKELL wins the set 58-33, losing most of those IMPs over the last few deals, and leads by 31, 126-95.

Set 4 Boards 46-60

Board 46. Neither Vul.

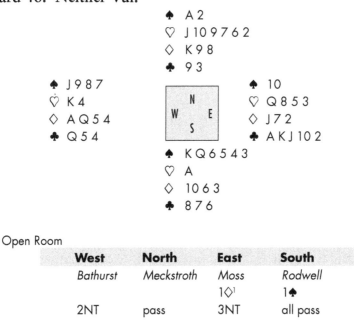

Open Room

	West	North	East	South
	Bathurst	Meckstroth	Moss	Rodwell
			1♢[1]	1♠
	2NT	pass	3NT	all pass

1. 2+ diamonds, 10-15.

If North starts on spades, the contract goes at least two down, as South can clear spades with his heart entry intact, but Meckstroth, very reasonably on the auction, leads the ♡10, Rusinow. Rodwell wins the ace and finds the vital switch to a diamond (else declarer can play on spades to build a trick or kill the defenders' communications), choosing the ten with the idea of discouraging a diamond continuation. Bathurst follows low, and when Meckstroth wins, it is essential to cash three spade tricks. However, still convinced that declarer has at least the ♠Q, he reverts to hearts, playing Rodwell for the ♣Q. Declarer claims ten tricks, +430.

Closed Room

	West	North	East	South
	Weinstein	Greco	Levin	Hampson
			1♣	1♠
	3◇[1]	pass	3♠[2]	pass
	5♣[3]	all pass		

1. Bid 3NT.
2. Spade shortness.
3. Not a great hand, one keycard.

Against 5♣, Hampson leads the ♡A, sees Greco follow with the suit-preference jack, and switches to the ♠3, which gets him his heart ruff. The ◇K is the second undertrick, -100, 11 IMPs for DIAMOND, 106-126.

The fact that neither South overcalls 2♠ at the prevailing vulnerability facing an unpassed hand gives us some idea of how weak the *best* hand for a weak jump overcall would be for their partnerships. At the same time, we might consider how weak these players could be to bid spades freely a second time at a low level.

On Board 47, East is dealt:

♠AQJ8 ♡J1062 ◇10976 ♣3

At both tables, West overcalls a strong club with a natural 2♣, passed back to opener, who has classic shape for his reopening double. North passes for penalty, and it is up to East. I am surprised to see both Moss and Levin redouble for rescue, which works an absolute treat when it gets them to an unbreakable 2♡ doubled (even against best defense at both tables) opposite:

♠54 ♡AQ94 ◇5 ♣KQ9862

No swing at East-West +470. FYI: 2♣ doubled would go one down.

Board 50. N-S Vul.

```
                    ♠ Q 7 4
                    ♡ J 10 6 4 3
                    ◇ Q 5 3
                    ♣ 10 3
      ♠ 6 5                         ♠ 10 8 3
      ♡ 7 2              N          ♡ K Q 9
      ◇ J 10 6 4 2   W     E       ◇ A 9
      ♣ K 9 6 4          S         ♣ A Q 7 5 2
                    ♠ A K J 9 2
                    ♡ A 8 5
                    ◇ K 8 7
                    ♣ J 8
```

Open Room

West	North	East	South
Bathurst	Meckstroth	Moss	Rodwell
		1NT	dbl[1]
2♣[2]	2♡	3♣	3♡
all pass			

1. 'Meckwell': one minor or both majors or a strong spade overcall or some other strong hand (not two-suited).
2. Natural, with a second suit.

Closed Room

West	North	East	South
Weinstein	Greco	Levin	Hampson
		1NT	dbl[1]
pass	2♣[2]	dbl	2♠
4♣	4♠	5♣	dbl
all pass			

1. 'Meckwell': one minor or both majors or a strong spade overcall or some other strong hand (not two-suited).
2. Please explain.

In these days of frequent upgrades and eccentric medium-plus notrump openings, both North-South pairs believe it's important to retain a double that can be used to introduce strong hands, which explains South's initial action.

Bathurst takes the opportunity to make a start on showing his suits, which convinces Meckstroth that the double of 1NT is one of the strong types (spades or ostensibly balanced). With support for spades, it should be safe enough to compete in hearts, but when Moss competes accurately to 3♣, there is no way for North-South to go plus: 3♡ down one, -100, is as good as anything, and better than anything doubled.

Facing a slightly higher minimum, Weinstein is not so keen to get involved, especially as North is almost certain to take out the multi-meaning double. Bobby's double of the artificial pass-or-correct 2♣ shows clubs, and Hampson follows through on his plan with 2♠, strong. Weinstein's 4♣ is theoretically wrong but practically exactly right as it forces Greco to guess. His under-pressure stab at 4♠ is also theoretically wrong, but practically very right. Once North-South reach 4♠ with only about half the deck in high cards, Levin considers it likely that Steve has a stiff spade so that 5♣ will be cheap even if it proves a trick wrong, so he saves, only to find that everything would have cashed. Also, 5♣ doubled is down 300; 9 IMPs to DIAMOND, 115-133.

For what it's worth, perhaps a double of 4♠ in this type of auction should best be defined as, 'I want to bid 5♣ and have nothing in their suit; can you make a better decision?'

Board 51. E-W Vul.

```
              ♠ K 6 2
              ♡ Q 4
              ◇ K J 8 6 3
              ♣ 8 6 3
♠ A Q 10 9 7 4              ♠ J 8 5
♡ A J 9 5         N         ♡ 10 6
◇ A Q        W       E      ◇ 7 2
♣ 2              S          ♣ J 10 9 7 5 4
              ♠ 3
              ♡ K 8 7 3 2
              ◇ 10 9 5 4
              ♣ A K Q
```

Closed Room

	West	North	East	South
	Weinstein	Greco	Levin	Hampson
				1♡
	2♠[1]	pass	pass	dbl
	rdbl	3◇	3♣	pass
	pass	4◇	all pass	

1. Intermediate.

Weinstein prefers a heavy intermediate jump overcall to a heavier simple overcall or an off-shape takeout double. He gets an opportunity to show his extra strength with a follow-up redouble and is well-placed to pass Levin's 3♠, but Greco judges correctly to forge on to 4◇ although he has decent defensive prospects against 3♠. Levin leads the ♣J, which convinces Weinstein to underlead the ♠A to try for a club ruff when he wins the first trump with the ace. Greco plays the ♠K, for +150.

Open Room

West	North	East	South
Bathurst	Meckstroth	Moss	Rodwell
			1♡
dbl	2♣[1]	pass	3◇
3♠	4◇	4♡	5♣
5◇	pass	5♠	all pass

1. Diamonds, natural, or lead-directing.

Bathurst's double-then-spades sequence convinces Moss to bid game, but it's not obvious why he chooses 4♡ over North's 4◇; could he be offering a choice of games if West has secondary clubs and only five spades? North-South have done very well already in the bidding, but there is still plenty of jeopardy for them, as North might well lead a diamond against 4♠ to let it make. Rodwell decides not to take that sort of chance and tries 5♣ to direct the lead should East-West bid on, and indeed, Bathurst, crediting Moss with rather more than he has, tries for slam *en route* to 5♠. Meckstroth leads the ♣2 to the jack and queen, and the diamond switch leads to four tricks for the defense, -200, and 2 IMPs to NICKELL, 135-115. Does East-West's strong bidding dissuade North-South from doubling 5♠? Well, maybe just a bit.

Kevin Bathurst

Board 53. N-S Vul.

```
                    ♠ K 4 3 2
                    ♡ A J 10 7 5 3
                    ◇ A 8
                    ♣ 10
    ♠ Q 10 7 6 5              ♠ 8
    ♡ K 4          N          ♡ 9 6
    ◇ 6 3 2      W   E        ◇ K Q J 10 7 4
    ♣ 7 5 3        S          ♣ K J 9 2
                    ♠ A J 9
                    ♡ Q 8 2
                    ◇ 9 5
                    ♣ A Q 8 6 4
```

Open Room

West	North	East	South
Bathurst	Meckstroth	Moss	Rodwell
	1♡	2◇	4♡¹
all pass			

1. Wide range.

Against 4♡, Moss leads the ♠8 (nine, ten, king). Meckstroth plays a second spade, which Moss gives a long look before ruffing in (five from Bathurst) to switch to the ◇K. Declarer takes the ace, cashes the ♡A, plays the ♣A, ruffs a club, ♠A, another club ruff and claims ten tricks when the ♣K does not surface, +620.

Closed Room

West	North	East	South
Weinstein	Greco	Levin	Hampson
	1♡	2◇	2NT¹
pass	3◇*	pass	3♠
dbl	4♠²	pass	5♡³
pass	6♡	all pass	

1. Limit raise plus in hearts.
2. RKCB for hearts.
3. 2 keycards + ♡Q.

Although there are no fast losers in 6♡, twelve tricks are far from assured, and this is the sort of slam you'd rather not bid at single dummy. Greco's 3◇

is a slam try, and once Hampson cooperates, Greco ignores the double of 3♠ to unleash RKCB and drive to slam. Levin leads his stiff spade, but with both rounded kings onside and the spades well located for the purposes of ruffing the last in dummy, 6♡ is cold on any lead: +1430, 13 IMPs to DIAMOND, now only 6 IMPs behind, 129-135. The deficit had been over 50 a dozen deals earlier.

Board 54. E-W Vul.

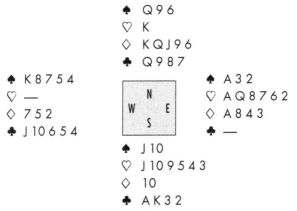

```
              ♠ Q 9 6
              ♡ K
              ◇ K Q J 9 6
              ♣ Q 9 8 7
♠ K 8 7 5 4                      ♠ A 3 2
♡ —              N              ♡ A Q 8 7 6 2
◇ 7 5 2      W       E          ◇ A 8 4 3
♣ J 10 6 5 4     S              ♣ —
              ♠ J 10
              ♡ J 10 9 5 4 3
              ◇ 10
              ♣ A K 3 2
```

Open Room

West	North	East	South
Bathurst	Meckstroth	Moss	Rodwell
		1♡	pass
1♠	2◇	dbl[1]	pass
2♠	pass	4♡	dbl
4♠	dbl	all pass	

1. Three-card spade support.

Closed Room

West	North	East	South
Weinstein	Greco	Levin	Hampson
		1♡	pass
1♠[1]	2◇	3◇	pass
3♠	pass	4♠	all pass

1. Nearly always at least five spades.

Both East players aggressively commit to game over a simple 1♠ response, at least in part because they hope to keep hearts in the picture. As Weinstein's 1♠, thanks to Flannery, would normally deliver at least five, the bold choice is more attractive for Levin than Moss, and in the Closed Room, doubling 4♠ is not really a consideration. In the Open Room, however, Moss's dalliance with hearts creates a doubling rhythm that costs his side 7 IMPs. Declarer has only one sure loser but is miles from piecing together ten winners, and with a minor divergence in the play, both come to eight tricks (-500 and -200). They win the diamond lead and then play the ♡A followed by the master ♡Q to discard diamonds; North ruffs and exits with the ♣9, and declarer crossruffs until he can't. NICKELL now up by 13, 142-129.

Board 57. E-W Vul.

```
              ♠ K J 10
              ♡ A K 7 5 2
              ◇ K 6
              ♣ 10 4 2
♠ 9 8 6 5 4 3              ♠ 7
♡ 9              N          ♡ J 6 4
◇ A 8 7 2   W     E        ◇ Q J 5 4
♣ J 3            S          ♣ A K 9 6 5
              ♠ A Q 2
              ♡ Q 10 8 3
              ◇ 10 9 3
              ♣ Q 8 7
```

	West	North	East	South
Open Room	Bathurst	Meckstroth	Moss	Rodwell
Closed Room	Weinstein	Greco	Levin	Hampson
		1NT	pass	3NT
	all pass			

Moss leads the ♣6, fourth-best, and Meckstroth, who also had to worry about the diamond suit, boldly calls for dummy's queen, bucking the two-to-one odds (♣AJ965 or ♣KJ965 versus the actual holding) in the suit taken in isolation, and is home with his ninth trick and +400.

As commentator Barnet Shenkin presciently volunteers on BBO, 'He just might guess it — he is Meckstroth, after all!'

Levin leads the 'attitude' ♣5, and Greco plays dummy's seven, the percentage play in clubs, but which here amounts to a wager that Weinstein, with king-low or ace-low in clubs, would not switch to diamonds when the ace is badly placed for declarer. When the ♣J takes the first trick, Greco is quickly two down, -100, 11 IMPs for NICKELL, 158-130.

Board 60. N-S Vul.

```
                    ♠ K 7 6 4 3
                    ♡ 10 7 6
                    ◇ 9 6 4
                    ♣ A 10
    ♠ A J 5 2                          ♠ —
    ♡ Q J 5 4 2      ┌─────────┐       ♡ A 3
    ◇ J 10           │    N    │       ◇ A K Q 7 3 2
    ♣ K 9            │ W     E │       ♣ Q J 8 7 6
                     │    S    │
                     └─────────┘
                    ♠ Q 10 9 8
                    ♡ K 9 8
                    ◇ 8 5
                    ♣ 5 4 3 2
```

Open Room

West	North	East	South
Bathurst	Meckstroth	Moss	Rodwell
1♡	pass	2◇	pass
2♠	pass	3♣[1]	pass
3◇	pass	3♡	pass
3NT	pass	6◇	all pass

1. Fourth suit.

Bathurst's careful 3◇, rather than the 'easy' 3NT, proves the key to the auction: when he subsequently shows a high card in clubs with his 3NT bid, Moss can take a practical shot at 6◇. South's lead of the ♣3 solves declarer's only problem. North puts in the ten, and declarer wins with the jack, crosses to the ◇10, cashes the jack, throws a heart on the ♠A, ruffs a spade high, draws trumps and claims, conceding the ♣A, +920.

It is worth noting that Moss's 3♣ would be the normal move with 3=2=5=3 shape lacking a club guard, but over 3◇ he would have an easy 3♡ or less-frequent 3♠ continuation available.

Closed Room

West	North	East	South
Weinstein	Greco	Levin	Hampson
2◇[1]	pass	2NT[2]	pass
3♡[3]	pass	4♣[4]	pass
4◇[5]	pass	5◇	all pass

1. Flannery: four spades plus five or six hearts, 11-15.
2. Inquiry, at least invitational.
3. 4=5=2=2 minimum.
4. Puppet to 4◇ to follow with a natural slam try.
5. Forced.

Levin would have liked to make his natural slam try a level lower to initiate control-showing and learn whether partner could provide a club honor, but system dictates that he must choose between his non-specific 5◇ slam try, 4♠ (RKCB for diamonds, multi-flawed and not a good idea) and a bash at slam. His choice is clearly best in that context, and has the advantage of allowing Weinstein, who has described his shape and strength accurately, to revalue his hand facing a slam try with long diamonds unsuitable for Blackwood. Although Weinstein likes his minor-suit holdings and ♠A, he doesn't like them enough to raise, so that is +420 (North leads the ♣A); 11 IMPs to DIAMOND for reaching this excellent slam. Deals that seem to depend on pure 'judgment' often generate strong feelings when a partnership gets them wrong, and this one is no exception.

DIAMOND wins the session, 46-39, but NICKELL is still a couple of game swings ahead at the halfway point in the match, 165-141.

Set 5 Boards 61-75

Board 64. Both Vul.

```
              ♠ J 8 4 2
              ♡ Q 8 7
              ◇ 7 5 4
              ♣ A 8 6
♠ 9 3                          ♠ A 7
♡ 10 4 3         N             ♡ A K 5
◇ 10 9 6 3   W       E         ◇ A 2
♣ K J 3 2        S             ♣ Q 10 9 7 5 4
              ♠ K Q 10 6 5
              ♡ J 9 6 2
              ◇ K Q J 8
              ♣ —
```

Open Room

West	North	East	South
Diamond	Levin	Platnick	Weinstein
pass	pass	1♣[1]	dbl[2]
pass[3]	2♠	3♣	3◇
4♣	pass	pass	4♠
5♣	dbl	all pass	

1. Precision.
2. Majors.
3. Negative.

Diamond's decision to bid 5♣ in front of his partner after raising to 4♣ is certainly a captaincy violation, but he is a bit unlucky that, given South's strong bidding, Platnick holds so little in clubs and so many side prime cards. There is no way to avoid a loser in each suit; two down, -500. Perhaps Diamond should make his wager a round earlier by bouncing to 5♣.

Closed Room

West	North	East	South
Katz	Greco	Nickell	Hampson
pass	pass	1♣	1♠
pass	2♠	3♣	3♡
4♣	4♠	dbl	all pass

The auction times out much better for East-West here. Hampson's 4♠ doubled is down one in top tricks, -200, and 12 IMPs for NICKELL, 179-146.

Board 66. E-W Vul.

```
                    ♠ K 9 7 3
                    ♡ A 4
                    ♢ Q J 5 4 2
                    ♣ Q 4
    ♠ Q J 6                        ♠ 4 2
    ♡ 8 6              N           ♡ Q J 9 5 3 2
    ♢ A 8 7 6 3    W     E         ♢ 10 9
    ♣ 9 6 3           S            ♣ 8 5 2
                    ♠ A 10 8 5
                    ♡ K 10 7
                    ♢ K
                    ♣ A K J 10 7
```

Open Room

West	North	East	South
Diamond	Levin	Platnick	Weinstein
		pass	1♣
pass	1♢[1]	pass	2NT
pass	3♡[2]	dbl	4♣
pass	4♠	pass	4NT[3]
pass	5♡[4]	pass	5♠
all pass			

1. Most often 5+ diamonds.
2. Four spades.
3. RKCB for spades.
4. 2 keycards, no ♠Q.

Levin's second-round transfer shows four spades, at least five diamonds, and at least a sound 11 HCP. When Weinstein agrees spades with an advance control-bid of 4♣, Levin's non-forcing 4♠ is not a pure signoff. When Blackwood reveals that a keycard and the trump queen are missing, a five-level spade contract is too high for comfort, but Levin loses only a diamond and a trump, +450.

	West	North	East	South
	Katz	*Greco*	*Nickell*	*Hampson*
			pass	2NT[1]
	pass	3♣	pass	3♠
	pass	4♡[2]	dbl	4♠
	pass	4NT[3]	pass	5♡[4]
	pass	6NT	all pass	

1. 19-21, ostensibly balanced.
2. Artificial slam try in spades.
3. RKCB for spades.
4. 2 keycards, no ♠Q.

Greco, knowing that the ♠Q is missing, and doubly deceived about partner's high-card strength and minimum diamond length, gambles that his diamond suit might provide enough winners in notrump.

West leads the ♡8, and Hampson takes East's jack with the king, and plays the ◊K. When that holds, he crosses to the ♣Q and leads the ◊Q, discarding the ♠5. If West takes his ace, the count will be rectified for declarer, who will have no trouble completing a simple spade-diamond squeeze against West (if East holds three spades he will be squeezed in the majors). Katz, very much alive to the squeeze possibilities, accurately ducks the second diamond, so declarer goes back to clubs, pitching a diamond from dummy on the third round, a spade on the fourth, and finally another diamond on the fifth. When he crosses to the ♡A, West (who has parted with his second heart) has to throw a diamond. Declarer exits with a diamond to West's ace. Back comes the ♠J, which Katz would lead from jack-third. Hampson knows that playing for split spade honors is the textbook restricted-choice play (with both queen and jack, West might lead either honor) in this matrix with nothing to go on, but relies instead on what he knows — that Katz is twice as likely as Nickell to hold any specific missing spade at this point. He runs the ♠J to his ace and finesses the nine on the way back for a magnificent +990, 11 IMPs to DIAMOND.

If Hampson places Katz with only two hearts, as his carding suggests, he could leave another diamond in dummy and come down to only two spades; then, when he crosses in hearts, Katz has to discard a diamond to keep his spades, and Hampson could concede a diamond to develop a diamond trick for his twelfth winner.

Board 72. N-S Vul.

```
              ♠ 6 2
              ♡ J 10 9
              ◇ K Q 9 3 2
              ♣ Q 10 9
♠ 4                          ♠ A K Q 10 9 5
♡ 7 5 4 2         N          ♡ A K 6 3
◇ 10 7 5      W     E        ◇ A 6
♣ K J 7 5 3       S          ♣ 6
              ♠ J 8 7 3
              ♡ Q 8
              ◇ J 8 4
              ♣ A 8 4 2
```

Closed Room

West	North	East	South
Katz	Greco	Nickell	Hampson
pass	pass	2♣	pass
2◇[1]	pass	2♠	pass
3♣	pass	3♡	pass
4♡	all pass		

1. 0 or 1 control.

With trumps 3-2, Nickell's 4♡ is easy enough to make, but the play is of some interest, as declarer must be concerned about 4-1 trumps. He wins the diamond lead, cashes the ♡A, and plays three high spades to discard dummy's diamonds. Greco ruffs, crosses to partner's ♣A, and overruffs dummy on a fourth round of spades. As there is only one trump out now, declarer can extract it when he regains the lead; +420.

Open Room

West	North	East	South
Diamond	Levin	Platnick	Weinstein
pass	pass	1♣*	pass
1◇*	pass	1♠[1]	pass
1NT[2]	pass	4♠	all pass

1. Forcing, at least four spades.
2. 0-5.

Platnick's 4♠ is not easy to make, but the defense needs to be accurate. Weinstein leads the ◇4 to the queen and ace, and declarer plays three high trumps. Levin follows deuce-six to suggest something good in clubs, then discards the ◇3 after dummy parts with the ◇7. Although North's diamond spot-card is a true remainder count, it is not routinely legible, but Levin is reluctant to part with the nine in case the opening lead was a singleton. When Platnick continues with the ♣6, Weinstein ducks. Unfortunately for his side, declarer has no guess. When the king holds, he concedes a trump, a heart and a diamond for +420 and a push.

DIAMOND wins the fifth set, 34-15, and closes to within 5 IMPs, 175-180.

Set 6 Boards 76-90

Board 76. E-W Vul.

```
                    ♠ K Q 8 6 3
                    ♡ 4
                    ◇ K J 7 2
                    ♣ 10 7 5
   ♠ 9 2                            ♠ 7 5 4
   ♡ J 10 6 5           N           ♡ 8
   ◇ Q 10 9 6 5     W       E       ◇ A 8 4
   ♣ 8 6                 S          ♣ Q J 9 4 3 2
                    ♠ A J 10
                    ♡ A K Q 9 7 3 2
                    ◇ 3
                    ♣ A K
```

Open Room

West	North	East	South
Diamond	Katz	Platnick	Nickell
pass	pass	pass	2♣[1]
pass	2♡[2]	pass	3♡
pass	3♠	pass	4♣[3]
pass	4◇[4]	pass	4NT[5]
pass	5◇[6]	pass	6♠
all pass			

1. Forcing to game, 2NT or three of a major.
2. 2 controls.
3. Ostensibly natural, but perhaps not.
4. Waiting, until further notice.
5. RKCB for spades.
6. 1 keycard.

As a raise to 4♠ would not be forcing (though it would be after a 2♠ response showing 3+ controls), Nickell continues with a nominally natural 4♣ hoping to buy time to sort out the strain choice between the majors. With no clear direction, Katz stalls with 4◇, but when Nickell continues with 4NT, Katz accurately interprets it as RKCB for spades, perhaps part of a planned auction to finish in a solid heart suit after clarifying the spade-honor situation. The two-control response to 2♣ marks Katz with either the ◇A or both the spade and diamond kings, so if the partnership is in sync, Nickell can check on the ♠Q by bidding 5♡ and stop in 5♠ if it is missing. However, he is aware that the auction has been less than straightforward and that 5♡ might be treated as natural and non-forcing, so he simplifies life for his partner by bidding a slam he knows will be reasonable opposite both possible control combinations, thanks to the ♠J10.

After losing Trick 1 to the ◇A, Katz wins the heart switch in dummy, cashes the ♠AJ, ruffs a heart high, crosses to the ♠10, and claims, +980.

Closed Room

West	North	East	South
Meckstroth	Greco	Rodwell	Hampson
pass	pass	pass	1♣[1]
pass	1♠	pass	2♣[2]
pass	2NT[3]	pass	3♡
pass	3♠	pass	4♠*
pass	4NT*	pass	6♡
all pass			

1. 16+ unbalanced or 18+ balanced.
2. At least five hearts.
3. Five spades, singleton or void in hearts.

Hampson could support spades early, but understandably prefers to 'rebid' hearts. That has the effect of making his 4♠ over Greco's 3♠ (values for hearts) RKCB for hearts. Because Hampson knows his partner would not 'like' his hand for hearts with at best king-queen fifth of spades, a suit that might be facing shortness if he were void in hearts, Hampson votes in the end for the 'solid' 7-1 fit. West leads the ◇10 and dummy's king loses to East's ace. The cruel 4-1 trump break leaves Hampson one down, -50. So 14 IMPs to NICKELL, 194-175.

Chip Martel, doing live commentary on BBO, notes that, 'DIAMOND has had 100 IMPs of slam luck in this match (or perhaps more) going into this board, so NICKELL will doubtless think they are due for a little luck.'

Or more than a little luck...

Board 77. Neither Vul.

```
              ♠ 10 9 8 4
              ♡ 5 4
              ◇ 10
              ♣ A 9 8 7 5 4
♠ K J 7 2                      ♠ A Q 6 3
♡ J 10          N              ♡ A 9
◇ K 9 7 4     W   E            ◇ A Q J 8 5 3
♣ Q J 6         S              ♣ K
              ♠ 5
              ♡ K Q 8 7 6 3 2
              ◇ 6 2
              ♣ 10 3 2
```

Open Room

West	North	East	South
Diamond	Katz	Platnick	Nickell
	pass	1♣[1]	2♡
dbl[2]	rdbl[3]	3◇	pass
3♡	pass	3♠	pass
4♠	all pass		

1. Strong.
2. 6-7 or a game force with no accurate bid.
3. Nominally a transfer to spades.

With spades 4-1, a heart lead would beat the excellent 6♠, so in theory Platnick and Diamond are in their best contract on this layout, perhaps sublimi-
nally influenced by Katz's strange redouble, which purports to show long or
lead-worthy spades. As Platnick remembers it, once the bidding tray was
passed, Katz wrote him a note saying that his redouble was an inadvertent
misbid, but that his explanation of the meaning of redouble was correct.
Nickell, who takes the redouble at face value and believes East-West are playing in North's suit, leads a trump, so Platnick coasts home with twelve tricks,
+480. Would that better-than-par result be a winner for DIAMOND?

Closed Room

West	North	East	South
Meckstroth	Greco	Rodwell	Hampson
	pass	1♣*	2◇[1]
dbl[2]	rdbl[3]	pass	2♡
3♡	pass	4◇	pass
5◇	pass	6◇	all pass

1. Hearts or spades.
2. 6-7 or a game force with no accurate bid.
3. Bid your suit.

When Rodwell does not bid his long suit over Greco's 'asking' redouble, he is obliged to show it at the four-level at his next turn, and spades get lost in the shuffle. It takes a heart lead to set 6◇, but as that would virtually require the suit to be 7-2-2-2, Hampson chooses the far more attractive spade lead, needing to find Greco with one of the pointed-suit aces. Not this time: Rodwell draws trumps and concedes a club for +920 and 10 IMPs to NICKELL, 204-175. Luck seems to have established residence in NICKELL's camp.

There are two main variations for advancer after the (increasingly-popular) Multi 2◇ overcall is doubled, the other being as follows:

- redouble forces 2♡ (sort of like Lebensohl) to allow advancer to play in his own long suit
- 2♡/2♠ and 3♡/3♠ are pass or correct
- minor-suit bids and 2NT accommodate partnership interests (lead direction, game tries, high-level transfers or requests to transfer)

The meaning of advancer's double of 3♡ in our auction would depend on his options over the double of 2◇. Whether Greco could get his clubs into the picture and whether it would make sense for him to do so are separate issues.

Board 80. Both Vul.

```
              ♠ 10 5 3
              ♡ 8 6
              ◇ A 7 6
              ♣ A J 6 5 4
  ♠ A J 8 2                    ♠ K
  ♡ J 9 7 4 3      N           ♡ A K 10 5
  ◇ —          W       E       ◇ K J 10 9 5 2
  ♣ K 10 7 2       S           ♣ 9 3
              ♠ Q 9 7 6 4
              ♡ Q 2
              ◇ Q 8 4 3
              ♣ Q 8
```

Open Room

West	North	East	South
Diamond	*Katz*	*Platnick*	*Nickell*
pass	pass	1◇[1]	pass
1♡	pass	4♡[2]	all pass

1. 2+ diamonds, 10-15.
2. Distributional.

Diamond takes quite a while to pass 4♡. As Katz knows declarer was think-ing of slam, he reasons that the only real chance to defeat game will be to arrange some ruffs, and that would logically need to be in dummy's known long-suit. Alas, West ruffs the lead of the ◇A, cashes dummy's top hearts and the ◇K, then runs the ◇J. All his clubs go away, +710.

Closed Room

West	North	East	South
Meckstroth	*Greco*	*Rodwell*	*Hampson*
pass	pass	1◇[1]	pass
1♡	pass	3♡	pass
3♠[2]	pass	3NT[3]	pass
4♣[4]	pass	4◇	pass
5◇[5]	pass	6♡	all pass

1. 2+ diamonds, 10-15.
2. Asking for shortage.
3. Short spades, probably singleton.
4-5. Control bids.

Although Rodwell settles for 3♡, Meckstroth treats that with great respect, going past game to show his diamond control, although shortness in his long suit would often not be what opener needs. It is not obvious whether Rodwell bids slam because of his strong trumps or because he expects Meckstroth to hold the ◊A. Against 6♡, Greco leads his lower trump, and declarer wins with dummy's ace, ruffs a diamond, plays a spade to the king, ruffs a diamond, cashes the ♠A to discard a club, ruffs a spade, and ruffs a diamond with the jack. When the ace appears, Meckstroth leads his remaining trump to the king, and claims twelve tricks when the queen drops (as expected once North follows); +1430.

After the trump lead, which points to North holding something of value in dummy's suit, Meckstroth is not about to adopt the alternative line in diamonds — two ruffing finesses against the ace-queen in South — but ruffing out ace-third of diamonds is still not much of a chance (less than 30%).

That's 12 IMPs to NICKELL, ahead by 35, 216-181, thanks to 36 IMPs in the plus column for those three slam deals.

DIAMOND does appreciably better on the non-slam hands in the rest of this set, only one of which is a game swing (on a superior line of play), and outscores NICKELL by 21 IMPs over those deals. Overall, DIAMOND loses Set 6 by a slender 9 IMPs, 32-41. With 30 boards to play, NICKELL is only 14 IMPs ahead, 221-207.

Set 7 Boards 91-105

Board 92. E-W Vul.

```
                    ♠ Q 10 4
                    ♡ 6 3
                    ◊ A J 7 5 3
                    ♣ A 3 2
     ♠ A J 9 5 3                      ♠ K 8 6 2
     ♡ 8 7 2            N             ♡ A 10
     ◊ K Q 10       W       E         ◊ 9 8 6
     ♣ J 5             S             ♣ 9 8 7 6
                    ♠ 7
                    ♡ K Q J 9 5 4
                    ◊ 4 2
                    ♣ K Q 10 4
```

Open Room

West	North	East	South
Greco	Levin	Hampson	Weinstein
1♠	pass	3♡[1]	4♡
all pass			

1. Mixed spade raise.

Closed Room

West	North	East	South
Meckstroth	Moss	Rodwell	Bathurst
1♠	pass	3♠[1]	4♡
all pass			

1. Mixed raise.

Both Easts, dealt a classic mixed raise, in the boss suit, no less, are pleased to use the treatment. South, under pressure, is more or less bullied into taking a stab at 4♡, which proves to be the right thing to do for North-South, as 4♡ can't be defeated while East-West would go for 800 in 4♠ doubled. No swing at North-South +420.

Would North-South get to 4♡ if East raised to 2♠? Maybe not, as 3♡ by South would almost universally be treated as a pre-balancing action these days. Sure, any East raising only to 2♠ would bid 3♠ if 3♡ comes around to him, but if North-South did not bid 4♡ earlier, they would sell out to 3♠ now, and North would not double. This is not to say that the mixed raise is a bad idea; it is not, and has clearly proven its value over time, but perhaps we too often ignore that there is a downside to even the best of treatments.

Board 95. E-W Vul.

```
                  ♠ J 9 8 7 3
                  ♡ J 9 5 4 2
                  ◇ A 5 4
                  ♣ —
    ♠ 6                            ♠ A Q 10 4 2
    ♡ A K 7 6          N           ♡ Q 10 8
    ◇ J 9 8        W       E       ◇ 6 2
    ♣ K J 8 7 5        S           ♣ A 4 3
                  ♠ K 5
                  ♡ 3
                  ◇ K Q 10 7 3
                  ♣ Q 10 9 6 2
```

Open Room

West	North	East	South
Greco	Levin	Hampson	Weinstein
			pass
1◇[1]	2♡[2]	dbl	2♠
3♡	pass	3NT	all pass

1. 2+ diamonds, 10-15.
2. Majors, non-forcing.

Levin's two-suited 2♡, though limited and at favorable vulnerability, is a stretch. Greco's 3♡ looks weird, but he is reluctant to defend 2♠ doubled (probably -300) without doing something about getting his unbid five-card suit into the mix, albeit indirectly. Hampson, deprived of his penalty double, can hardly do anything but bid 3NT, which is not a lovely contract. However, when Weinstein, who holds a remarkably strong hand on the auction, leads the ♠K, Hampson's prospects have improved. He wins with the ace, and cashes the ♣A, North discarding the ♡4. A club to the nine and jack is followed by the ♡A, and a heart to the ten. Hampson cashes out for +600.

Closed Room

West	North	East	South
Meckstroth	Moss	Rodwell	Bathurst
			1◇[1]
1♡	1♠	2♣[2]	pass[3]
2♡	pass	pass	2♠
dbl	pass	pass	rdbl
pass	3◇	pass	pass
dbl	all pass		

1. 2+ diamonds, 10-15.
2. Transfer cuebid, showing heart support.
3. Fewer than three spades.

Having opened a shapely 10-count, and seen Moss limit his hand by passing West's retreat to 2♡ after a strength-showing move by East, let's settle for describing South's reopening 2♠ as simply 'bold.' Meckstroth, having signed off at his previous turn, feels he can afford to compete further and hopes his flexible double will not get him to 3♡ with only seven combined trumps. Indeed, double is just the bidding card Rodwell wants to see, but Bathurst isn't quite done; he redoubles for rescue, and finds Moss with both a three-card minor and a void in the other. With all the side suits locked up, Meckstroth is willing to double 3◇, although North-South are likely to have eight or nine trumps.

It's surprising that he does not start trumps, but Rodwell takes the opening spade lead with the ace and switches to the ◇2. Bathurst wins with dummy's ace and plays a heart, East winning with the eight to return a second trump. Declarer wins with the king, ruffs a club, ruffs a heart (West unblocking the ace), draws the outstanding trump, and plays the ♣Q. West takes the king and exits with the ♡7. Declarer ruffs away East's queen with his last trump, and leads the ♣10. What to make of that? The bidding has not clearly established whether South or East holds the ♣A. As playing low on the ♣10 would allow the contract to make if declarer holds it, Meckstroth goes in with the jack to ensure a set. When East's ace appears, as Meckstroth suspected it would, Bathurst can claim one down, -100. That is 11 IMPs for DIAMOND, just a fraction behind now at 218-221.

DIAMOND was due to gain significantly in any case; the second undertrick would have saved NICKELL only 4 IMPs on one of the stranger deals so far in the match.

Board 96. Both Vul.

```
                    ♠ J 9 3 2
                    ♡ A Q 10 9
                    ◇ A 7 3
                    ♣ A 8
      ♠ A Q 8                        ♠ K 10 6 5
      ♡ K J 7 5 4 3 2      N         ♡ 8 6
      ◇ J 5 2          W       E     ◇ Q 9
      ♣ —                  S         ♣ 10 9 5 4 2
                    ♠ 7 4
                    ♡ —
                    ◇ K 10 8 6 4
                    ♣ K Q J 7 6 3
```

Open Room

West	North	East	South
Greco	Levin	Hampson	Weinstein
1♡	1NT	pass	2♠[1]
pass	2NT[2]	pass	3◇[3]
pass	3♡[4]	pass	3♠[5]
pass	3NT	all pass	

1. Artificial range ask, or clubs.
2. Minimum.
3. At least 5-5 minors.
4. Relay.

Although North's bidding has not announced *four* stoppers in opener's suit, Hampson backs his judgment and attacks with the ♠5, from a modest four-card suit. And right he is. Greco makes the textbook play of the queen, and is in a strong position to cash out the suit, declarer pitching two diamonds from dummy (as who would not?) as West parts with his middle heart, neutral. This is still not so easy for Hampson, but he continues his good work by switching to the ◇Q, and declarer wins with the ace to cash the ♣A, preparing to claim, which leads to... 'You're kidding me,' from Levin, who is soon two down, -200.

Please don't write to tell us that 3NT can be made. That would require taking an inconceivable, unnatural line of play on what seems to be a straightforward deal. Declarer must discard no more than one diamond from dummy on the run of the spades, essentially discarding his ninth winner — a club — to retain a dubious threat. East is endplayed, and depending on which unsafe exit he chooses, declarer can either squeeze West in the reds or make four diamond tricks without losing one.

Closed Room

	West	North	East	South
	Meckstroth	Moss	Rodwell	Bathurst
	1♡	pass	1♠	3♣
	dbl[1]	pass	3♠	pass
	pass	dbl	pass	pass
	4♡	dbl	all pass	

1. Three-card spade support, decent hand in context.

Moss's decision to pass on the first round works spectacularly well. Meckstroth does not have to get involved over 3♣, but it wouldn't take much from partner to offer a good play for game in a major. Offering preference to 3♡ probably would have worked better for Rodwell, but Moss is clearly ready to double everything. As 3♠ would be dreadful on a trump lead, Meckstroth saves something by going back to hearts. Moss leads the ♠2 against 4♡ doubled, and when dummy's ten holds, declarer plays a heart. South's discard lets declarer know he is booked for three down, -800.

If declarer divines that South is void in trumps he can escape for two down by never touching the suit — he can ruff a diamond in dummy and ruff clubs in hand, and eventually, North will be endplayed. Triumphs like -500 are not the stuff of victory photos, however. DIAMOND gains 14 IMPs and takes the lead in style, 232-221.

Brad Moss

Board 100. Neither Vul.

```
                  ♠ A K 10 9
                  ♡ A 4 2
                  ◇ 10 6 5 4 3
                  ♣ 2
    ♠ J 8 7 6 3                      ♠ Q 2
    ♡ J 7              N             ♡ K 5 3
    ◇ Q 7         W         E        ◇ A 9 8
    ♣ K Q 7 3          S            ♣ J 10 8 6 4
                  ♠ 5 4
                  ♡ Q 10 9 8 6
                  ◇ K J 2
                  ♣ A 9 5
```

Open Room

West	North	East	South
Greco	Levin	Hampson	Weinstein
pass	1◇	pass	1♡
pass	2♡	pass	4♡
all pass			

Rather than risk overstating his strength by supporting hearts voluntarily later, Levin suppresses his spades and raises directly. Greco leads the ♣K: deuce, jack, ace. Weinstein crosses to the ♠A to lead a diamond down. Hampson goes in with the ace and forces dummy with a club. Declarer continues with a diamond to the jack, but West wins the queen to exit with a spade. Declarer takes dummy's king, ruffs a spade (diamond from East), ruffs a club, ruffs a spade, crosses to the ♡A and plays a diamond. East ruffs in front of his partner, and plays a club, but declarer accurately ruffs with the queen for one down, -50.

Closed Room

West	North	East	South
Meckstroth	Moss	Rodwell	Bathurst
pass	1◇[1]	pass	1♡
dbl	rdbl[2]	3♣	3♡
pass	4♡	all pass	

1. 2+ diamonds, 10-15.
2. Three-card heart support.

West leads a Rusinow ♣Q, and Bathurst wins with the ace, ruffs a club and plays a diamond. When East follows with the nine, declarer, who can place West with ♣KQ and (surely) a spade honor, goes up with the king — with the ◇A, Meckstroth would have opened. Now come three rounds of spades, ruffing (♣8 from East). A club ruff is followed by another spade ruff (♣4 from East), and declarer exits with the ◇J. West wins with the queen and plays the ♡7 to dummy's blank ace, but declarer plays a diamond to East's ace then goes up with the queen on the forced heart return — with the ♡K, Meckstroth would have opened — for a beautifully-played +420, and 10 more IMPs to DIAMOND, now ahead by 20, 246-226.

Board 105. Both Vul.

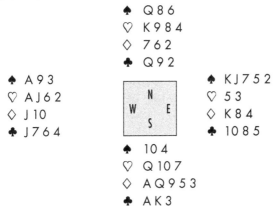

```
              ♠ Q 8 6
              ♡ K 9 8 4
              ◇ 7 6 2
              ♣ Q 9 2
♠ A 9 3                      ♠ K J 7 5 2
♡ A J 6 2          N         ♡ 5 3
◇ J 10         W       E     ◇ K 8 4
♣ J 7 6 4          S         ♣ 10 8 5
              ♠ 10 4
              ♡ Q 10 7
              ◇ A Q 9 5 3
              ♣ A K 3
```

At both tables, South's third-seat 1NT is passed out. Do you have a strong view about what West should lead?

There was a time when the ♡2 would have been a nearly-unanimous choice, but it's been many years since that was so, at least in strong competition. Meckstroth's choice is the ◇J, showing either a long queen-jack holding or a short jack-ten holding. The idea is to avoid blowing a cheap trick, combining safety with the possibility of establishing winners. Rodwell innocently encourages with the four, and Bathurst, declarer, does likewise by following lowest. You can see what happens next: Meckstroth continues diamonds, and declarer runs for cover with four diamonds and three clubs for +90.

Greco, too, does not lead his best suit, but chooses his fourth-best club, from a holding that for many years was low on the pecking order of desirable combinations, only slightly less unattractive against notrump than suits. That works remarkably well in a subtle way, as it makes it difficult for declarer to conceal his holding in the suit on the way to establishing diamonds. One possibility is to play dummy's nine, hoping to take the ten or jack with the king to play a low diamond (although that gives up on jack-ten doubleton onside), intending to use the ♣Q later to lead a diamond to the queen. Weinstein opts to cater to *all* the obvious diamond positions by winning with the ♣Q at Trick 1 (ten from East) to lead a diamond to the queen, which holds (eight from East, jack from West). Weinstein continues with a low diamond, and Greco is permitted to hold the trick with the ten. Those diamond plays by East are by agreement suit preference, so you can see what happens next at this table, too: Greco switches to ace and another spade and the defense soon takes five spades and the ♡A to set the contract: -100, and 5 IMPs to DIAMOND.

Declarer can make 1NT legitimately by playing West for the ♡J, a line that has far less appeal at Bathurst's table.

DIAMOND wins the set convincingly, 47-6, to turn the match around, and with one 15-board set remaining, leads by 27 IMPs, 254-227.

Set 8 Boards 106-120

There aren't many opportunities to generate swings on the first nine deals, but both East-West pairs (Bathurst-Moss and Levin-Weinstein) earn a handful of IMPs on partials by competing accurately to the three-level to nudge their opponents a level higher...

On Board 106, East holds:

♠Q972 ♡A3 ◇1084 ♣KQ108

with neither side vulnerable. Both Easts open in a minor and see partner respond at the two-level with a bid that shows five spades and at least four hearts, less than invitational strength. RHO overcalls 3◇. Well — 3♠ or not 3♠? Bathurst's 3♠ is the winner as it can't be defeated, and bidding induces the opponents to overbid to 5◇, two down, -100. Levin's pass is the last chance for his side, and 3◇ yields +110, 5 IMPs to DIAMOND

On Board 109, West holds:

♠97 ♡87 ◇AQ10875 ♣752

with neither side vulnerable. At both tables, North opens a strong club and South responds 1◇. At Moss's table, Bathurst (East) has doubled 1♣ to show the majors and the voluntary 1◇ response from South shows 5-7. Moss passes, then sells out to 1NT, which yields +120 on a non-diamond lead. At Weinstein's table, Levin has passed as East and 1◇ is 0-7. Weinstein overcalls 2◇ and eventually defends 3♡ on a 4-3 fit, down 100, 6 IMPs to NICKELL.

Board 111. E-W Vul.

```
              ♠ K 10 9 7
              ♡ K Q 6 4
              ◇ 10 3
              ♣ 8 5 3
♠ 8 5 4 3                    ♠ J 6
♡ 7 2            N           ♡ J 10 9 8 5
◇ 5 4        W     E         ◇ J 7 6
♣ A J 10 9 2     S           ♣ K 7 6
              ♠ A Q 2
              ♡ A 3
              ◇ A K Q 9 8 2
              ♣ Q 4
```

Open Room

West	North	East	South
Moss	Meckstroth	Bathurst	Rodwell
			1♣¹
pass	2◇²	pass	3◇³
pass	3♡⁴	pass	3NT⁵
all pass			

1. Strong.
2. Balanced, 8-10.
3. Puppet to 3♡: one-suited diamonds or secondary major with splinter in the other major.
4. Forced.
5. 6+ diamonds, balanced, offer to play.

Closed Room

West	North	East	South
Weinstein	Greco	Levin	Hampson
			1♣¹
pass	1♡²	pass	2◇
pass	2♡³	pass	2NT
pass	3NT	all pass	

1. Strong.
2. 8-11, denies 5+ spades.
3. Waiting, no good five-card suit.

At both tables West leads the ♣10 and the defense cashes five club tricks for an unhappy (for North-South) push at -50.

Although North-South have two balanced hands and 29 combined HCP with no weak doubleton, 3NT is not their best contract, and they pay heavily for not conducting a more thorough investigation that might lead to 5◊ or 4♠. For Meckstroth and Rodwell, it appears that system gets in the way, but in the Closed Room, South's two-step to 2NT implies 6-3-2-2 with stoppers of the actual ilk. It's difficult to see why North should get involved with stopper-showing in this context.

This is actually a good combination for strong club partnerships who needn't treat the South hand as some strong balanced range without mentioning diamonds cheaply. However, it seems straightforward for South, after showing his suit, to represent his hand as otherwise balanced with values everywhere. Just a very tough combination.

Board 114 is a fairly-normal 4♡ for North-South that might on a good day be bid to a lucky six. Both pairs stop in four, +450. The deal is noteworthy, however, because Weinstein, at unfavorable colors, facing a passed partner, overcalls RHO's strong club with 1♠ on:

♠9763 ♡K3 ◊Q1053 ♣AK10

When Levin innocently raises to 2♠ on king-third and a jack, a penalty double would extract a penalty of 1400 or so... and on this deal an opponent has been dealt ♠AQJ82! Did Weinstein misread the bidding tray and believe it was *Levin* who had opened 1♠?

So, Steve-o, what really happened?

Steve Weinstein

'I psyched. I had visions of running the clubs against 3NT. Hampson and Greco were in a groove and seemed incredibly comfortable. I felt like the risk/reward with Bobby being a passed hand was there, given the spot we were in, with the likely score and number of boards left.'

Thanks. Now back to Anderson Cooper in Kabul.

NICKELL has gained 1 IMP so far (the set score is 9-8), so DIAMOND leads by 26 with only six deals remaining.

Board 115. Both Vul.

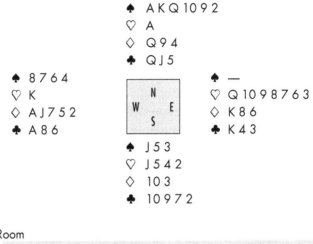

Open Room

West	North	East	South
Moss	Meckstroth	Bathurst	Rodwell
			pass
1◇[1]	4♠	5♡	pass
pass	dbl	all pass	

1. 2+ diamonds, 10-15.

Meckstroth, facing a passed partner, opts to bash 4♠, giving up on 3NT or a partscore. Bathurst, who has a pressure guess over 4♠, buys a rather good dummy for a Precision 1◇ noise. In 5♡ doubled, he ruffs the opening spade lead, and leads a trump to the king and ace. North's best move now is to switch to a club honor, but that is not without risk, and Meckstroth plays another spade. Declarer ruffs, cashes the ♡Q (♠2 from North), and plays a diamond to the jack and queen. A third spade reduces declarer's trumps to South's length, but Bathurst can drive out the ♡J and get back to hand safely to draw the last trump. The club loser goes on a diamond winner, and he is only one down, -200.

West	North	East	South
Weinstein	Greco	Levin	Hampson
			pass
1◇	dbl	4♡	pass
pass	4♠	dbl	all pass

After the natural 1◇, Greco settles for a double-then-spades strategy to show a strong hand. Levin's 4♡ (somewhat ironically the same tactical approach as teammate Meckstroth's) virtually forces Greco to bid 4♠, and Levin, with peculiar values for his preempt, doubles to say that he believes the deal belongs to his side and to invite cooperation. It is far from clear that West should pass the double with three keycards and a combining jack, plus no wasted strength in spades, but Weinstein judges well, counting on his spade length to be a nuisance for declarer.

After a heart lead to the king and ace, Greco can ensure one down by staying off trumps, but he cashes the ♠A before broaching clubs, and is now in down-two territory when West wins the first club and plays a second trump around to dummy. When declarer calls for the ◇3, West can go in with the ace to play a third trump, after which East would wait to win the *third* round of clubs before exiting safely with the ♡Q, leaving declarer to lose to both the jack and king of diamonds. West plays low on the first round of diamonds, however, and East takes the nine with his king, and leads the ♡Q for West to discard a club. With the ♡J high now, Greco draws trumps and leads the ♣J. Whenever East takes his ♣K, he must give dummy the ♡J or the long club, or give declarer the ◇Q, so Greco escapes for down one after all, -200 and 9 IMPs for NICKELL, 17 behind at 245-262.

Having won the deal at both tables in the bidding, perfect defense in difficult positions by both NICKELL pairs would have brought in another 5 IMPs.

Board 117. E-W Vul.

```
                  ♠ 10 9 7 2
                  ♡ A 3
                  ◇ 10 3 2
                  ♣ 10 6 5 4
  ♠ K 4                              ♠ Q J 8 6 3
  ♡ K J 10 9 7        N              ♡ 8 4
  ◇ A J 7 6       W       E          ◇ K 4
  ♣ 9 7               S              ♣ A Q 3 2
                  ♠ A 5
                  ♡ Q 6 5 2
                  ◇ Q 9 8 5
                  ♣ K J 8
```

Open Room

West	North	East	South
Moss	Meckstroth	Bathurst	Rodwell
	pass	1♠	dbl
2◇[1]	pass	2♡	pass
3◇	pass	3♡	pass
4♡	all pass		

1. Hearts.

Rather than look for a non-vulnerable penalty after Rodwell's aggressive takeout double, Moss decides to start showing his hand to investigate the best vulnerable game. As Bathurst would usually jump with three-card heart support, it might have been better for Moss to show his spade support at his third turn, which would have led to 3NT, a contract that offers some chances for a make.

Against the uncomfortable 4♡, South does well to stay off a club lead, instead choosing the six of trumps, a card that he hopes will convince declarer he doesn't hold the queen and that might be read by Meckstroth as reverse suit preference for clubs when it matters. Bathurst expects the takeout doubler to hold the ♡A, and can stand two trump losers if he can avoid a club loser. If the ♡K wins Trick 1, Bathurst intends to start on spades, but Meckstroth takes the ♡K with the ace and returns a club, which leaves declarer with four losers, for one down, -100.

West	North	East	South
Weinstein	*Greco*	*Levin*	*Hampson*
	pass	1♠	dbl
rdbl	pass	pass	1NT
dbl	2♣	dbl	rdbl
pass	2◇	pass	pass
dbl	all pass		

Here too, South is willing to double for takeout facing a passed partner, but unlike Rodwell, Hampson finds trouble when Weinstein redoubles and North-South have nowhere to run ('... to, baby, nowhere to hide' — Martha and the Vandellas, 1965). Delighted to defend with a minimum opening and a balanced hand, Levin leads the king of trumps to make a start towards protecting the defenders' high cards.

After three rounds of trumps, East discarding the ♣3 (standard count, reverse attitude, but a tough card to read with confidence), Weinstein switches to the ♡10, as East is likely to hold the ♡A, and if he does, that is likely to produce the biggest penalty. Greco runs that to dummy's queen, draws the last trump, and calls for the ♠5. Weinstein takes his king and drives out the ♡A, but Greco has time for a club trick. As Levin can win the ace and tuck dummy in with a spade, the ♣K is declarer's last trick; three down, -500, and 12 IMPs to NICKELL, only 5 IMPs behind with three deals to go.

Board 118. Both Vul.

```
              ♠ A 9 8 3
              ♡ 8 7 6 3
              ◇ Q 10 8 4
              ♣ 9
  ♠ K 7                        ♠ Q J 6 2
  ♡ K J 4          N           ♡ A Q
  ◇ A J 5 3     W     E        ◇ K 9 6
  ♣ A K J 3        S           ♣ 8 7 6 5
              ♠ 10 5 4
              ♡ 10 9 5 2
              ◇ 7 2
              ♣ Q 10 4 2
```

	West	North	East	South
	Moss	Meckstroth	Bathurst	Rodwell
			1◇[1]	pass
	2♣	pass	2♡[2]	pass
	4♠[3]	pass	5NT	pass
	6◇	pass	6NT	all pass

1. 2+ diamonds, 10-15.
2. 11-13 balanced.
3. Intended to show 4-4 in the minors with the values for 4NT, as over a 1NT opening.

Bathurst has an idea about what Moss would have for his undiscussed 4♠ bid, and might well bid 6♣ as Moss has made a natural 2♣ response, but he is swayed by his heart tenace, and overbids slightly to offer a choice of slams.

Against 6NT, South leads the ♡10, which declarer takes with the ace to play a spade to the king and ace (it might be better for North to duck, and play low again on the second round of spades). Declarer wins the spade continuation with the queen, plays a club to the ace, a heart to the queen, and, after long thought, a club to the jack, North discarding the ♡8. After cashing the ♣K, declarer comes to hand with the ◇K, cashes the ♠J and takes the losing diamond finesse for two down, -200.

It's not so easy to see why, but declarer's timing for possible squeezes is better if he crosses to the ♣A at Trick 2. When North's nine appears, declarer comes to hand with a heart, and will see South follow to the second club with the remaining low club. Assuming North does not have a sure club trick, his meaningful original holdings are singleton nine, ten-nine doubleton, and queen-nine. Finessing the jack works on only one of these. As South could play ten-four-deuce in any order but most often would play low-ten, while from ♣Q1042 could safely only follow low twice, restricted choice comes into play. The deep finesse — passing the eight — turns out to be the odds play. Of course, taking only three club tricks might be enough if diamonds run, but four club tricks improves the chances for twelve tricks significantly.

Had Bathurst found the winning play in clubs, cashing two more rounds of clubs would force North to throw a diamond and two hearts. Then the ♡K finishes North, who does best to discard a spade and duck two rounds of spades. Declarer still is obliged to guess that North has blanked the ♠A, but will almost certainly do so.

	West	North	East	South
	Weinstein	Greco	Levin	Hampson
			1♣	pass
	2♣[1]	pass	3♣[2]	pass
	4◇[3]	pass	4♡[4]	pass
	4♠[5]	pass	5♣[6]	all pass

1. Inverted raise; forcing to 3♣.
2. Minimum, usually 4+ clubs.
3. RKCB for clubs.
4. 1 keycard.
5. Asking about the ♣Q.
6. No ♣Q.

Off an ace and the ♣Q, and with no source of tricks, Weinstein wants to retreat to 4NT, but it is too late for that, and he passes 5♣, aware that despite his prime 20-count, this might be too high. South leads the ♡10, and declarer wins with the queen, plays a club to the ace, a heart to the ace and a club to the jack. He loses a club and spade, but has the rest, for +600 and 13 IMPs, more than enough to give NICKELL the lead, 270-262, on the strength of a 34-0 run.

Board 119 is a dull 2♠ for North-South on a chunky 6-2 fit with 22 combined HCP. It is dull because even if they get uncomfortably high in 3♠ they can't go down in that, so a push at North-South +140.

Would the final deal have some life in it?

Well, it is a slam...

Board 120. N-S Vul.

```
                    ♠ Q 9 4
                    ♡ A Q 10
                    ◇ K Q 5 4 2
                    ♣ K 2
  ♠ 10 7 5 2                        ♠ J 8 3
  ♡ 8 7 5 2            N            ♡ 9 6 4
  ◇ 10              W     E         ◇ 8 6
  ♣ 9 8 5 4            S            ♣ A 10 7 6 3
                    ♠ A K 6
                    ♡ K J 3
                    ◇ A J 9 7 3
                    ♣ Q J
```

Open Room

West	North	East	South
Moss	*Meckstroth*	*Bathurst*	*Rodwell*
pass	1NT	pass	2NT[1]
pass	3♣[2]	pass	4◇[3]
pass	4♡[4]	pass	5♣[5]
pass	6◇	pass	6NT
all pass			

1. Puppet Stayman.
2. No five-card major.
3. Natural, slam try or stronger.
4. RKCB for diamonds.
5. 2 keycards, no ◇Q.

Closed Room

West	North	East	South
Weinstein	*Greco*	*Levin*	*Hampson*
pass	1♣*	pass	2◇
pass	3◇	pass	4♡[1]
pass	5◇[2]	pass	6NT
all pass			

1. RKCB for diamonds.
2. 2 keycards and the ◇Q.

No, it is a mama-papa Blackwood hand for either North, South, or both, a push at North-South +1440.

NICKELL has taken the last set 43-8 to prevail 270-262, and would be USA 1 in the 2015 Bermuda Bowl.

It was just coincidence, of course, that NICKELL had scored 34 unanswered IMPs on the deals immediately following Weinstein's tactical 1♠ 'undercall' on Board 114. Can we help but wonder whether Weinstein would have opened 1♠ with the West hand on Board 120 had he picked it up earlier in the session?

2014 Gunfight Winners NICKELL
(l-r) Weinstein, Rodwell, Meckstroth, Katz, Levin, Nickell, Kokish

Epilogue

DIAMOND, with Justin Lall replacing Moss, would have a second chance to qualify for Chennai in the 2015 Trials to select USA 2.

With a bye to the round of 16, DIAMOND started the 2015 Trials as the top seed and, to no one's surprise, made it through to the final, where they encountered team FIREMAN (Paul Fireman, Gavin Wolpert, John Kranyak, Vince Demuy, John Hurd, Joel Wooldridge). This time 48 IMPs behind with one set remaining, DIAMOND's aggressive late-match tactics earned fewer IMPs than they lost, and FIREMAN won by 68 IMPs, 297-229.

So DIAMOND had the distinction, but not the pleasure, of finishing second to both USA 1 and USA 2.

4. 2017 (The) Lyon in Summer

Bridge has its share of fitness and nutrition adherents and more than its share of players following or intending to follow one diet plan or another, but as a group we love our good food. It is widely anticipated that Lyon, the venue for the 2017 World Bridge Championships and one of the great culinary capitals of the world, will be a special treat for the visiting bridge community. The flagship restaurant of Paul Bocuse, 'chef of the century', and several satellite branches are on everyone's lists, and there are any number of excellent bistros, some with Michelin stars.[**]

Less widely anticipated is the unavoidable truth that August is the month in which many (well, most) French restaurants close for vacation. This is indeed the case for most of the best establishments in Lyon. However, it is still possible to dine well with a little research, a wise concierge, and an activated Uber app.

The playing area and the two main tournament hotels, no more than a five-minute walk away, adjoin a gorgeous park and overlook the Rhône River. Indeed, if the tournament could be scheduled in September, Lyon would be a near-perfect venue for the players, though not the directors, who are billeted in far less salubrious accommodations a good twenty-minute walk from the site.

But I digress, as I am prone to do. Bridge and life don't always fit into separate compartments for me, even when I'm playing, which might help explain why I have almost never played in the current millennium.

At the end of nearly two weeks of play, the Bermuda Bowl field is down to two teams. Let's meet them before the showdown for the world title gets under way.

In late 2013, the French Bridge Federation decided to get serious about selecting and supporting its Open teams for international competition. Rather than rely on one Trials format or another, a new strategy was put in play: create a squad of no more than seven pairs, ideally fairly young, hungry, talented players, who would be expected to build their partnerships, participate in team training sessions, and commit to staying together. The training staff would determine which pairs would represent France in major European and World events based on their performance in French events and practice sessions. As a French Open team had last earned a world title in 1997, it's easy to see why the financially sound Federation would want to be more proactive

---

[**] Primary author Eric Kokish

in restoring the country to the elite status in the world bridge community it had enjoyed in the nineties.

The project was a success from the outset, and France has quickly become one of the favorites every time out. Lyon is the third major competition in succession for these three pairs: Thomas Bessis - Frederic Volcker, Jean-Christophe Quantin - Cedric Lorenzini, and Jerome Rombaut - Francois Combescure, with each new opportunity building valuable experience and team chemistry. France wins the round robin, handles China in their quarterfinal, and then crushes New Zealand — who are perhaps still basking in the euphoria of an upset win over the Netherlands — in the semifinal. The French are playing with great confidence and will be formidable opponents.

Team France (l-r): Combescure, Bessis, Volcker,
Quantin, Lorenzini, Rombaut

USA 2 struggles towards the end of the round robin, eventually finishing fifth, which buys them a tough draw against Sweden for their quarterfinal match. The Americans prevail 193-170, then draw Bulgaria, fresh off a dramatic win against favored USA 1 and primed to claim another scalp. USA 2 wins the semifinal, 216-182. Two of the American partnerships, Chip Martel-Marty Fleisher and Brad Moss-Joe Grue have been playing together for a few years, but Michael Rosenberg-Jacek Pszczola (mercifully for bridge writers and Vu-Graph commentators, better known as 'Pepsi') are a marriage of more recent vintage. Lots of World Championship experience in this group, but probably more important is the battlefield experience gained so far in Lyon.

Of the six pairs in the final, only Moss and Grue play a strong club system, but only when not vulnerable, which is their strategy to make the opponents pay for the privilege of interfering too aggressively. Spectators can look forward to some exciting bridge as most of the protagonists play a busy game.

As all the players know each other well from their participation in the three North American Championships each year, and there are some real international friendships here, we can expect the match will be played in the best traditions of camaraderie and sportsmanship.

Session One (Boards 1-16)

After two boards USA 2 leads 8-0, mostly due to a successful Grue penalty double of an overbid game. Then:

Board 3. E-W Vul.

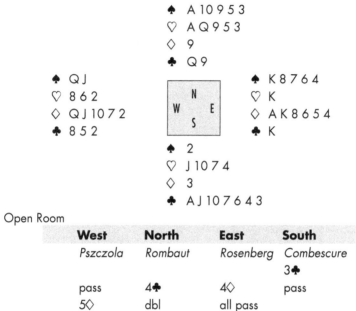

Open Room

West	North	East	South
Pszczola	Rombaut	Rosenberg	Combescure
			3♣
pass	4♣	4◇	pass
5◇	dbl	all pass	

Neither South sees enough flaws in his hand to pass up an opportunity to open at the three-level as dealer at the delicious vulnerability.

Rombaut is willing to increase the preempt, since 4♣ figures to be safe enough and might induce a major-suit misjudgment by fourth hand. Rosenberg is dealt a hand that my good friend, the late Stephen Howard Labins, would often deem suitable for a natural bid in notrump, but I am not surprised to see that Michael prefers a natural bid in his long suit. Pepsi, aware that 5◇ may be too high, does his best to look confident when he raises, but Rombaut, who was planning to double any game, takes his chances here.

Combescure, living somewhat dangerously, leads the ♣A, and is pleased to see it survive. He switches to his singleton spade, and Rombaut wins, then cashes the ♡A; when Combescure does not show out, he gives him his spade ruff for two down, -500.

West	**North**	**East**	**South**
Lorenzini	*Grue*	*Quantin*	*Moss*
			3♣
pass	pass	3◇	3♡
4◇	4♡	4♣	pass
5◇	5♡	all pass	

Grue passes 3♣, which shows us that he doesn't think 4♣ should be secure. Perhaps Moss believes his hand is too strong for 3♣, for he volunteers 3♡, unsolicited. Perhaps he is convinced Grue won't play him for a fifth heart; perhaps this is the way the game is played in 2017. Grue, enjoying this deal a lot more now, competes to 5♡ rather than guess how many hearts and clubs will cash on defense. Moss wins the spade lead to start clubs. When East covers the queen, declarer wins and leads a trump to the ace for +510. Our first push is a strange one!

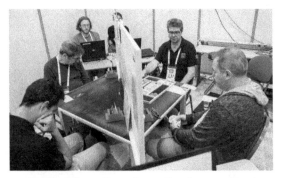

(l-r) Rombaut, Rosenberg, Combescure, Pepsi

Board 5. N-S Vul.

```
              ♠ Q J 10 7 5 2
              ♡ J 5
              ◇ 2
              ♣ K Q 10 8
  ♠ 8                         ♠ A K
  ♡ A 10 6 3       N          ♡ Q 9 7 2
  ◇ A J 7 6 4 3  W   E        ◇ K 10 8
  ♣ 9 6            S          ♣ A J 5 3
              ♠ 9 6 4 3
              ♡ K 8 4
              ◇ Q 9 5
              ♣ 7 4 2
```

West	North	East	South
Pszczola	Rombaut	Rosenberg	Combescure
	2♢[1]	2NT	pass
3♣*	dbl	3♡[2]	pass
3♠[3]	pass	3NT[4]	pass
4♡[5]	pass	4NT	pass
5♡	pass	6♡	all pass

1. Weak 2♡ or weak 2♠.
2. 4+ hearts and clubs stopped.
3. Either unbalanced with five spades (game only) or a slam try in hearts.
4. Doubleton spade.
5. Mild slam try in hearts (stronger slam tries cuebid, although 4♣ would be suspect).

Closed Room

West	North	East	South
Lorenzini	Grue	Quantin	Moss
	2♠	2NT	pass
3♣[1]	pass	3♢[2]	pass
3♠[3]	pass	3NT	all pass

1. Puppet Stayman.
2. One four-card major.
3. Four hearts.

Pepsi's 3♣ is simple Stayman while Lorenzini's is Puppet Stayman, which leads to subtly different scenarios. Rombaut is willing to double 3♣ where Grue is not, but the main difference is that Rosenberg shows his hearts explicitly (handily, along with a club stopper), allowing Pepsi the opportunity to try for a heart slam without going past game. Quantin is obliged to bid 3♢ to show a four-card major, and Lorenzini's 3♠ shows four hearts. It is unclear whether Quantin would admit to a major with four cards in opener's weak-two suit to help advancer with his evaluation, but it does seem certain that Quantin believes his 3NT is a strain choice between hearts and notrump. Lorenzini can honor that opinion with his source of tricks, but as his hand is strongly suit-oriented with some hope for a heart slam, perhaps the inference about Quantin's hearts is not so clear after all. On a spade lead, Quantin guesses diamonds early, then leads the ♡Q, which is covered: +490.

Against 6♡, Combescure dutifully leads the ♣2 to the queen and ace. Rosenberg takes a club discard from dummy on the second high spade, and, like Quantin, starts hearts by leading the queen, which is covered. When

North wins the second heart, he forces dummy with the ♣K, but Rosenberg draws South's remaining trump, cashes the ◇K, and passes the ten successfully, issuing a small silent vote of thanks to North for squealing on the distribution. Achieving +980 requires a bit of decent luck, but it's fair game to take your clues where you find them. That's 10 IMPs to USA 2, 18-1.

I confess to being mystified by Quantin's pessimistic approach on Board 7, where he holds:

♠ 10 9 8 3　♡ A K 9 5 2　◇ A J 2　♣ 7

Over Lorenzini's 15-17 1NT, he starts with Stayman, then jumps to 4♠ over the 2♣ reply, giving up on slam. As Lorenzini has a slightly off-center 15-17 notrump opening: ♠AQ65 ♡Q3 ◇65 ♣AQ1032, slam is not very good, though makeable. After the more normal 1♣ at the other table, the Americans conduct a thorough investigation in which Rosenberg can show his singleton club and slam interest, but they too stop at 4♠. An overtrick IMP to France, 2-18.

Board 8. Neither Vul.

♠ J 9 8 6
♡ 9 6
◇ J 3
♣ A K J 7 3

♠ K Q 10 5 4		♠ A
♡ 10	N	♡ K Q 8 3
◇ K 9 8 6	W E	◇ A Q 10 5
♣ Q 5 2	S	♣ 10 9 6 4

♠ 7 3 2
♡ A J 7 5 4 2
◇ 7 4 2
♣ 8

Open Room

West	North	East	South
Pszczola	Rombaut	Rosenberg	Combescure
pass	1NT[1]	dbl	2♡
3♡[2]	pass	3NT	pass
4♠	all pass		

1. 10-12.
2. No agreement other than artificial game force with no better bid.

The dreaded 10-12 notrump doesn't seem to hurt its opponents… until Pepsi converts 3NT to 4♠. He believes his spade length is limited by his failure to open a Multi 2◇, and his distribution by his failure to open a two-suited 2♠. He thinks slam is not out of the question, and is hopeful that Rosenberg will read him for something like this, perhaps 5=0=4=4.

Rosenberg (much later): 'I knew it was almost certainly a five-one fit, but hoped he had very good spades (like ♠QJ109x), that my heart holding would stop the tap, and that my 'fast' diamond holding would produce ten tricks. Maybe I should bid 4NT, but as it happens, that would not have made. Passing 3NT had to be a practical alternative for Pepsi, but it was still unlucky that 4♠ worked so badly. I considered passing 1NT; that would work if Pepsi overcalled 2♠ over 2♡, and I bid 3NT.'

For what it's worth, Pepsi also has a forcing pass available over 2♡. His 4♠ is quickly down with a third-round club ruff, and the ♡A, with a trump trick coming: -100

Closed Room

West	North	East	South
Lorenzini	Grue	Quantin	Moss
	1◇[1]	pass	1♡
1♠	pass	2NT	pass
3NT	all pass		

1. 2+ diamonds, 10-15.

When Moss innocently leads a low heart against 3NT, dummy's ten is declarer's ninth trick. He comes to the ◇Q to drive out the ♡A. Moss carefully switches to his club, but Grue is not gracious enough to hold the ten to go with his otherwise impressive club holding. Quantin has nine tricks and 11 IMPs. USA 2 leads 18-13.

So tell us, Joe, how light do you open when you are not vulnerable (i.e., Precision mode)?

'Ask Brad. Look at Board 9, where he doesn't force to game over my first-seat 1♡ with:

♠9 2   ♡J   ◇A K 2   ♣K Q 10 8 6 3 2

but starts with 1♠, which is like a forcing limited 1NT for other guys.'

Got it, thanks.

Board 10. Both Vul.

```
              ♠ A 10 8 3 2
              ♡ J 7 3
              ◇ 6 4
              ♣ Q J 6
   ♠ 7                        ♠ Q 9 4
   ♡ A 9           N          ♡ Q 2
   ◇ K 9 8 5 3 2  W   E       ◇ A Q J 7
   ♣ 10 8 3 2        S        ♣ K 9 5 4
              ♠ K J 6 5
              ♡ K 10 8 6 5 4
              ◇ 10
              ♣ A 7
```

Open Room

West	North	East	South
Pszczola	Rombaut	Rosenberg	Combescure
		1◇	1♡
2♡[1]	3♡	pass	4♡
all pass			

1. At least a limit raise.

Closed Room

West	North	East	South
Lorenzini	Grue	Quantin	Moss
		1◇	1♡
3◇[1]	3♡	pass	4♡
all pass			

1. Limit raise.

At both tables, West leads the ♠7, which is bound to be a singleton. Both declarers want to start trumps from dummy, so win with the ♠A, counting on finding a way back there later. When East follows to the trump with the deuce, declarer is not going to have the entries to neutralize East's ♡AQ2, so must play East for ace-low or queen-low.

Combescure puts in the ten, perhaps convinced that with ace-deuce Rosenberg would have gone in with the ace to give his partner the marked spade ruff. That works well, as Pepsi takes his ace, switches to a diamond, and gets his ruff (Combescure puts in the jack on the spade return, of course), but that's all for the defense, as declarer extracts the ♡Q when he ruffs the second diamond: +620.

Moss, who has seen West jump-raise to 3◊, has more reason to place East with the ♡A, and does not rely on Combescure's inference about East rising with the ♡A; he plays the ♡K, only to find worse coming to worst. Lorenzini gets his spade ruff with the outstanding low trump, and the trump queen is the setting trick; -100. France gains 12 IMPs and takes the lead, 25-18.

Board 11. Neither Vul.

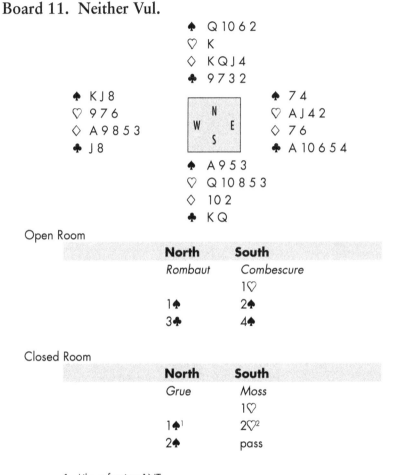

♠ Q 10 6 2
♡ K
◊ K Q J 4
♣ 9 7 3 2

♠ K J 8
♡ 9 7 6
◊ A 9 8 5 3
♣ J 8

♠ 7 4
♡ A J 4 2
◊ 7 6
♣ A 10 6 5 4

♠ A 9 5 3
♡ Q 10 8 5 3
◊ 10 2
♣ K Q

Open Room

North	South
Rombaut	Combescure
	1♡
1♠	2♠
3♣	4♠

Closed Room

North	South
Grue	Moss
	1♡
1♠[1]	2♡[2]
2♠	pass

1. Like a forcing 1NT.
2. 5+ hearts and 4 spades.

Grue earns 7 IMPs for USA 2 when he makes no move towards a non-vulnerable game facing a limited (10-15) opening bid with four spades and at least five hearts. Even 3♠ might fail, but he chalks up +140 when Quantin, East, breaks trumps to simplify declarer's task. Rombaut finishes three down in 4♠ after Combescure accepts his 3♣ trial bid, misguessing everything. That ties the match at 25.

On Board 12, at unfavorable vulnerability, the South players, Combescure and Moss, hold:

♠ A Q 9 4   ♡ 5 4   ◇ A 9 4 3   ♣ K J 9

They each see (1◇) P (1♡), both natural bids. Both Souths bite the bullet and plunge in with a double despite the missing fourth club. Nothing terrible happens in the bidding, but Rosenberg and Quantin, declaring a touch-and-go 4♡, can both place the honor cards with some confidence, something they could not do had South passed, and make their games.

Board 13. Both Vul.

```
                    ♠ Q J 7
                    ♡ 6 2
                    ◇ 6 5
                    ♣ K J 10 6 5 4
   ♠ 8 6 4                          ♠ 3
   ♡ J 7 4          N               ♡ A 10 9 8
   ◇ K J 10 4 3   W   E             ◇ A Q 8 7
   ♣ A Q            S               ♣ 9 8 7 2
                    ♠ A K 10 9 5 2
                    ♡ K Q 5 3
                    ◇ 9 2
                    ♣ 3
```

Open Room

West	North	East	South
Pszczola	Rombaut	Rosenberg	Combescure
	pass	pass	1♠
pass	2♠	dbl	3♡
4◇	all pass		

Closed Room

West	North	East	South
Lorenzini	Grue	Quantin	Moss
	pass	pass	1♠
pass	2♣[1]	pass	4♠
all pass			

1. Three-card spade support, at least a constructive raise.

In an era where opening disgusting balanced 11-counts has become routine it is mildly surprising that neither East opens, despite an impending rebid problem. Rosenberg, as he had hoped, gets a chance to describe his hand perfectly on the next round, and Pepsi, with excellent cards that might combine for a decent 5◇ opposite a passed partner, is able to avoid a higher-level decision when Combescure settles for a game try. However, the quiet 4◇ is already too high. Pepsi wins the heart lead with dummy's ace and tries a club to the queen, but loses a club, a club ruff, two hearts and a spade for two down, -200.

As a double of the Drury 2♣ would show clubs for Quantin, he is obliged to pass, and Moss's practical jump to 4♠ finishes him off. Serendipitously, this is best for France as Moss has four losers against accurate defense: trump lead, heart to the king, club taken by West to switch to the ◇3, East taking the ♡A before returning a diamond. That's -100 and 7 IMPs to France, 32-25.

Board 14. Neither Vul.

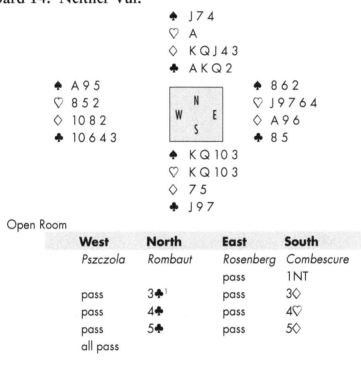

```
                    ♠ J 7 4
                    ♡ A
                    ◇ K Q J 4 3
                    ♣ A K Q 2
   ♠ A 9 5                          ♠ 8 6 2
   ♡ 8 5 2              N           ♡ J 9 7 6 4
   ◇ 10 8 2         W     E         ◇ A 9 6
   ♣ 10 6 4 3          S            ♣ 8 5
                    ♠ K Q 10 3
                    ♡ K Q 10 3
                    ◇ 7 5
                    ♣ J 9 7
```

Open Room

West	North	East	South
Pszczola	Rombaut	Rosenberg	Combescure
		pass	1NT
pass	3♣[1]	pass	3◇
pass	4♣	pass	4♡
pass	5♣	pass	5◇
all pass			

1. Diamonds.

With trumps 3-3, there is no defeating the ugly 5◇, and North-South record +400. Rombaut wants to treat his hand as 2=2=5=4, but there is no system sequence to do that; in theory he would have to transfer and jump in notrump, and wriggle into clubs later. Indeed, he later reveals that he had intended to rebid 4NT, but then risked 4♣ intending it as natural even though he was unsure how it would be interpreted. Combescure (correctly) reads it as club shortage with long diamonds, which explains his motivation in not retreating to 4NT. Over the 4♡ slam try, Rombaut bids a hopeful 5♣ to keep the ball rolling while denying a spade control, but in the end Combescure does not feel he is obliged to bid slam facing what should be a club void. The last sigh we hear is one of relief.

Closed Room

West	North	East	South
Lorenzini	Grue	Quantin	Moss
		pass	1◊[1]
pass	2◊[2]	pass	2♡[3]
pass	2♠[4]	pass	2NT[5]
pass	3♣	pass	3NT
pass	4NT	all pass	

1. 2+ diamonds, 10-15.
2. Natural game force.
3. 11-13 balanced.
4. Puppet to 2NT.
5. Forced.

The bidding is always under control here, and in the end Moss knows enough to decline Grue's natural slam invitation, +460. Rombaut and Combescure are fortunate to survive their mini-notrump auction and the American gain is only 2 IMPs, 27-32.

Board 16. E-W Vul.

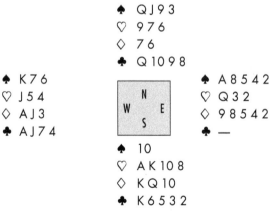

Open Room

West	North	East	South
Pszczola	*Rombaut*	*Rosenberg*	*Combescure*
1♣	pass	1♠	dbl
rdbl[1]	pass	2♠	all pass

1. Three-card spade support.

Closed Room

West	North	East	South
Lorenzini	*Grue*	*Quantin*	*Moss*
1♣	pass	1♠	dbl
rdbl[1]	1NT	2♠	3♣
all pass			

1. Three-card spade support.

As was the case on Board 12, South must decide whether to make a two-suit takeout double with only three cards in one of the unbid suits, and again, both Combescure and Moss accept the risk. When both Wests contribute a support redouble, North is off the hook. Rombaut retires and is not unhappy to defend 2♠, but he can't quite defeat that: +110 for Rosenberg.

In contrast, Grue sticks out his neck and volunteers 1NT. For his partnership, as with so many of the most successful pairs today, favorable vulnerability covers almost any sin. Here, Grue hits an unanticipated home run when Moss is both able and willing to compete in clubs, a suit for which he now expects to find support, thanks to Grue's bid. Lorenzini, trying to get two-for-one for each trump play, leads a low club and dummy wins. A low spade is taken by the ace for a diamond switch to the queen and ace. Lorenzini leads another low trump, Moss wins in dummy and passes the ♠Q, discarding a heart, and when Lorenzini takes his king, he plays the ♣A and another club. That is +110 for Moss, 6 IMPs to USA 2, tying the match at 33 after the first set.

Session Two (Boards 17-32)

Board 17. Neither Vul.

```
                  ♠ J 2
                  ♡ A K J 8 7 4
                  ◇ K 8
                  ♣ 8 3 2
  ♠ K 8                          ♠ 10 6 5 4
  ♡ Q 5 3            N           ♡ 6 2
  ◇ J 10 9 3 2   W     E         ◇ A Q 5 4
  ♣ A Q 5            S           ♣ K J 6
                  ♠ A Q 9 7 3
                  ♡ 10 9
                  ◇ 7 6
                  ♣ 10 9 7 4
```

Open Room

West	North	East	South
Moss	Bessis	Grue	Volcker
	1♡	pass	1♠
pass	2♡	all pass	

Grue leads the ♠5, third from even: low, *eight*, jack. Although the defense had six tricks — three clubs, two diamonds, and a spade — Moss's spade play has a lot going for it as declarer is marked with two or three spades if the opening lead was a true card. Indeed, Bessis cashes ace-king of trumps, then leads a spade to the queen and king, and goes two down, -100.

Closed Room

West	North	East	South
Combescure	Fleisher	Rombaut	Martel
	1♡	pass	1♠
pass	2◇[1]	pass	2♡
all pass			

1. 6+ hearts.

Against the same contract, Rombaut attacks instead with the ♣6. Combescure wins with the ace and switches to a trump. Fleisher wins with the ace and leads the ♠J: six, three, *eight*. Declarer exits with a club, retaining his options in the majors and threatening to establish the long club. West leaves East on play with the ♣J, and Rombaut continues with the ♣4. Fleisher does the right thing by calling for the ace, felling the king. When he leads the ♠3 now, Combescure ruffs high with the ♡Q as his partner might have started with jack-low in trumps, but Fleisher overruffs, and plays a third club. Now he can enter dummy with the ♡10 to cash the thirteenth club, but Rombaut cashes the ◇A to shorten the play. That +140 is a rather sexy result, and USA 2 gains 6 IMPs, 39-33.

In case you're interested in such things, take note that as dealer at favorable colors on Board 18, one of our Easts opens 3♣ with:

♠765 ♡K10 ◇J10 ♣J97543

Is it (a) Joe Grue, or (b) Jerome Rombaut?

The correct answer is (b): it is very much a suitable *trois trèfles* for Mr. FUNBRIDGE. It gets him to 4♣ when Combescure, with:

♠KJ32 ♡J976 ◇AQ2 ♣A6

employs a conventional sequence to reach 3NT that shows uncertainty, and finds Rombaut equally concerned. In the end, 4♣ proves difficult to double, but finishes three down, -150. As Grue, after cravenly passing as dealer, can't play in clubs below the three-level after Moss's third-seat 12-16 1NT, and finishes two down, -100, France loses only 2 IMPs, 8 IMPs behind now, 33-41.

Although Moss-Grue's wide-ranging third-seat non-vulnerable 1NT openings are often more than a bit imaginative, Bessis is not tempted to double (treating 1NT as weak) or overcall 2♣ (majors) at unfavorable, facing a passed partner, holding:

♠AQ109 ♡A432 ◇85 ♣K82

'Pass' is not a dirty word.

Joe Grue

Board 19. E-W Vul.

```
                    ♠  9 8 5 4 2
                    ♡  J
                    ◇  7 5
                    ♣  Q 10 7 4 3
   ♠  A K Q 10                        ♠  J 7 6 3
   ♡  A 10 4 3          N             ♡  K 7 6 5
   ◇  8 4 3          W     E          ◇  J 6
   ♣  A 5               S             ♣  K 8 6
                    ♠  —
                    ♡  Q 9 8 2
                    ◇  A K Q 10 9 2
                    ♣  J 9 2
```

Open Room

West	North	East	South
Moss	Bessis	Grue	Volcker
			1◇
dbl	pass	1♡	2◇
4♡	all pass		

You can get a feel for style by watching men at work.

There was a time when Moss's hand would be a routine raise to 2♡, as partner could be very weak. These days, everyone raises to 2♡ on a minimum with four trumps and a singleton, and some don't wait for the singleton. Who worries about advancer holding a three-card suit? Easier to assume he has at least a little something and make it harder for the opponents to get together. That style has the effect of making a raise to 3♡ a significantly weaker action than it once was. Check? Check.

So why does Brad jump to 4♡? Because he wants to entice the opponents to save when 4♡ is too high. Where the best players used to play down the middle of the fairway and wait for their opponents to err, that style has been replaced, perhaps surprisingly frequently, by a more proactive approach: take risks to help the bad guys do the wrong thing. Moss catches Grue with a maximum, but no one bites, and 4♡ is left to play. The defense can defeat this by arranging an uppercut on the third diamond with the singleton jack of trumps, but Bessis discards a spade after Volcker's ace, king then queen of diamonds. Perhaps because of this Grue assumes the trump position is different (but wouldn't North ruff in with queen-jack doubleton?), and plays the ♡K and a heart to the ace, fatally.

	West	North	East	South
	Combescure	Fleisher	Rombaut	Martel
				1◇
	dbl	pass	1♠	2◇
	3◇	pass	4♡	pass
	4♠	dbl	all pass	

USA 2 gains 3 IMPs on the deal, however, when Rombaut responds 1♠ to the double to preserve a same-level rebid in hearts, and finishes in 4♠ doubled (after Combescure, like Moss, bids a lot), where he is beaten by the very unlucky 5-0 trump break. USA 2 leads by 44-33.

Board 20: Second seat, both vulnerable, North holds:

♠4 ♡964 ◇3 ♣AKJ107432

Pick your number of clubs. 'Four,' says Fleisher; 'Five,' says Bessis.

If East finds the winning lead from:

♠KQ872 ♡J105 ◇Q92 ♣Q6

declarer can be held to nine tricks, but as that lead would need to be the ♡J, not a high spade, it is not surprising to see that Bessis is +600 and Fleisher +190 (discarding issues result in declarer's ♡964 all becoming winners!). France gains 9 IMPs, 42-44.

On Board 22, Bessis holds:

♠A10 ♡QJ87 ◇A1062 ♣AQ2

and sees Moss open 1NT in front of him in third seat, unfavorable, nominally strong. As double would show a four-card major and a longer minor, he must pass, anticipating some vulnerable undertricks. As on Board 18, Grue (who has not opened 3♣ as dealer) uses a two-step route to sign off at 3♣. Bessis likes his chances on defense, but can't double for penalty even if he wants to, and the contract goes two down, -200. Again, 'Pass' is not a dirty word.

Sure enough, Moss has opened on a chunky (the opposite of junky) 14, ♠Q984 ♡AK109 ◇KQ9 ♣65, which his counterpart, Combescure, considers more appropriate for 1◇. Now Fleisher, with Bessis' cards, can overcall 1NT, and is transferred into 2♠, which can't be made, -50. That gives France 6 IMPs and the lead, 48-44.

After Board 26, it is 51-48, France.

On Board 27, neither vulnerable, East is dealt:

♠ J 9 2   ♡ K 2   ◇ K J 5   ♣ A K J 7 2

LHO opens a strong notrump and RHO transfers to 2♠. After two passes, Grue, who tends to be conservative in competition with balanced hands, lets it go, but Rombaut protects with 3♣, which would probably make, and pushes opener up a level. Both 2♠ and 3♣ go one down, so the board is a push at -50.

Board 28. N-S Vul.

```
              ♠ —
              ♡ K 10 6 5
              ◇ J 7 5 2
              ♣ K J 9 6 2
♠ K 10 9                      ♠ Q 8 5 3
♡ —               N          ♡ A Q 8 4 3 2
◇ K Q 10 6 4 3  W    E       ◇ A 9 8
♣ Q 8 5 3          S         ♣ —
              ♠ A J 7 6 4 2
              ♡ J 9 7
              ◇ —
              ♣ A 10 7 4
```

Open Room

West	North	East	South
Moss	Bessis	Grue	Volcker
1◇	pass	1♡	1♠
2◇	pass	2♠	pass
3♣	pass	3◇	pass
3NT	all pass		

Closed Room

West	North	East	South
Combescure	Fleisher	Rombaut	Martel
1◇	pass	1♡	1♠
2♣	pass	2♠	pass
3◇	pass	3♡	pass
3NT	all pass		

When West opens with a one-bid and bids again freely, it's not realistic for East to stop short of game. At least Grue has a chance to support diamonds below 3NT, due to the order in which Moss has shown his 6-4, but in the end both East-West pairs land in 3NT on a club lead. Martel, whose partner had led the fourth-best ♣6, returns the ♣10 at Trick 2, making it easy to run the suit; Volcker, whose partner had sagely led the ♣2, playing fourth-best, prefers to return the seven, a hedge of sorts, but when Bessis takes the eight with the nine, he is endplayed. Both Norths (Fleisher after taking the setting trick, Bessis at Trick 3) exit with a heart, and both declarers reject the finesse, discarding spades. When diamonds break 4-0, the play gets messy in different ways, and both declarers finish down four, -200.

Board 29. Both Vul.

```
                    ♠ J 10 8
                    ♡ K Q J 4
                    ◇ K J 7 4
                    ♣ A 9
    ♠ A 6 5 4                        ♠ K 9
    ♡ 10 5 3            N            ♡ A 7 2
    ◇ 9 8 2        W       E         ◇ Q 5 3
    ♣ J 7 4            S            ♣ Q 10 6 3 2
                    ♠ Q 7 3 2
                    ♡ 9 8 6
                    ◇ A 10 6
                    ♣ K 8 5
```

Open Room

West	North	East	South
Moss	Bessis	Grue	Volcker
	1NT	pass	3♣[1]
pass	3◇[2]	pass	3NT
all pass			

1. Puppet Stayman.
2. Some four-card major.

Closed Room

West	North	East	South
Combescure	Fleisher	Rombaut	Martel
	1NT	pass	3NT
all pass			

Both 1NT openings are strong, so the Souths are willing to commit to game, vulnerable, with an unexceptional balanced 9-count. They like their ◇10, of course, and on this layout, that will be a crucial card. Both pairs open 1NT freely with a five-card major, but only Volcker gets involved, intending to play in 4♠ only if Bessis has five of those. Both Easts lead their long suit, but Rombaut, with many possible entries, tries to create a false picture for declarer by starting with the deuce, feigning four.

Fleisher takes that at its face value and does not duck a round of clubs in the process of driving out the ♡A. On the long heart, Rombaut discards the ◇5, both to keep all his black cards and to help declarer go wrong in diamonds should he have a guess in the suit. Combescure discards the ♠6, encouraging. With entries to the North hand no longer fluid, the best play in the diamond suit taken in isolation would be low to the ten, picking up doubleton queen with East as the upside. But after the diamond discard, that is no longer a relevant holding (the queen would come up on the first round). Now the crafty fourth-best club lead comes back to haunt Rombaut, as Fleisher sensibly plays him for 2=3=4=4, believes he would not discard a diamond if he did *not* hold the queen, and leads a diamond to the ten to chalk up +600. So much for enterprise!

Grue leads an honest fourth-best ♠3. Bessis ducks the first round, and has an accurate read on the suit after knocking out the ♡A. He plays with the 'vacant spaces' odds by starting diamonds with dummy's ten, a thoughtful play that would allow him to pick up West's queen-nine-fourth or queen-eight-fourth with a later finesse if West covers the ten. East's ◇Q is a disappointment, and Bessis is three down, -300. 14 IMPs to USA 2, ahead by 11, 62-51.

Board 31. N-S Vul.

```
              ♠ 7 5
              ♡ Q 10 8 5 3 2
              ◇ 10 4
              ♣ A 8 7
♠ Q 9                        ♠ 10 8 6 4
♡ A K            N           ♡ 9
◇ J 9 8 3    W     E         ◇ A K Q 7 5
♣ 10 9 5 3 2    S            ♣ K Q 4
              ♠ A K J 3 2
              ♡ J 7 6 4
              ◇ 6 2
              ♣ J 6
```

Closed Room

West	North	East	South
Combescure	Fleisher	Rombaut	Martel
			pass
1NT	pass	2♣	pass
2◇	pass	2NT	all pass

Rombaut can't show his shape or his diamonds without forcing to game, and so settles for an uncomfortable (facing 10-12, now with fewer than four hearts) invitational sequence. Since 2NT is impregnable on a heart lead, Combescure can play a second club safely, leading the ten. Fleisher follows low, but declarer guesses correctly for +150.

Open Room

West	North	East	South
Moss	Bessis	Grue	Volcker
			pass
1♢[1]	1♡	dbl*	2♠[2]
pass	3♡	dbl*	pass
3NT	pass	pass	dbl
all pass			

1. 2+ diamonds, 10-15.
2. Fit jump (spades and hearts).

Moss can't resist opening at favorable vulnerability, but 1♢ lets Bessis in, and the French compete to 3♡, which essentially commits East-West to 3NT under duress. This is doubled by Volcker on general principles: neither East nor West has advertised a long suit. Although Moss can't be happy and Grue must have thoughts about 5♢, both sit for the double.

With the ♣A certain to be in the North hand after South's initial pass, the revealing spade lead to the king and the strongly auction-indicated switch to the ♡J, Moss has time for two club tricks for a lovely +550. So 9 IMPs to USA 2, up 20, 71-51.

It must be exceptionally painful for Volcker when he realizes that his alternative significantly anti-percentage line of defense — ducking the opening spade lead, which amounts to playing Bessis for the ♣A — would have beaten the pushy contract.

Board 32. E-W Vul.

```
                    ♠ Q 6
                    ♡ K J 5 3
                    ◇ A K 10 5 2
                    ♣ A 4
     ♠ 9 7 5                          ♠ J 10 4
     ♡ A 9 8 6 4        N             ♡ 10 2
     ◇ 8 4          W       E         ◇ 9 7 3
     ♣ Q 9 2            S             ♣ K J 8 6 5
                    ♠ A K 8 3 2
                    ♡ Q 7
                    ◇ Q J 6
                    ♣ 10 7 3
```

Open Room

West	North	East	South
Moss	Bessis	Grue	Volcker
pass	1◇	pass	1♠
pass	2♡	pass	3◇[1]
pass	3NT	pass	4◇
pass	4♡[2]	pass	4♠[3]
pass	5♣[4]	pass	6◇
all pass			

1. Forcing to game.
2-4. Control-showing.

There are several sensible ways to treat the North hand: open 1NT, open 1◇ and jump to 2NT over 1♠ or open 1◇ and reverse into hearts. Bessis's strategy works beautifully here as Volcker can value his red honors accurately. In 6◇, Bessis wins the club lead, plays the ◇Q and ◇A, and with trumps 3-2, starts on spades, ruffing the third high before drawing the last trump with dummy's jack for +920, conceding the ♡A. If trumps were 4-1, he would need spades 3-3, so slam is excellent.

Thomas Bessis

Closed Room

West	North	East	South
Combescure	Fleisher	Rombaut	Martel
pass	1♣	pass	1♡[1]
pass	1NT[2]	pass	2♡[3]
pass	2♠	pass	3NT
all pass			

1. At least four spades.
2. 17-19 balanced.
3. At least five spades.

In theory, the Americans are ahead of the game when their system enables North to show his strong balanced hand at the 1NT level and South can get his hand type across in some comfort. But in practice, the focus on balanced ranges and spades versus notrump has effectively buried both diamonds and North's 2=4=5=2 pattern. Indeed, with a balanced 17-count including something in both doubletons, opening or rebidding in notrump is a far more popular expert approach than a minimum reverse, in no small measure because reversing can lead to an awkward third bid, particularly when responder is weak.

Even if you believe it's worth the price to treat this sort of hand as balanced, it would be foolish to pretend that the alternative plan adopted by Bessis will not be superior some of the time, and can lead to a big gain when it works.

On these North-South hands, France earns its 10 IMPs, and USA 2 leads only by 10, 71-61, after 32 deals, winning the set 38-28.

Board 33. Neither Vul.

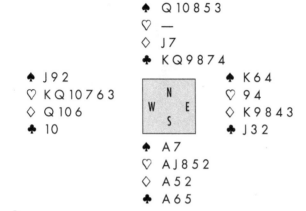

```
                    ♠ Q 10 8 5 3
                    ♡ —
                    ◊ J 7
                    ♣ K Q 9 8 7 4
    ♠ J 9 2                        ♠ K 6 4
    ♡ K Q 10 7 6 3      N          ♡ 9 4
    ◊ Q 10 6       W        E      ◊ K 9 8 4 3
    ♣ 10               S          ♣ J 3 2
                    ♠ A 7
                    ♡ A J 8 5 2
                    ◊ A 5 2
                    ♣ A 6 5
```

Open Room

West	North	East	South
Pszczola	Lorenzini	Rosenberg	Quantin
	pass	pass	1♡
pass	1♠	pass	2♣[1]
pass	2◊[2]	pass	3NT[3]
all pass			

1. Natural, or most possible strong hands.
2. Artificial, 8+.
3. Presumably 2=5=3=3, 18(17)-19.

As Lorenzini has not begun to describe his hand, it is surprising to see him pass the descriptive 3NT. Rosenberg might double the artificial Gazzilli 2◊ rebid, but believes North is alerting fourth-suit forcing. Whether that would keep North-South out of 3NT is uncertain, but it would help with the lead... Pepsi's choice is the increasingly popular expert lead of the ♠J (rather than guess which heart to lead). When that is covered all around and Quantin finesses against the ♠9 after testing clubs, the defense gets no tricks: +520. The legendary S.J. Simon would have added 'unlucky' somewhere in the description of the lead.

Jacek "Pepsi" Pszczola

Closed Room

West	North	East	South
Volcker	Fleisher	Bessis	Martel
	pass	pass	1♥
pass	1♠[1]	pass	2NT
pass	3♠[2]	pass	4♣
pass	4NT[3]	pass	5♣
all pass			

1. Usually at least five spades.
2. At least five clubs.
3. 'Good' 5♣ bid, no reference to diamond control.

The Americans investigate slam more comprehensively, but quit at 5♣, where Martel gets a diamond lead and eventually ruffs out spades for +420. So 3 IMPs to France, 64-71.

Even if clubs are not 4-0, 6♣ needs a bit of luck in the black suits to avoid a trump loser in the handling, but it's the sort of contract you don't mind reaching. With all the aces, South instinctively leans towards accepting a slam invitation, but the lack of fillers is a significant negative.

On Board 34 we are treated to another showcase of different styles. At unfavorable, North holds:

♠A853 ♥J963 ◇KJ8 ♣A10

RHO opens 1♠ in third seat. Lorenzini passes, which is still the normal bid in many circles in 2017. Fleisher not only doubles for takeout, but accepts Martel's game-invitational jump to 3♥, as his hand seems to have improved. The eventual 4♥ needs trumps to come in for no losers (Martel's hearts are AQ752), but not this time, -100. Lorenzini defends 2♠, scoring +50. France gains 4 IMPs, 68-71.

Board 37. N-S Vul.

```
              ♠ K 9 5
              ♡ K 8 5
              ◇ Q 10 8 5
              ♣ Q 7 2
   ♠ A J 4 3              ♠ 10 8 6 2
   ♡ 10 3         N        ♡ 7 4
   ◇ A        W       E    ◇ 4 3 2
   ♣ A K J 10 6 4   S      ♣ 9 8 5 3
              ♠ Q 7
              ♡ A Q J 9 6 2
              ◇ K J 9 7 6
              ♣ —
```

Open Room

West	North	East	South
Pszczola	Lorenzini	Rosenberg	Quantin
	pass	pass	1♡
dbl	2◇¹	pass	4♡
5♣	dbl	all pass	

1. Constructive heart raise.

This board highlights different approaches by Pepsi and Volcker.

Pepsi's double is probably the bid that scores 100 on most bidding panels. At his next turn, he could double again or bid 5♣, and chooses to rely on the long suit, not anxious to see a 5◇ reply to 'double'. The final 5♣ is doubled on his left.

Closed Room

West	North	East	South
Volcker	Fleisher	Bessis	Martel
	pass	pass	1♡
2♣	2♡	pass	4♡
4♠	dbl	all pass	

Volcker settles for 2♣, avoiding an unwanted response in diamonds that might not allow him to show his hand type unambiguously. He follows through with 4♠, which gives a fine picture of his hand (with 5-5 or 5-6 he would start with 2♡). When 4♠ is doubled and Bessis passes, showing preference for spades, Volcker naturally stands his ground.

As North-South have eleven tricks in hearts, it's good for East-West to buy the contract. Unluckily for Volcker, the ten-card club fit handles more comfortably than the 4-4 spade fit, with clubs 3-0 offside. He goes three down to Pepsi's two, and USA 2 gains 5 IMPs, 78-68. I confess that I prefer Volcker's strategy.

Board 38. E-W Vul.

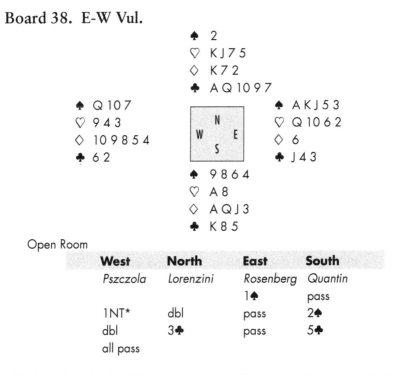

	♠	2
	♡	K J 7 5
	◇	K 7 2
	♣	A Q 10 9 7

♠ Q 10 7		♠ A K J 5 3
♡ 9 4 3		♡ Q 10 6 2
◇ 10 9 8 5 4		◇ 6
♣ 6 2		♣ J 4 3

	♠	9 8 6 4
	♡	A 8
	◇	A Q J 3
	♣	K 8 5

Open Room

West	**North**	**East**	**South**
Pszczola	Lorenzini	Rosenberg	Quantin
		1♠	pass
1NT*	dbl	pass	2♠
dbl	3♣	pass	5♣
all pass			

This is a fine 6♣ for North-South, but West gives them a hard time by responding 1NT, which, at least initially, prevents South from counting on short spades opposite. Quantin could pass the double, of course, but prefers to make a start on finding his side's best strain for game or slam. Pepsi presses his luck by doubling the cuebid, but Quantin gives up prematurely once Lorenzini's voluntary 3♣ strongly implies 1=4=3=5 or 1=3=4=5, scoring +420.

Closed Room

West	**North**	**East**	**South**
Volcker	Fleisher	Bessis	Martel
		1♠	pass
1NT	dbl	pass	pass
2♠	pass	pass	dbl
all pass			

Martel has reason to expect Fleisher to be short in spades when Volcker runs to 2♠, but at the prevailing vulnerability, he likes his chances for 500 or perhaps 800 with slam a long way off. When Martel leads the ♣4, declarer has a nasty guess: if the seven gets covered by the eight or nine, the defense can get 800, so in those cases, he needs to play the ten or queen at Trick 1. Bessis does the right thing and plays the seven, perhaps because he believes Martel might have all five missing trumps. With the ♡J onside for declarer, there is no denying him a sixth trick now, so 500 it is. 2 IMPs to USA 2, 80-68.

On Board 39, both vulnerable, West holds:

♠ A K 8 7 5 4   ♡ 6 3   ◇ Q 8 3   ♣ A 2

and overcalls 1♣ with 1♠. Partner advances with 1NT. What now?

Although both Pepsi and Volcker play weak jump overcalls, neither feels a 2♠ rebid does the hand justice, which confirms that some hands with six-card majors are not *strong* enough to make a vulnerable weak jump overcall (see Board 31, for example). Volcker jumps to 3♠ but Pepsi can take advantage of a specialized sequence: a 2♣ cuebid followed by an invitational 2♠ over a red-suit reply. As so often happens, 2♠ makes three but 3♠ makes only two (more accurate defense by Martel and Fleisher), so USA 2 gains 6 IMPs, 86-68.

Board 40. Neither Vul.

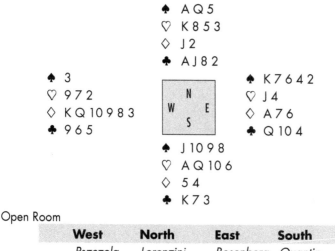

Open Room

	West	North	East	South
	Pszczola	Lorenzini	Rosenberg	Quantin
	3◇	dbl	4◇	dbl
	all pass			

West	North	East	South
Volcker	Fleisher	Bessis	Martel
pass	1NT	pass	2♣
2◇	2♡	3◇	4♡
all pass			

Neither West has a weak 2◇ available, so they cope in different ways. Pepsi's 3◇ fares badly when Rosenberg raises and Lorenzini judges immaculately to pass his partner's responsive double. Pepsi is down two, -300. Volcker does much better by waiting a round, which lets Martel and Fleisher find their heart fit painlessly and bid game; doubling 3◇ is not a live possibility. Fleisher goes two down after ◇A, diamond, spade switch to the queen and king, spade ruff, with a club still to come. So 9 IMPs to France, 77-86.

Cedric Lorenzini

Just to keep you in touch with how bridge at the top is played these days, Lorenzini, as dealer at favorable vulnerability, opens 2♡ on Board 41 with:

♠Q9876 ♡10854 ◇102 ♣Q7

Their card describes this as '4+ hearts and 4+ spades', which strikes me as less than responsible in the 'full disclosure' department. No effect on the result this time.

While we're discussing obstructive openings, the next deal features different approaches by the two Easts.

Board 42. Both Vul.

```
              ♠ A Q J 8 6 4 3
              ♡ 7
              ◊ 3
              ♣ A K 5 3
  ♠ 9 7 2                          ♠ 5
  ♡ J 8 4          N               ♡ K Q 10 6 5 3 2
  ◊ K Q 10 7 6  W     E            ◊ J 9
  ♣ J 2             S              ♣ Q 9 4
              ♠ K 10
              ♡ A 9
              ◊ A 8 5 4 2
              ♣ 10 8 7 6
```

Open Room

West	North	East	South
Pszczola	Lorenzini	Rosenberg	Quantin
		2◊[1]	pass
3♡[2]	4♠	pass	4NT
pass	5♠	pass	6♠
all pass			

1. Weak 2♡ or weak 2♠.
2. Pass or correct.

Closed Room

West	North	East	South
Volcker	Fleisher	Bessis	Martel
		3♡	pass
4♡	4♠	all pass	

It's human nature not to pass with the East hand, so it comes down to whether you consider the weak intermediates in the long suit adequate reason *not* to open 3♡, or whether opening 2♡ with a seventh heart is the lesser sin, notwithstanding the possible gain from having partner declare by starting with a Multi 2◊. The relevance of the missing ♡9 is a matter of perception.

Bessis's 3♡ proves especially effective when Volcker can raise; if you believe either Fleisher or Martel should do differently, the person staring you in the face in your mirror is a result merchant. We have seen enough so far in this match to know that Pepsi is no shrinking violet in the obstruction arena, but he can hardly do more than bounce to the three-level. That leaves room for Lorenzini to show a big suit in a big hand by jumping to 4♠, which is enough to stimulate Quantin, the proud owner of three keycards. In 6♠, the heart lead kills the possibility of establishing dummy's long diamond (if the suit is 4-3) and cashing it, but with clubs behaving, twelve tricks are secure. France wins 13 IMPs and takes the lead, 90-86.

Obviously, 6♠ is a desirable contract, and Blackwood works very well for Quantin, but might not North jump to 4♠ without the ♣K? Perhaps 5♡ would be enough encouragement.

Board 43. Neither Vul.

```
              ♠ K J 9 4
              ♡ 10 5 4
              ◇ A 7
              ♣ K 8 7 6
♠ 7                          ♠ Q 10 8 6 5
♡ A 6 2          N           ♡ K 9 8
◇ J 10 6 5 4   W   E         ◇ 3 2
♣ A Q 9 5        S           ♣ 10 4 2
              ♠ A 3 2
              ♡ Q J 7 3
              ◇ K Q 9 8
              ♣ J 3
```

Open Room

West	North	East	South
Pszczola	Lorenzini	Rosenberg	Quantin
			1◇
pass	1♠	pass	1NT
pass	2NT	pass	3NT
all pass			

Closed Room

West	North	East	South
Volcker	Fleisher	Bessis	Martel
			1♣[1]
1◇	1♡[2]	pass	1NT
all pass			

1. Natural or 2+ clubs, balanced.
2. At least four spades.

Martel's 1NT is limited to 13 HCP, so Fleisher is not tempted to raise, non-vulnerable, despite his dearth of twos and threes. In contrast, Quantin could have as much as 14, so Lorenzini invites and Quantin, who is not minimum, accepts, which is one way to play: the other is to accept only with a maximum.

West's ◇5 lead at both tables concedes a *fourth* diamond trick. Quantin, in game, leads a heart to the ten and king. If East switches to clubs, declarer's ♣J prevents the defense from untangling its third club winner, but Rosenberg continues diamonds. When Pepsi ducks the ♡J, Quantin, with fragile communications, misjudges by changing tack; a spade to the jack would succeed if he can take four spades or a club and three spades, but here East's club switch establishes five tricks for the defense before declarer can take a ninth, -50. Martel finishes +120 in 1NT. That's 5 IMPs to USA 2, back in front, 91-90, but the score is tied at 91 going into Board 46:

Board 46. Neither Vul.

```
               ♠ 10 5 2
               ♡ A 7 5
               ◇ K 7 4
               ♣ K J 9 4
  ♠ 8 3                        ♠ A K 4
  ♡ Q 6 3           N          ♡ K 9 8 2
  ◇ Q 9 6       W     E        ◇ 10 8 5 2
  ♣ A 10 7 5 3       S         ♣ Q 2
               ♠ Q J 9 7 6
               ♡ J 10 4
               ◇ A J 3
               ♣ 8 6
```

Closed Room

West	North	East	South
Volcker	Fleisher	Bessis	Martel
		1◇	pass
1NT	pass	pass	2♠
all pass			

Martel, with a modest balanced hand suitable for play in hearts, declines the opportunity to overcall 1♠ with neither side vulnerable. When he reopens over Volcker's 1NT response with 2♠, he buys well, and scores +140 when the defense breaks hearts and he gets clubs right late in the play.

Open Room

West	North	East	South
Pszczola	Lorenzini	Rosenberg	Quantin
		1◇	1♠
pass	2◇	pass	2♠
2NT	pass	3♣	pass
pass	dbl	pass	3♠
all pass			

Quantin, after overcalling 1♠, is able to stop safely in 2♠, but is not able to buy it cheaply. Pepsi pre-balances with 2NT, showing three diamonds and five or six clubs, with fewer than four hearts. With so much high-card strength, he has reason to believe that Lorenzini will be passing 2♠, so is willing to accept the risk to compete for the partscore. He is perhaps unlucky to find his partner with 3=4=4=2 shape, and when Rosenberg wriggles into clubs on queen-deuce doubleton, Lorenzini is waiting with the axe. At first glance, 3♣ doubled figures to go for 300, 5 IMPs to France, but with hearts frozen for the defense and diamonds favorable, declarer can use his fourth diamond effectively to escape for -100, which would be 1 IMP to USA 2.

All of that is moot, however, because Quantin apparently misreads the double and pulls to 3♠, where he goes one down after a trump lead and diamond switch, West breaking hearts when he gains the lead with the ◇Q. That is 5 IMPs to USA 2, 96-91.

The East-West pairs do very well on Board 47, where North-South are vulnerable. After (1♠) P (1NT), Rosenberg and Bessis double for takeout with this minimum balanced East hand:

♠A 6 ♡A 8 6 2 ◇A 9 7 2 ♣9 8 2

Pepsi and Volcker pass for penalty with:

♠K 9 8 4 ♡Q 5 4 ◇5 3 ♣Q 10 5 4

Neither of those actions is routine. When North escapes to 2◇, East doubles for penalty, hoping the ◇9 will come into its own. Not to mention that 2◇ doubled is not game, which is a subtle downside to escaping to a minor. At both tables, the price is -500, as that promising nine of trumps takes a trick on a promotion. No swing, but no lack of excitement.

The final deal of a very interesting set features another doubling opportunity. East, at unfavorable colors, holds:

♠J 3 ♡8 6 4 ◇A Q J 7 ♣Q 9 6 2

At both tables, the auction proceeds:

West	North	East	South
1♠	pass	1NT	2♣
2♡	3♣	?	

Rosenberg, whose double would be penalty, passes; Bessis, who believes his double is cards, not penalty, doubles. Volcker interprets double as penalty and passes. Both declarers take seven tricks so France gains 5 IMPs for +300 and -100, a handsome reward for a misunderstanding.

France wins the set 68-58 (a total of 126 IMPs scored — no kidding!) and the match is tied at 96, which is a fair reflection of the bridge so far.

Session Four (Boards 49-64)

Board 49. Neither Vul.

```
              ♠ K8764
              ♡ 3
              ◇ Q92
              ♣ QJ102
♠ QJ                         ♠ 95
♡ AQ1092         N           ♡ J865
◇ J3          W     E        ◇ AK1076
♣ K983           S           ♣ 74
              ♠ A1032
              ♡ K74
              ◇ 854
              ♣ A65
```

Open Room

West	North	East	South
Pszczola	Bessis	Rosenberg	Volcker
	pass	pass	1♣
1♡	dbl¹	3♣²	pass
3♡	dbl	pass	3♠
all pass			

1. At least four spades.
2. As 3◇ would be a mixed raise, 3♣ is a surrogate fit-showing jump with diamonds.

Closed Room

West	North	East	South
Lorenzini	Moss	Quantin	Grue
	pass	pass	1♠
2♡	4♠	5♡	all pass

If you're going to open in third seat, as most non-vulnerable players do these days, 1♣ is safer and caters best to hearts, while 1♠ steals the one-level and allows an easy pass over any non-forcing response. I'm big on 1♠ and dislike 1♣, but recognize that this is a minority view. The biggest upside for 1♠

is highlighted by the Closed Room auction, which leads nearly inevitably to East competing to 5♡, down one, -50, on a club lead and timely spade switch.

Meanwhile, Volcker's 1♣ leaves lots of room for East-West to *miss* their unbreakable sub-25% game and sell out to 3♠ (Bessis refusing to go quietly), where declarer guesses trumps after the indicated lead of the ◊J to go one down, -50. That's a lot of ink for a 3-IMP swing, but it's the sort of deal I love, so please indulge me. USA 2, 99-96.

Board 51. E-W Vul.

```
              ♠ 6 4
              ♡ A 9 7 6 3
              ◊ K Q 8 7 2
              ♣ 5
♠ K Q 3                      ♠ J 10 8 7 5
♡ Q 8 5          N           ♡ J 10
◊ J 6 5 3      W   E         ◊ 9
♣ K J 9          S           ♣ A Q 8 7 3
              ♠ A 9 2
              ♡ K 4 2
              ◊ A 10 4
              ♣ 10 6 4 2
```

Open Room

West	North	East	South
Pszczola	Bessis	Rosenberg	Volcker
			pass
1◊	1♡	1♠[1]	2◊*
2♣	3♡	dbl[2]	pass
3♠	all pass		

1. At least five spades.
2. Artificial game try.

Closed Room

West	North	East	South
Lorenzini	Moss	Quantin	Grue
			1◊[1]
pass	1♡	1♠	dbl[2]
2♡*	3◊	3♠	all pass

1. 2+ diamonds, 10-15.
2. Three-card heart support.

There are several points of interest here, including the 1◇ openings by Grue (normal for him, not vulnerable) and Pepsi ('We open all balanced 12 counts') where passing would not be a great sin.

Although the rest of the auction at both tables is understandable, it would not have been surprising to see North or East (or both) bid game as a two-way shot. As 4♡ is cold with trumps 3-2, selling out to 3♠ at both tables is bad for North-South. It turns out to be worse for the French when Volcker, after a heart lead to the ace and a switch to the ♣5, ducks the first trump and so does not give Bessis his club ruff. That's +140 for Rosenberg, -100 for Quantin, 6 IMPs to USA 2, 105-96.

Board 52. Both Vul.

```
                    ♠ 10 5
                    ♡ K 6 4 3 2
                    ◇ 7 4
                    ♣ K 9 4 2
   ♠ K 9 7 6                         ♠ A Q J
   ♡ J 10 8            N             ♡ Q 5
   ◇ A Q 10 9 8 2   W     E          ◇ K J 6 3
   ♣ —                  S            ♣ Q 8 5 3
                    ♠ 8 4 3 2
                    ♡ A 9 7
                    ◇ 5
                    ♣ A J 10 7 6
```

Open Room

West	North	East	South
Pszczola	Bessis	Rosenberg	Volcker
1◇	pass	2◇[1]	pass
3♣[2]	pass	3◇	pass
3♠	pass	4♠	pass
5◇	all pass		

1. Game-forcing raise.
2. Club shortness.

Rosenberg's game-forcing 2◇ denies a four-card major in principle, which allows him to offer 4♠ as a contract later while denying a heart control. He fears that 5◇ would have two hearts and a club to lose off the top, but expects Pepsi to correct to 5◇ most of the time. Indeed, he does so here, and the result is +600, losing only the first two tricks in hearts.

West	North	East	South
Lorenzini	*Moss*	*Quantin*	*Grue*
1◇	pass	2♣	pass
2◇	pass	2♠	pass
3♠	pass	4♠	all pass

Quantin needs a fifth diamond for an inverted raise, so starts with 2♣ (2NT would be invitational). Although he could force with a raise to 3◇ on the next round, he prefers to show his spade values, aiming for 3NT. The raise to 3♠ is awkward for him, and he raises himself to 4♠, which amounts to the same 'three losers in diamonds' analysis as Rosenberg employed. The difference here is that he has strongly implied holding four spades. With spades 4-2, USA 2 has a chance to defeat 4♠ by leading a club, or by finding a timely switch to clubs after leading hearts and defending accurately after that. Grue leads a trump, however, expecting his opponents to be on a 4-4 fit. Quantin has time to draw all of those, overtaking on the third round when the ten appears on the second: +620 and 1 IMP to France, 97-105, when it might well have been 13 IMPs to the other team. I can envision all my friends in France exhaling in unison.

Board 53. N-S Vul.

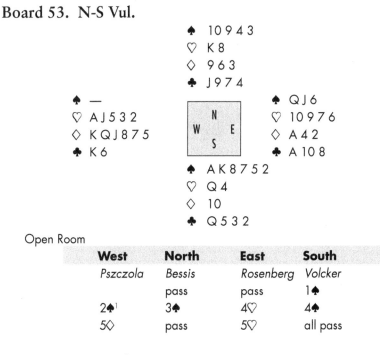

West	North	East	South
Pszczola	*Bessis*	*Rosenberg*	*Volcker*
	pass	pass	1♠
2♠¹	3♠	4♡	4♠
5◇	pass	5♡	all pass

1. Hearts and a minor.

Closed Room

West	North	East	South
Lorenzini	Moss	Quantin	Grue
	pass	pass	1♠
3♣[1]	3♠	4♡	4♠
5◇	pass	5♡	all pass

1. Hearts and diamonds.

As Lorenzini has already specified his minor, perhaps his 5◇ should be a slam suggestion. Quantin does not seem to read much into it, and signs off. Rosenberg is in a different position, as Pepsi may be naming his minor to help with a decision over 5♠ or even 6♠, so he too retreats to 5♡ with a splendid hand for his bidding, and both teams miss an 11-IMP opportunity.

Michael Rosenberg

There is a clue that West is void in spades: North-South have bid up to 4♠ at unfavorable vulnerability and are apparently not loaded in high cards, so a ten-card spade fit is likely. No swing at +480 for East-West.

Board 54. E-W Vul.

```
                  ♠ Q J 10 5
                  ♡ A 7 3
                  ◇ K 8
                  ♣ J 8 4 3
  ♠ 9 7 6 2                      ♠ 4
  ♡ Q J              N           ♡ K 10 8 6 4 2
  ◇ 10 7 4 2     W     E         ◇ J 9 5
  ♣ A 7 6           S            ♣ K 9 2
                  ♠ A K 8 3
                  ♡ 9 5
                  ◇ A Q 6 3
                  ♣ Q 10 5
```

Open Room

West	North	East	South
Pszczola	Bessis	Rosenberg	Volcker
		2◇[1]	pass
3♡[2]	pass	pass	dbl
pass	4♠	all pass	

Closed Room

West	North	East	South
Lorenzini	Moss	Quantin	Grue
		2◇[1]	dbl
2♡[2]	dbl	pass	2♠
pass	3♠	pass	4♠
all pass			

1. Weak 2♡ or weak 2♠.
2. Pass or correct.

Different defensive schemes versus the Multi lead to the North-South pairs declaring 4♠ from different sides of the table.

Rosenberg, who I believe steps out a bit to open 2◇ at unfavorable colors, leads a low heart to the jack and ace. Bessis plays the ♠A and ♠Q, learning of the bad break, then starts on clubs, losing the ten to West's ace. Pepsi plays two-for-one in trumps, Bessis winning in dummy to continue clubs. Rosenberg wins the second club and leads the ♡10 to Pepsi's jack. He plays a fourth round of trumps but declarer has ten winners in top cards for +420. Two rounds of hearts from Rosenberg would not help: Bessis ruffs with the ♠K, and crosses in diamonds to draw the last trump.

The early play is the same in the Closed Room after West leads the ♡Q, but when Lorenzini wins the first club with the ace, he continues hearts, and Quantin overtakes to continue with the suit-preference eight. Although Grue can ruff safely with the king, Lorenzini can discard a club. Declarer can't afford to draw trumps because he needs a club trick, and if he cashes his top cards, East will keep the ♣K and a heart winner in the endgame, so Grue must play another club. Quantin wins, and has the remaining club to give Lorenzini the killing club ruff to set the contract: -50 and 10 IMPs to France, reclaiming the lead, 107-105.

Jean-Christophe Quantin

On this layout, after winning the first heart, declarer can get home legitimately by cashing one of North's top spades at Trick 2, then playing three rounds of diamonds to discard a heart before turning to clubs. That's a line that smacks of double dummy, though, since if trumps were 3-2, allowing the defenders to arrange a club ruff would be a mistake.

Ducking the first round of hearts is a more intuitive strategy, and would work well for declarer here. While the risk of the defenders changing tack to negotiate a club ruff is no less real, it may not be obvious for them to do so, and on any other return, declarer can test trumps and will have a much smoother ride with trumps dividing poorly and clubs 3-3.

Board 55. Both Vul.

```
              ♠ A Q J 8 4
              ♡ A 8 4 2
              ◇ J 9 4
              ♣ 10
  ♠ 10 9 7 3              ♠ 6
  ♡ K Q 10         N      ♡ 9 6 5 3
  ◇ 2          W       E  ◇ 5 3
  ♣ K Q 8 7 3      S      ♣ A 9 6 5 4 2
              ♠ K 5 2
              ♡ J 7
              ◇ A K Q 10 8 7 6
              ♣ J
```

Open Room

West	North	East	South
Pszczola	*Bessis*	*Rosenberg*	*Volcker*
			1◇
pass	1♠	pass	3◇
pass	4◇	pass	4NT
pass	5♡	pass	6◇
all pass			

Unless there is something special about Bessis's slam-try 4◇, Volcker's Black-wood seems like a gamble on the heart control; perhaps 4♠ would have been non-forcing and 5♣ would have shown the ace. Volcker scores an easy +1390 on the lead of the ♡K.

Closed Room

West	North	East	South
Lorenzini	*Moss*	*Quantin*	*Grue*
			1◇[1]
dbl	1♠	2♣	dbl[2]
pass	3♡	pass	3♠
5♣	dbl	pass	5◇
pass	6◇	all pass	

1. 2+ diamonds, 10-15.
2. Three-card spade support.

Lorenzini gets busy with the West cards; not only does he risk a light vulnerable takeout double, but then he jumps to 5♣ *after* his opponents' bidding pinpoints Quantin's spade shortness. As East-West have an 800-point save in 7♣, the effectiveness of Lorenzini's enterprise is highlighted, but it's understandable that they don't save after forcing their opponents to guess under pressure. Here too, West leads the ♡K, so North-South are +1390 for a push.

Board 56: Neither vulnerable, North has a straightforward 1NT overcall of a 1♣ opening at both tables, but catches his partner with only a jack in a balanced hand. East, with:

♠K987 ♡72 ♢Q6 ♣K10765

would do well to double, but in these times of depreciated opening bids, neither does so. Instead, Rosenberg jumps to 3♣; Quantin bids 2♠, a transfer to clubs. As it happens, opener is 3=4=3=3 with a fair 14-count:

♠Q65 ♡AQ94 ♢A95 ♣Q83

Pepsi, in 3♣, is pleased to learn that North is endplayed on lead, and the result is +110. Lorenzini responds to 2♠ by bidding what he thinks is a 'choice of partscores' 2NT, but Quantin thinks 2NT is strong and shows his four-card spade suit. Lorenzini convinces himself that Quantin has forgotten their agreement and has only long spades, so he passes 3♠, which is fortunate to go only one down, -50. So 4 IMPs to USA 2, back in the lead, 109-107. Ping-pong.

Board 57. E-W Vul.

```
                    ♠ A Q J 5 3
                    ♡ 3
                    ♢ A K J 8 5 3
                    ♣ 8
        ♠ 8 7                         ♠ 10 9 6 4
        ♡ K 10 5          N           ♡ 8 7 6 4
        ♢ Q 9 7      W         E      ♢ 10 6
        ♣ A Q 9 6 3       S          ♣ 10 5 2
                    ♠ K 2
                    ♡ A Q J 9 2
                    ♢ 4 2
                    ♣ K J 7 4
```

Closed Room

West	North	East	South
Lorenzini	Moss	Quantin	Grue
	1♣[1]	pass	1♠[2]
pass	2◇	pass	3♣
pass	3♠	pass	4◇
pass	5◇	pass	6◇
all pass			

1. Strong.
2. Positive with at least five hearts.

Six is a lot of diamonds, but with trumps 3-2 and the queen onside, the slam is bound to make. Moss actually makes seven on the dangerous-looking lead of the ♠10 by winning in hand, playing the ♡A, ♡Q (covered and ruffed), a hopeful spade to the king, ♡J to pitch the club loser, and finally, a trump to the jack. With so many layouts leading to failure in 6◇, Moss can appreciate that his +940 must be attributed to clean living.

Open Room

West	North	East	South
Pszczola	Bessis	Rosenberg	Volcker
	1◇	pass	1♡
pass	2♠	pass	2NT
pass	3♠	pass	4♣
dbl	4◇	pass	4♡
pass	4♠	all pass	

After Bessis's first two bids, Volcker will have to show restraint to avoid the poor slam (Hamman would call it 'good' because it makes, tongue only slightly in cheek). The French supporters are hoping Volcker will feel unrestrained. No, when Pepsi doubles 4♣, Volcker correctly decides that Bessis would go past 4♠ if the pointed suits were solid, and so settles for the ten-trick game. That is a close decision, as 5◇ might be safer with a club lead threatening to shorten declarer's five-card trump suit. Rosenberg leads the illegible ♣5, the partnership card from three, or from doubleton five-deuce. Pepsi takes the jack with the queen and continues with the ♣A, which doesn't figure to hurt the defense. With a master club in dummy now, Bessis draws all the trumps, discarding losers, cashes the ◇AK to see if the queen appears, and when it does not, leads a heart to the queen and king. Pepsi can cash the ◇Q, but dummy has the rest for +420.

USA 2 gains 11 IMPs and leads 120-107.

On Board 58, both vulnerable, East, with:

♠ Q 8 7 3 ♡ Q 8 ◇ 6 4 2 ♣ A K 10 4

must decide whether to try for game after partner opens 1♣ and rebids 1NT. Rosenberg, who knows Pepsi won't have a 'good' 14 once he does not open 1NT, passes; Quantin, whose card describes a 1NT opening as 15-17, raises to 2NT and plays there. Even 1NT is in danger at single dummy, but there are nine tricks this time, a push at +150.

It's easy to brush past quiet flat boards like that one, both in comparing scores after a session and in reviewing a match, but there is often something to be gleaned from a closer look; it might be nothing more than gaining an insight about evaluation or tactics or how system can affect a marginal decision.

Board 59. Neither Vul.

```
              ♠ A 5
              ♡ 4
              ◇ J 10 9 5 4
              ♣ A Q 7 4 2
♠ J 9 8 3                      ♠ Q 7 4 2
♡ Q 8 7 6 2        N           ♡ 9 5 3
◇ 8 6 2        W       E       ◇ A K 7
♣ 10               S           ♣ K 9 5
              ♠ K 10 6
              ♡ A K J 10
              ◇ Q 3
              ♣ J 8 6 3
```

Open Room

West	North	East	South
Pszczola	Bessis	Rosenberg	Volcker
			1NT
pass	2♠[1]	pass	2NT
pass	3◇	pass	3♡
pass	3♠	pass	4♣
pass	5♣	all pass	

1. Clubs.

Closed Room

West	North	East	South
Lorenzini	Moss	Quantin	Grue
			1NT
pass	2◇[1]	pass	2♡
pass	2♠[2]	pass	3♣
pass	3♡[3]	pass	3NT
all pass			

1. Hearts, or game force with both minors.
2. Minors.
3. Shortness.

Volcker borrows a point to open 1NT; Grue needn't. The space saved by the American methods allows North to show his heart shortage *after* South shows real club support, so Grue is in a strong position to bid 3NT where Volcker has a close decision.

Since 5♣ fails on any lead, Pepsi's heart lead does not cost, -50. The lead matters against 3NT, however, but Lorenzini also leads a heart, so 3NT has nine easy tricks after the ♣J (declarer can guard against K1095 only in the West hand) runs to the king. Grue has time for a safe tenth trick when East continues hearts, but switches to spades after winning the first diamond, +430, and 10 IMPs to USA 2, opening some daylight now, 130-107.

On a spade lead, declarer in 3NT is likely to take the losing heart finesse after developing one minor or the other. When declarer bids 3NT into the teeth of known shortness in dummy, opening leader never really knows how many stoppers he will find in the closed hand. Declarer might have a holding like king-third (worthless in a minor-suit game) and strong fillers in responder's suits, for example. It makes some sense to adopt a consistent strategy for choosing the lead on such auctions, but the truth is that we tend to think we will do better on a case-by-case basis by examining our holdings in the key suits in the context of partner's not doubling the shortness-showing bid.

Board 60. N-S Vul.

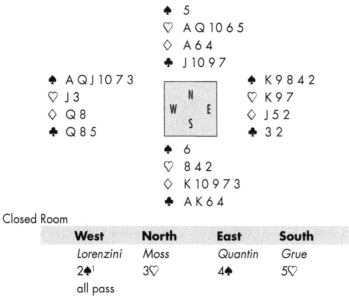

```
                    ♠ 5
                    ♡ A Q 10 6 5
                    ◇ A 6 4
                    ♣ J 10 9 7
 ♠ A Q J 10 7 3              ♠ K 9 8 4 2
 ♡ J 3            N          ♡ K 9 7
 ◇ Q 8       W        E      ◇ J 5 2
 ♣ Q 8 5          S          ♣ 3 2
                    ♠ 6
                    ♡ 8 4 2
                    ◇ K 10 9 7 3
                    ♣ A K 6 4
```

Closed Room

West	North	East	South
Lorenzini	Moss	Quantin	Grue
2♠[1]	3♡	4♠	5♡
all pass			

1. Six spades, 10-14.

Lorenzini's tailor-made constructive 2♠ opening works particularly well when it bullies Moss into an aggressive but pragmatic three-level overcall, and Grue takes the push to 5♡ under pressure. After a count spade lead and low-trump switch to the ten and king, Moss eventually loses a diamond trick for one down, -100.

Open Room

West	North	East	South
Pszczola	Bessis	Rosenberg	Volcker
1♠	2♡	4♠	dbl
all pass			

Pepsi's 'standard' 1♠ fares less well when Volcker is unwilling to commit to the five-level, facing a two-level overcall, and expands the strain discussion with a flexible responsive double. Bessis could be forgiven for taking it out with good offensive prospects in three suits, but makes the winning decision by passing. Declarer has five unavoidable losers for two down and -300. France earns 9 IMPs, 116-130.

Board 61. Both Vul.

```
                    ♠ A 10 6 2
                    ♡ J
                    ◇ 10 7 6
                    ♣ A Q 10 8 2
  ♠ K 8 7 4                          ♠ 3
  ♡ A 6 2            N               ♡ K 8 7 5 3
  ◇ K Q 3       W        E           ◇ J 4 2
  ♣ K 9 6            S               ♣ 7 5 4 3
                    ♠ Q J 9 5
                    ♡ Q 10 9 4
                    ◇ A 9 8 5
                    ♣ J
```

Open Room

West	North	East	South
Pszczola	Bessis	Rosenberg	Volcker
	1♣	pass	1♡
dbl	pass	2◇	all pass

Closed Room

West	North	East	South
Lorenzini	Moss	Quantin	Grue
	1♣	pass	1♡
dbl	1♠[1]	pass	3♠
all pass			

1. Natural, with at least five clubs.

For the third time in the match we encounter a deal where a player is willing to make a two-suit takeout double with only three cards in one of the unbid suits and an unexceptional hand, vulnerability be damned. As the doublers expect their partners to bid aggressively with a four-card fit in one of the expected suits, the fact that 'double' seems to be both acceptable and perhaps even indicated gives us some idea of the concern the defensive-bidding side has for coping with very light opening bids and responses. That concern does not seem to extend to risking an even-more dangerous 1NT overcall.

Moss and Grue prefer to bid naturally over this type of double, and here they find their spade fit painlessly and quit at 3♠, both partners treading carefully as they expect West to hold four trumps. Moss takes the lead of the ◇2 with dummy's ace, passes the ♠Q, and calls for the ♡4. Lorenzini accurately goes in with the ace, and after some thought, returns the ♠K, hoping to get a trump winner back if declarer ruffs clubs with the jack and nine. Moss wins and concedes a diamond, and Lorenzini, rather than establish dummy's long card, continues trumps. Moss wins in dummy and passes the ♡9 to the king, discarding his remaining diamond. Quantin wins the third defensive trick and exits in diamonds, aiming to force Moss to use his remaining trump, which would allow Lorenzini to score his ♠7 *en passant* to set the contract. Moss avoids this fatal ending by discarding on the third round of diamonds, keeping his ♠10 to lead to dummy's jack to remove that evil lurker and claim those red winners, +140.

Bessis sees no reason to bid one of West's suits when East-West might be in trouble, and indeed, Rosenberg, badly placed, settles for 2♢. Volcker has no penalty double available, but does just fine by passing. His lead of the ♣J holds the first trick, and he switches to the ♢5. The defense is poised for a four-trick set, but a trick gets away and Rosenberg escapes gratefully for -300. But 4 IMPs to France, just the same, closer at 120-130.

Board 62. Neither Vul.

```
                    ♠ 9 8 4 3
                    ♡ 8 5 2
                    ♢ Q 9 4
                    ♣ J 8 7
     ♠ A K 6                        ♠ Q J 10 7
     ♡ 10 4 3          N            ♡ Q 9
     ♢ K 10 2      W       E        ♢ A J 8 5 3
     ♣ 10 9 6 5        S            ♣ A K
                    ♠ 5 2
                    ♡ A K J 7 6
                    ♢ 7 6
                    ♣ Q 4 3 2
```

Open Room

West	North	East	South
Pszczola	Bessis	Rosenberg	Volcker
		1♢	1♡
dbl[1]	pass	3♠	pass
4♠	all pass		

1. Expected to deliver four spades.

	West	North	East	South
	Lorenzini	Moss	Quantin	Grue
			1◇	1♡
	1♠¹	pass	2♠	pass
	3◇	pass	3NT	all pass

1. Denies as many as four spades.

This is a tricky deal for East-West after South's 1♡ overcall, and neither pair finishes in 5◇, which needs only to avoid a trump loser.

In the French auction, Quantin's 2♠ is a natural reverse, with the 3◇ preference game-forcing. Perhaps Quantin believes he would have bid notrump earlier with a full stopper so his delayed 3NT suggests only a half stopper, but we've all been in worse contracts than 3NT. Here, however, Grue has an easy 'strong king' heart lead, asking for count or unblock, and he cashes out the suit for one down, -50.

Pepsi's negative double is a spade short, but that doesn't concern him enough to look elsewhere when Rosenberg invites in spades. After three rounds of hearts, Rosenberg accepts the force, leaving North with the long trump. At first glance, it seems that Rosenberg needs to find the ◇Q to get home in 4♠, but that's why second glances were invented. Rosenberg cashes the ◇A, then leads a second round through South, who would be ruffing a loser if he were short. When the ◇K stands up, declarer cashes the ♣AK, and exits in diamonds, showing his hand; he can win any return and make the rest on a high crossruff for a very pretty +420. USA 2 has worked hard to earn these 10 IMPs, 140-120.

On Board 63, West, second seat favorable, holds:

♠ A 2   ♡ J 10 8 7 6 2   ◇ Q 7 6 2   ♣ K

That doesn't look like a one-bid or a two-bid, and Lorenzini duly passes, happy to see his LHO open 1♡. After double (1♠), he volunteers 1NT, which essentially turns on which defender holds the ♠8. Although 1NT survives for +90, a diamond partial would have been much safer.

Pepsi is not dissuaded by all the negative features of his hand, opens 1♡, and is soon confronted by one of the more subtle but easy-to-anticipate downsides when he is obliged to find a rebid over partner's 1♠. Although he has methods in place to untangle weak 6-4 hands after 1♡-1♠; 2♦-2NT, and partner can separate courtesy diamond raises (3◇) from stronger ones (3♣), Pepsi tries 2♡ with the hope that showing a sixth heart early will be the right strategy. He buys a heart void in dummy, and slowly loses six tricks, -50. That's 4 IMPs to France, 124-140.

Board 64. E-W Vul.

```
                    ♠ A Q J 4 3
                    ♡ A K 10 9
                    ◇ 6 3 2
                    ♣ 9
    ♠ 8 2                            ♠ K 10 9 7 6
    ♡ Q 7 6 5          N             ♡ 8 3 2
    ◇ A J 10       W       E         ◇ 5
    ♣ Q 10 7 2         S             ♣ A 6 5 4
                    ♠ 5
                    ♡ J 4
                    ◇ K Q 9 8 7 4
                    ♣ K J 8 3
```

Open Room

West	North	East	South
Pszczola	Bessis	Rosenberg	Volcker
pass	1♠	pass	3◇[1]
pass	5◇	all pass	

1. Invitational, decent suit.

Closed Room

West	North	East	South
Lorenzini	Moss	Quantin	Grue
pass	1♠	pass	1NT[1]
pass	2♡	pass	3♣[2]
pass	3◇[3]	all pass	

1. Forcing, but limited.
2. Good raise in hearts, or a hand with long diamonds.
3. Forced, unless an excellent non-strong-club hand for diamonds.

The Open Room 5◇ needs more luck than it gets, and Volcker is one down, -50, after a club lead. Moss, playing 3◇ from the short side, makes four on the stiff trump lead, +130. USA 2 gains 5 IMPs, and wins the set, 51-28. At the halfway point in the match, the Americans lead by 21 IMPs, 145-124.

Session Five (Boards 65-80)

Board 65: With the points evenly divided, Rombaut's 10-12 1NT is passed out, -50. In theory, Moss-Grue do better by finding their 4-4 heart fit via: 1◇-1♡; 2♡, but Bessis, with ♠A965 ♡J6 ◇A87 ♣QJ53, risks a "live position" double. Volcker, with ♠KQ84 ♡532 ◇62 ♣K1096, declares 3♠ for +140. 3 IMPs to France, 127-145.

Board 66. N-S Vul.

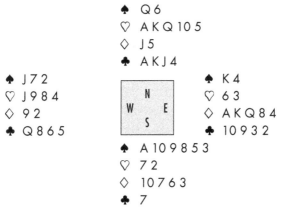

```
              ♠  Q 6
              ♡  A K Q 10 5
              ◇  J 5
              ♣  A K J 4
♠ J 7 2                        ♠  K 4
♡ J 9 8 4         N            ♡  6 3
◇ 9 2          W     E         ◇  A K Q 8 4
♣ Q 8 6 5         S            ♣  10 9 3 2
              ♠  A 10 9 8 5 3
              ♡  7 2
              ◇  10 7 6 3
              ♣  7
```

No IMPs are scored on this one, but the bidding and play at both tables is interesting.

Open Room

West	North	East	South
Martel	Rombaut	Fleisher	Combescure
		1◇[1]	pass
1♡	dbl	pass	1♠
pass	2♡	pass	3♠
pass	4♠	all pass	

1. Usually 5+ diamonds, usually unbalanced.

When Combescure is not willing to overcall 1♠ or 2♠ at unfavorable, Rombaut must deal with Martel's light 1♡ response. Although 2♡ would be natural (stronger than bidding hearts later), with all those high cards, Rombaut feels he can afford to double, but in the end takes a hopeful shot at 4♠ when diamonds seem to be a problem for notrump. Combescure's cautious 1♠ seems to cater to the sort of hand Rombaud has, but not so accurately to the more normal 'spades and clubs' hands. This is the fourth deal in the match involving a two-suit takeout double with unexpected lengths in those suits.

Martel leads the ◇9 against 4♠, and Fleisher plays queen-king-ace, West ruffing the third in front of dummy with the seven. Declarer overruffs and leads the ♠6 (four, ten, jack), and later ruffs himself in with a club to cash the ♠A with the desired result, +620.

Closed Room

	West	North	East	South
	Volcker	*Moss*	*Bessis*	*Grue*
			1◇	1♠
	pass	2◇¹	pass	2♠
	pass	3♡²	pass	3♠
	pass	4◇³	pass	4♡
	all pass			

1. Hearts.
2. Forcing.
3. Choice of games.

For Grue, the South hand falls into the category of 'not strong enough for a weak jump overcall but too dangerous to pass'. Moss has the tools to describe his hand very well and Grue eventually admits to two-card heart support with only mediocre spades in context. Against 4♡, Bessis cashes the ◇Q and ◇A, then switches to a trump, neutralizing Volcker's jack. Moss plays the ♣A, ruffs a club, ruffs a diamond (♠2 from West), draws all the trumps and cashes the ♣K. The good news for declarer is that East has parted with the long diamond, so if the clubs are not 2-0 at this stage, he will have a chance in spades. He exits with the ♣J, won by Volcker, who returns the ♠7. Moss knows where the king is, so follows low and makes his contract when the jack is on his right, +620.

USA 2 leads by 16 IMPs, 150-134, on the brink of Board 72, which is everyone's 3NT, South declaring.

Board 72. Neither Vul.

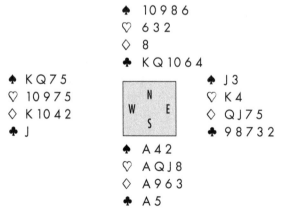

```
                  ♠ 10 9 8 6
                  ♡ 6 3 2
                  ◇ 8
                  ♣ K Q 10 6 4
 ♠ K Q 7 5                          ♠ J 3
 ♡ 10 9 7 5          N              ♡ K 4
 ◇ K 10 4 2      W       E          ◇ Q J 7 5
 ♣ J                 S              ♣ 9 8 7 3 2
                  ♠ A 4 2
                  ♡ A Q J 8
                  ◇ A 9 6 3
                  ♣ A 5
```

At both tables South shows four hearts and North implies four spades, so West leads the ◇2 (fourth-best leads). Combescure takes the jack with the ace, cashes four clubs (West discards three spades) and leads a heart to the queen. Those spade discards strongly suggest West is 4=4=4=1, and Combescure is not surprised to see the ♡K fall under his ace. The ♡J is his ninth winner, +400.

Grue ducks the first diamond, plays low on East's ◇5 continuation, but takes West's king on the third round (discarding a heart and a spade from dummy). Confident that diamonds are 4-4, he leads the ♡J, which might slip past West and perhaps lay the groundwork for an endplay or a squeeze. This is not the layout Joe is hoping for. Bessis takes the ♡K, cashes the ◇Q, and exits carefully with the ♠3: the jack would be fatal — when declarer cashes his club winners, West would be squeezed in the majors, dummy's ♠10 becoming the threat. Here Bessis can maintain parity with dummy's clubs, discarding the ♠J when Grue cashes the ace-queen of hearts, so the ♣9 takes the last trick for down one, -50. That's 10 IMPs to France, closing to 144-150.

Board 73. E-W Vul.

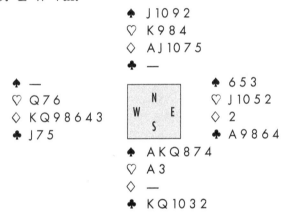

	West	**North**	**East**	**South**
Open Room	Martel	Rombaut	Fleisher	Combescure
Closed Room	Volcker	Moss	Bessis	Grue
		1◇[1]	pass	1♠
	pass	2♠	pass	5◇*
	pass	5♡*	pass	6♠
	all pass			

1. For Moss, 2+ diamonds, 10-15.

It's rare to have an opportunity to use Exclusion RKCB in partner's suit, and both Souths are pleased to have that club in their bag when North's 5♡ reply reveals the ♣A is missing.

Combescure makes six on the lead of the ♣5, discarding from dummy and losing to the ♣A. Grue makes seven on the lead of the ◊Q, winning the ace, crossruffing in the minors in the process of drawing trumps, and eventually coming a thirteenth trick on a double squeeze, with hearts the middle suit. Just 1 IMP to USA 2, 151-144.

Without a trump lead, declarer can cash his high hearts and crossruff, but as West would lead a trump if he had one, seven is not a favorite at single dummy.

Of some interest — at least to me — is the idea of responder to Exclusion showing a void of his own. Using similar responses to traditional RKCB, that would mean using step five to show an even number of working keycards plus a void, and steps six and seven (or a surrogate) to show an odd number of keycards plus a specific void. Doing this is hardly a free lunch, however: the void may be of no value and the method may get the partnership too high outright or too high to check on the trump queen when that is important. It's always nice to have a real deal to refer to when considering something new, and I'm filing this one away for a rainy day.

Board 74. Both Vul.

```
                    ♠ J 9 4
                    ♡ A J 8 5
                    ◊ 10 9
                    ♣ J 8 6 2
       ♠ 3 2                        ♠ A K Q 8 7
       ♡ Q               N          ♡ K 4 3 2
       ◊ A K Q 8 7 5  W     E       ◊ 3 2
       ♣ A 7 5 3          S         ♣ K 10
                    ♠ 10 6 5
                    ♡ 10 9 7 6
                    ◊ J 6 4
                    ♣ Q 9 4
```

This is a very worthwhile 6NT or 6◊, but not at all easy to bid.

Open Room

West	North	East	South
Martel	Rombaut	Fleisher	Combescure
		1♠	pass
2◊	pass	2♡	pass
3◊	pass	3NT	all pass

Martel's forcing 3◇ seems like a good start, but it inflicts a strain decision on Fleisher, who can stop clubs but also has a suitable hand for a high diamond contract. Fleisher's 3NT produces +720 on a club lead.

Closed Room

	West	North	East	South
	Volcker	Moss	Bessis	Grue
			1♠	pass
	2◇	pass	2♡	pass
	2♠[1]	pass	2NT[2]	pass
	3◇	pass	3♠	pass
	3NT	pass	4♣	pass
	4◇	pass	4♡	pass
	6◇	all pass		

1. Relay.
2. 5=4=2=2.

The difference in the Closed Room is that Volcker learns of two-card diamond support *before* rebidding his suit. Still, Bessis's problem over 3◇ is similar to Fleisher's. With extra values and primes, he is confident that 5◇ should be safe if there is no slam, so he goes past game to show controls in all the side suits. Volcker, after offering 3NT, can hardly stay out of slam now, and in the end Bessis passes 6◇ rather than convert to 6NT to protect his ♡K. Moss leads the ♡A, but Volcker has the rest for +1370. France earns these 12 IMPs to take the lead, 156-151.

Frederic Volcker

Board 75. Neither Vul.

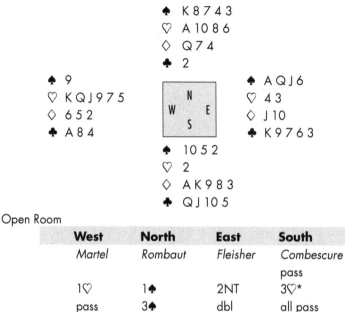

West	North	East	South
Martel	Rombaut	Fleisher	Combescure
			pass
1♡	1♠	2NT	3♡*
pass	3♠	dbl	all pass

Although Combescure's cuebid raise in a dangerous auction is quite a strong action, Fleisher can't resist doubling 3♠ for penalty facing a second-seat one-bid with neither side vulnerable. His analysis is correct, as 3♠ can be defeated, but only by one trick, so that's a lot of potential angst for an extra 50 points.

Rombaut wins the heart lead and plays a club to the queen and ace. Martel makes the essential switch to the ♠9, ducked to the jack. Fleisher can defeat the contract without much complexity by cashing the ♠A and exiting with a diamond, or, more exotically, by continuing with the ♠6. Instead, he switches to a diamond, which also should be good enough. Rombaut wins the ◊A (deuce from Martel, nominally reverse attitude), comes to the ◊Q (revealing that Martel's ◊2 was not what it seemed), ruffs a heart (nine from Martel, even number of hearts remaining), ruffs a club, and leads the ♡10 towards dummy's bare ♠10, concealing the ♡8. Fleisher can prevail by discarding a club or (again more exotically) by ruffing low, but when he ruffs in with the ♠Q, he has no good move. He cashes the ♠A and declarer claims the remaining tricks for +530.

Closed Room

West	North	East	South
Volcker	Moss	Bessis	Grue
			1◇¹
1♡	1♠²	1NT	2♠
3♡	3♠	all pass	

1. 2+ diamonds, 10-15.
2. At least five spades.

Facing a Precision 1◇ opening, and what could be a three-card raise, it's far from clear for Moss to compete to 3♠ when he has such promising defense against 3♡, and indeed, it would be easier to go plus by passing 3♡. The first three tricks here are as in the Open Room, but here Bessis plays a second round of hearts when he wins the ♠J. Moss ruffs in dummy, and passes the ♠10 to East's queen. He wins the diamond switch in hand, and drives out the trump ace and can extract East's last trump when he regains the lead, +140. So another 9 IMPs to France, suddenly 14 IMPs ahead, 165-151 on the strength of a 31-1 run.

Before we leave Board 75, we owe the deal a final look. It may not be obvious, but the truth is that both Moss and Bessis have missed an opportunity, and on the same trick. Bessis can set the contract by letting the ♠10 hold, which amounts to reaching the same sort of position we've seen in the Open Room. However, Moss can prevent that clever duck by overtaking the ♠10 with the king, as he retains the eight-seven as equals against the queen-six without having to shorten himself.

Brad Moss

Board 76. N-S Vul.

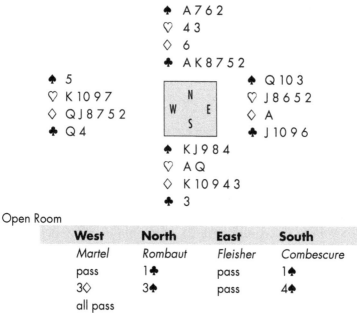

West	North	East	South
Martel	*Rombaut*	*Fleisher*	*Combescure*
pass	1♣	pass	1♠
3◇	3♠	pass	4♠
all pass			

Combescure, warned about the diamond position, decides not to try for slam. Just as well, as there's too much work to do in 6♠. Fleisher takes the lead of the ◇Q with the ace to switch to the ♡8. Although there are no more top losers, there is still some work to do to ensure ten winners. He takes the ♡A, discards the ♡Q on the second high club, and finesses against East's ♠Q. He can ruff one diamond after drawing trumps, and can build another diamond trick with the ten-nine for +650.

Closed Room

West	North	East	South
Volcker	*Moss*	*Bessis*	*Grue*
pass	1♣	1♡	1♠[1]
4◇[2]	4♠	pass	5♡
pass	6♠	pass	pass
7♡	dbl	all pass	

1. At least five spades.
2. Fit-showing raise to 4♡.

Channeling the popular Canadian commercial for Alexander Keith's India Pale Ale, those who like East's 1♡ overcall (seem to) like it a lot. I'm not sure Volcker is expected to worry about Bessis holding the sort of hand he holds just because of the vulnerability, but saving at the seven-level after stealing so much of the opponents' bidding space is always dangerous, especially after describing the character of your hand earlier. Moss, who has bid a lot on his promising but modest values, can't be terribly disappointed to double 7♡.

Grue leads the ♠K to determine how best to continue after holding the lead. There are several ways to secure a fifth undertrick, including a simple spade continuation, but when he switches to the ♣3, Moss must win and underlead his remaining honor to get the job done. Not surprisingly, he cashes the ♣A, and Bessis eventually neutralizes the ♡Q to escape for -800. The American gain is only 4 IMPs, but that is significantly better than the potential 13-IMP loss for -100 in 6♠. The French lead is down to 10 IMPs, 165-155.

Board 78. Neither Vul.

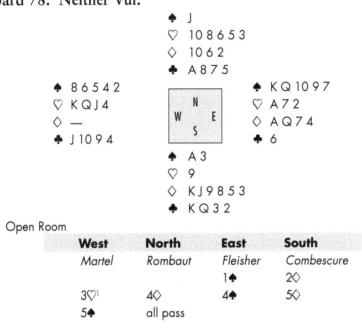

```
                    ♠ J
                    ♡ 10 8 6 5 3
                    ◇ 10 6 2
                    ♣ A 8 7 5
   ♠ 8 6 5 4 2              ♠ K Q 10 9 7
   ♡ K Q J 4        N       ♡ A 7 2
   ◇ —          W       E   ◇ A Q 7 4
   ♣ J 10 9 4         S       ♣ 6
                    ♠ A 3
                    ♡ 9
                    ◇ K J 9 8 5 3
                    ♣ K Q 3 2
```

Open Room

West	North	East	South
Martel	Rombaut	Fleisher	Combescure
		1♠	2◇
3♡[1]	4◇	4♠	5◇
5♠	all pass		

1. Mixed raise in spades.

It seems that Martel is intending to bid 4♠ over a potential 3♠ signoff with his peculiar hand and wants to give Fleisher an accurate picture of his high-card strength *en route*, but the auction gets away from him, and over 5◇, he feels he can't afford to pass when he has so much extra offense. It happens that 5♠ is a good contract, but fails on best defense: singleton heart lead, suit preference ♡3 from North under dummy's king, trump to the king and ace, ♣Q to the ace, heart ruff. One down, -50, a dignified result all around.

Closed Room

West	North	East	South
Volcker	Moss	Bessis	Grue
		1♠	2◇
4◇[1]	dbl	4♠	5◇
pass	pass	dbl	all pass

1. Splinter spade raise.

Volcker's splinter raise (neither 3♡ nor 4♡ is available as a fit bid) does not promise much defense at this vulnerability, while Moss's 'raise' double, like Rombaut's brave 4◇ in the Open Room, apparently doesn't promise much offense. Clearly, Bessis is not expecting much, for he makes no slam move over the double; he intends his 4♠ as 'extra offense, minimum but happy', which would be consistent with partnership policy in situations where forced to a level below game in a suit higher-ranking than the opponents' suit. As there is no firm agreement in 'game-forcing-but-still-below-game' situations like this one, Bessis hopes Volcker will interpret 4♠ the same way. Although Volcker has very little defense, an extra trump and a void, he is not sure he is invited to bid in front of his partner. Bessis's double is unambiguously a penalty opinion, but he is only too aware that 5◇ doubled might be down only one, with 5♠ cold.

Bessis overtakes the lead of the ♡K to play ace and another trump. Grue wins cheaply, takes his spade ruff, ruffs a heart, and plays the ◇K and another diamond. Volcker has been discarding spades at every opportunity but now must part with a heart honor, choosing the jack. Grue shows him his hand, and claims the rest on a heart-club squeeze to get out for one down, -100. In the end, 4 IMPs to France, 169-156. Curiously, best defense is a second round of hearts, as declarer will need to use the ♣A to enter dummy for a second trump play, and that takes West off the hook in discarding.

France wins the set, 45-11 and leads by 13 IMPs, 169-156, with 48 boards remaining.

Board 82. N-S Vul.

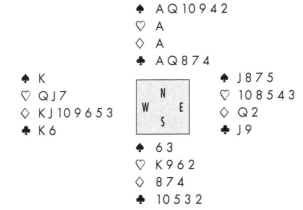

West	North	East	South
Pszczola	Rombaut	Rosenberg	Combescure
		pass	pass
1♢	dbl	pass	1♡
2♢	dbl	pass	2♡
3♢	dbl	pass	4♣
pass	6♣	all pass	

When Rosenberg can't find a reason to open the East hand, I am expecting Pepsi to do something sexier than 1♢ at this vulnerability (3♢, 4♢, 1NT, 2NT?), but I am not expecting him to volunteer a third bid either, so maybe I need to update my files for future scouting reports. Rosenberg, despite an impressive diamond holding, resists the temptation to raise to 4♢.

No one has written a manual about how to deal with hands like North's, but Rombaut's approach — three takeout doubles and a unilateral raise to slam after extracting a strained club preference from partner — works surprisingly well in real life. In 6♣, Combescure can do no better than play ace and another trump at his earliest opportunity. With a third-round trump entry, he can lead spades from the right hand, only to find that he needn't have bothered: he can take the marked third-round ruffing finesse against the ♠J to establish the suit and claim his remarkable slam, +1370.

West	North	East	South
Lorenzini	*Moss*	*Quantin*	*Grue*
		2♡¹	pass
pass	dbl	pass	2NT²
pass	3♣	all pass	

1. At least four hearts and four spades, weak.
2. Lebensohl puppet to 3♣, usually some weak hand.

Quantin's weak-majors 2♡ is no thing of beauty, but it lives up to its reputation as a creator of headaches, in this case for the opponents. Even the most thorough of countermeasures can't cover everything, and although Moss could have bid a strong 3♠ or stronger 4♠, he does not have a forcing 4♣ (clubs and a major) available to start his huge two-suiter. His double-then-spades sequence is natural and very strong, but is not forcing. Whether Grue is expected to raise with a couple of trumps and a probably-wasted king is a partnership matter. Moss loses a trump and a club for an unsatisfying +200.

That is 15 IMPs to France, who lead now by 28 IMPs, 184-156. Moss and Grue can console themselves with the knowledge that they could have saved only 3 IMPs by reaching 4♠.

Board 83. E-W Vul.

```
            ♠ 7 4 2
            ♡ K 8 4 3 2
            ◇ J
            ♣ A 10 7 2
♠ K J 10 6 5          ♠ 9 8
♡ 5            N      ♡ A 10 9 7 6
◇ Q 9 8 2   W   E    ◇ 7 6
♣ Q J 5         S    ♣ 9 8 6 3
            ♠ A Q 3
            ♡ Q J
            ◇ A K 10 5 4 3
            ♣ K 4
```

Open Room

West	North	East	South
Pszczola	Rombaut	Rosenberg	Combescure
			2NT
pass	3◇[1]	pass	3NT[2]
all pass			

1. At least five hearts.
2. Normally fewer than three hearts.

Closed Room

West	North	East	South
Lorenzini	Moss	Quantin	Grue
			1♣*
pass	1♠[1]	pass	1NT[2]
pass	2◇[3]	pass	2♡
pass	3◇[4]	pass	3NT
all pass			

1. Positive, at least five hearts.
2. Relay for shape.
3-4. 3=5=1=4.

Both Souths get the lead of the ♠J against 3NT. Combescure has an easy ride after winning with the queen. When he leads a low diamond, Pepsi goes in with the ◇Q to continue spades, and declarer can claim nine tricks when both follow to the second diamond: +400.

Grue seems to have a blind spot, for he ducks the opening lead when Quantin follows with the nine, nominally encouraging. While declarer's play will not cost and might gain if spades are continued as he expects (buying time for two heart tricks if diamonds are foul), this time it gives West the opportunity to find the killing heart switch for a spade return. Indeed, Lorenzini believes his partner would have played the ♠Q at Trick 1 had he started with queen-nine-low, so places Grue with that card, and switches at Trick 2... but to the ♣Q, not to the singleton heart. It is not over for the defense yet, however, when declarer wins with dummy's ♣A to pass the ◇J, which Lorenzini ducks. Declarer calls for a heart, but Quantin goes in with the ace to return... a club, not the ♠8. Grue, gratefully, wins with the king and clears diamonds. Lorenzini cashes the ♣J, but declarer can safely discard the ♠Q, and claim: five diamonds, two clubs, and one trick in each major, +400 the hard way for a flat board.

Joe Grue, still a young dude, ages a couple of years on that one.

Board 84. Both Vul.

```
              ♠ 9 6 5 4 3 2
              ♡ 9
              ◇ A 10 5 4
              ♣ J 4
  ♠ K                         ♠ Q 8 7
  ♡ A 6 3 2          N        ♡ J 10 7 5
  ◇ K 3          W       E    ◇ J 8 7
  ♣ A 8 7 5 3 2      S        ♣ Q 10 6
              ♠ A J 10
              ♡ K Q 8 4
              ◇ Q 9 6 2
              ♣ K 9
```

Open Room

West	North	East	South
Pszczola	Rombaut	Rosenberg	Combescure
1♣	pass	1♡	pass
3◇[1]	pass	3♡	all pass

1. Light raise to 3♡ with short spades or diamonds.

When Rombaut passes over 1♣ and Combescure sensibly does not come in with a 16-19 1NT overcall on a terrible 15, the Americans have the auction to themselves and finish in 3♡, where Rosenberg does well to go down only one, -100.

Closed Room

West	North	East	South
Lorenzini	Moss	Quantin	Grue
1♣	1♠	pass	2♣
pass	2♠	pass	3NT
pass	4♠	all pass	

Meanwhile, in the Closed Room, we are treated to yet another episode in the continuing saga of very light vulnerable six-card-major overcalls with a hand 'too weak for a weak jump overcall but too dangerous to pass'. Grue's two-step to 3NT offers Moss a choice of games, which is how Brad comes to declare a seemingly hopeless 4♠.

As is often the case, 'hopeless' is an overstatement of woe. Quantin leads the ♡J, innocently enough: king, ace, nine. Lorenzini, hoping for heart shortness, elects to continue hearts, and that is effectively the end of the defense. Moss has two discards for his clubs now, and has time to get diamonds going in the course of drawing trumps (ace first). That's +620 and 11 IMPs to USA 2; France lead 184-167.

Board 86. E-W Vul.

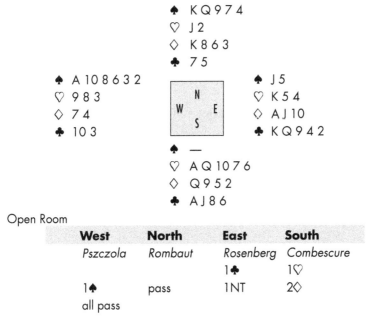

```
                    ♠ K Q 9 7 4
                    ♡ J 2
                    ◇ K 8 6 3
                    ♣ 7 5
  ♠ A 10 8 6 3 2              ♠ J 5
  ♡ 9 8 3          N          ♡ K 5 4
  ◇ 7 4         W     E       ◇ A J 10
  ♣ 10 3           S          ♣ K Q 9 4 2
                    ♠ —
                    ♡ A Q 10 7 6
                    ◇ Q 9 5 2
                    ♣ A J 8 6
```

Open Room

West	North	East	South
Pszczola	Rombaut	Rosenberg	Combescure
		1♣	1♡
1♠	pass	1NT	2◇
all pass			

Combescure's 2◇ implies that he could not double 1NT either as takeout of spades or simply to show four diamonds rather than five, but Rombaut does not offer a courtesy raise. The French 2◇ handles comfortably for +130 on the lead of the ♣10.

Closed Room

West	North	East	South
Lorenzini	Moss	Quantin	Grue
		1NT	2◇[1]
2♠	pass	pass	dbl
all pass			

1. Hearts.

Quantin is willing to upgrade to a strong notrump at unfavorable vulnerability, where Rosenberg is not, which generates a dramatically different competitive scenario in which Grue gets to show his main suit followed by support for the minors. His takeout double of 2♠ works particularly well when Moss can pass for penalty and lead the ♡J. On the third round of hearts Moss discards a club, then takes a second-round club ruff and switches to diamonds. Lorenzini can lose a diamond trick or allow Moss to score another low trump by discarding a diamond on a high club. He chooses the latter and soon concedes three down, -800; 12 IMPs to USA 2, now within 5, 179-184.

It might seem that borrowing a point to open a strong notrump (probably the norm with a hand like East's in 2017) is responsible for the big French loss, but that is not so. Had it started as in the Open Room, I am sure Grue would have doubled 1NT rather than bidding 2◊, and someone would have doubled West's retreat to 2♠.

Board 88. Neither Vul.

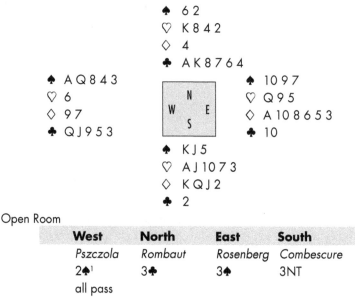

Open Room

West	North	East	South
Pszczola	Rombaut	Rosenberg	Combescure
2♠¹	3♣	3♠	3NT
all pass			

1. 5+ spades and 5+ in a minor, 6-10.

Pepsi has a descriptive two-bid at his disposal, and his 2♠ opening forces Rombaut to overcall at the three-level to get his suit into play. If Rosenberg passes, Combescure can choose between 3NT and a forcing 3♡, and if he reaches 4♡, would be a favorite to get the trumps right, excellent for France. But Rosenberg makes sure that can't happen by raising to 3♠; now Combescure must choose between 3NT, a responsive double and a hopeful shot at 4♡ with only a modest five-card suit; he votes for 3NT.

Pepsi leads his fourth-best spade to the nine and jack, and it looks as though declarer won't have time for a ninth trick even if he plays East for the ♡Q, which he does. Although, strictly speaking, that is true, because on the run of the hearts West can part with two clubs, a diamond, and a spade, Pepsi is spared this discarding challenge when Combescure, after the ♡J holds, tries the ◊J; he hopes to find West with the ace, which would give him everyone's favorable-vulnerability one-bid. It can't be much of a surprise when Rosenberg wins the ◊A and leads through the ♠K to set the contract, -50.

Closed Room

West	North	East	South
Lorenzini	Moss	Quantin	Grue
pass	2♣[1]	pass	2◊[2]
pass	2♡[3]	pass	2NT[4]
pass	3♣[5]	pass	3♡
pass	4♡	all pass	

1. 6+ clubs, 10-15.
2. Artificial inquiry, at least invitational.
3. Four hearts or four spades.
4. Game-forcing relay.
5. Hearts.

When Lorenzini passes as dealer, he gets no further chance to bid with any safety, but his silence proves serendipitous when Moss has no clue about the distribution as declarer in 4♡, after revealing the essential parts of his own shape.

Quantin leads the ♠10 (jack, queen, six), and when Lorenzini continues with the ♠A, Quantin follows with the seven. So-called 'standard' practice is to follow with the higher of two remaining cards, so following with the lowest would promise an original doubleton, but these guys have recently added this wrinkle, 'if we follow with a card we are 'known' to have (here the nine if the lead is from a ♠109 holding), that confirms an original doubleton'. So, Quantin must *not* play the nine, but the seven *could* be from ♠107 doubleton, of course. This is a possible moment of truth for West, as declarer could be 3=4=0=6 and switching to a diamond would deprive East of his spade ruff, although perhaps not fatally for the defense. Perhaps a stronger clue for West is that with 2=3=7=1 with the ◊A, it is partnership style to overcall directly, for Lorenzini switches at Trick 3 to the ◊7, doing what he can to paint a false picture of his distribution when he follows with the nine on Quantin's continuation of the ◊10 after taking his ace. Moss leads a heart to the king, and heart to the... ace, for one down, -50, and a push.

Board 89. E-W Vul.

```
                    ♠ 7 5 4 3
                    ♡ J 4 3
                    ◇ 9 6 3
                    ♣ 6 4 2
      ♠ A 9 6 2                      ♠ K Q
      ♡ 7 2              N           ♡ K Q 10 8 6
      ◇ Q J         W       E        ◇ K 7 5 2
      ♣ Q J 8 7 5         S          ♣ 10 3
                    ♠ J 10 8
                    ♡ A 9 5
                    ◇ A 10 8 4
                    ♣ A K 9
```

Open Room

West	North	East	South
Pszczola	Rombaut	Rosenberg	Combescure
	pass	1♡	1NT
dbl	all pass		

Closed Room

West	North	East	South
Lorenzini	Moss	Quantin	Grue
	pass	1♡	dbl
1♠	pass	2◇	pass
2♡	all pass		

Whether you have a strong opinion about the superiority of a takeout double versus a 1NT overcall of 1♡, you are forced to take a position with imperfect hands like South's. I'm with Grue, and by a wide margin, so I'm unable to empathize with Combescure. If Pepsi leads a heart or switches to a heart when he gains the lead in diamonds, he can hold declarer to his four top cards, but he leads and continues clubs, and declarer has time to clear diamonds to establish a second trick in the suit to escape for two down, -300.

Not that a takeout double has to work well on this layout, but when Lorenzini prefers to make a start on his suits at his first turn rather than try for a penalty by redoubling, Grue can retire from the auction safely. He leads the ♣K against 2♡, and switches to the ♠J. Quantin takes his high spades, and starts on diamonds. Grue takes his ace, cashes the ♣A, and gets off play with a diamond. Quantin wins in dummy, ruffs a club (relying on Moss's count card at Trick 1), ruffs the ◇7, discards the ◇K on the ♠A, and leads a trump to the ten and ace. When Grue produces the thirteenth diamond, Moss can uppercut with the ♡J and Grue takes the last trick with the ♡9. That's +110 for Quantin, but 5 IMPs to USA 2, back in front by a nose, 185-184.

Board 90. Both Vul.

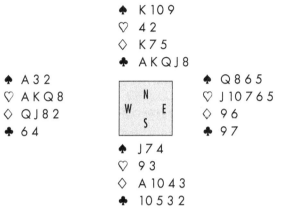

```
                        ♠ K 10 9
                        ♡ 4 2
                        ◇ K 7 5
                        ♣ A K Q J 8
        ♠ A 3 2                         ♠ Q 8 6 5
        ♡ A K Q 8              N         ♡ J 10 7 6 5
        ◇ Q J 8 2          W       E     ◇ 9 6
        ♣ 6 4                 S         ♣ 9 7
                        ♠ J 7 4
                        ♡ 9 3
                        ◇ A 10 4 3
                        ♣ 10 5 3 2
```

Open Room

West	North	East	South
Pszczola	Rombaut	Rosenberg	Combescure
		pass	pass
1NT	pass	2♣	pass
2♡	all pass		

System constraints deprive Rombaut of a sensible way into the auction over Pepsi's strong notrump opening, and 2♡ yields +110.

Closed Room

West	North	East	South
Lorenzini	Moss	Quantin	Grue
		pass	pass
1NT	dbl	rdbl	pass
2◇	pass	2♡	dbl*
pass	3♣	pass	3◇
all pass			

Moss, however, can double 1NT for penalty. Quantin escapes with a two-suited (not clubs) redouble, and East-West find their heart fit after opener first bids diamonds in case there is a fit there. Grue has just enough to double 2♡ for takeout and the nine-card club fit is located. That would be one down, -100, for a push, but Grue forges on with 3◇, trying for 3NT. Moss misreads that and passes, and is fortunate to be in a seven-card fit that goes only two down, -200. France gains 3 IMPs and leads once more, 187-185.

On Board 91, Pepsi misses an unlikely opportunity to punish the mini-notrump when he is dealt, neither vulnerable:

♠ K 7 5 ♡ J 5 ◇ Q 9 6 4 3 2 ♣ 8 4

When Rosenberg reopens over 1NT with a double, Pepsi takes out to 2◇, normally enough (although 1NT doubled is not game if it makes), and pushes the board at +130. If he passes the double, however, so will his LHO, who is 3=4=3=3 with two aces, a J108 suit, and a wealth of intermediates. The defense can take six diamonds and four spades before relinquishing the lead, for 800.

Whether it's worth the trouble to go after the intrepid weakies and minis remains a little-discussed strategy matter, but in my experience working with serious partnerships, most prefer to look after their own best contract unless it's obvious to decide to defend. The alternative position, at least when not doubling a partscore into game, is to punish them when they might be in trouble, making up for the suffering inflicted by their aggressive openings.

Board 92, North-South vulnerable, Quantin wins the board for France by opening the East hand with 1♣ in third seat on:

♠ Q 8 5 4 ♡ 5 3 ◇ A 3 ♣ A 9 8 7 6

where Rosenberg does not. That gets him to a cold 3♣ in a competitive auction, and coaxes Grue into a 'total-tricks' 3◇, where he is not doubled in his nine-card fit but goes -200 (it could have been 300). As the deal is passed out at the other table, France gains 5 IMPs, 192-185.

For what it's worth, neither Rombaut nor Moss opens:

♠ A 9 6 2 ♡ 9 7 6 ◇ K J 10 8 ♣ K 2

in second seat, unfavorable.

Board 93. Both Vul.

```
                     ♠ J 8 3
                     ♡ 10 9 7 4 2
                     ◇ —
                     ♣ A Q J 8 4
  ♠ A Q 10 9 2                        ♠ K 7 6
  ♡ Q 3            ┌─────────┐         ♡ K J 8
  ◇ 10 6 3 2      │    N    │         ◇ K Q J 9 8 4
  ♣ K 6           │ W     E │         ♣ 3
                  │    S    │
                  └─────────┘
                     ♠ 5 4
                     ♡ A 6 5
                     ◇ A 7 5
                     ♣ 10 9 7 5 2
```

Open Room

West	North	East	South
Pszczola	Rombaut	Rosenberg	Combescure
	pass	1◇	pass
1♠	2◇*	2♡[1]	4♡
4♠	pass	pass	5♣
dbl	all pass		

1. Three-card spade support.

Closed Room

West	North	East	South
Lorenzini	Moss	Quantin	Grue
	pass	1◇	pass
1♠	1NT*	2◇	2♡
dbl	pass	2♠	pass
4♠	all pass		

Both Norths, after passing originally, show their two-suiters. Style and judgment are highlighted in the reactions of the South players, Grue's conservative 2♡ implying his reluctance to fight the spades too vigorously with both sides having a double fit.

In theory, Grue is right to sell out to 4♠, as the defense can prevail by negotiating a diamond ruff, but in practice, that does not happen. Moss leads the count ♡2: cunning king, ace, three. As Grue can place declarer with two hearts and one or two clubs on the auction, and Moss would lead a singleton diamond, the actual layout is certainly in play, but Grue returns a heart; +620 for Lorenzini.

Combescure likes his double fit enough to try to steal the pot with a bounce to 4♡, then does the wrong thing — at least in theory — by competing to 5♣ over 4♠, a dread phantom save that seems destined for two down, not cheap at all.

Pepsi leads a diamond, spade from dummy, jack and ace. Declarer passes the ♣10 successfully, ruffs a diamond, cashes the ♣A, and leads a spade. The defense takes two spade winners ending in the East hand and Rosenberg exits with a diamond, ruffed in dummy, completing declarer's elimination. When Combescure leads the ♡10 from dummy, it is safe for Rosenberg to cover (with the jack to let West know who has it!) as he holds the eight. Perhaps Pepsi should realize that and dump the ♡Q when Combescure takes the ace, but Pepsi keeps his queen and is endplayed with it on the next trick, forced to concede a ruff and discard to let declarer out for down one, -200.

Thanks to the Closed Room result, France gains 9 IMPs, 201-185. Securing the second undertrick would save 6 IMPs for the Americans.

There is no swing on Board 94, but my eye catches Moss being Moss. Neither vulnerable, holding:

♠ A 10 8 5   ♡ 8 7   ◇ K 8 6 5   ♣ A Q 5

when LHO's strong notrump comes around to him, he does not go quietly; he reopens with 2◇, diamonds and a major, and corrects Grue's pass-or-correct 2♡ to 2♠, a 4-2 fit that goes two down, -100. Is this what the game is all about these days, neither vulnerable, at IMPs? I feel so old! Fortunately for Moss's side, at the other table Rosenberg negotiates 1NT with 16 opposite 3 on normal but gentle defense.

Board 96. E-W Vul.

```
                    ♠ A 10 8
                    ♡ 10 9 8 5
                    ◇ 10 7 5
                    ♣ A 9 8
      ♠ K J 9 4                      ♠ Q 5 2
      ♡ A 6 3             N          ♡ Q J 7 4 2
      ◇ A Q 3         W     E        ◇ 8 4
      ♣ Q 5 2             S          ♣ 10 6 3
                    ♠ 7 6 3
                    ♡ K
                    ◇ K J 9 6 2
                    ♣ K J 7 4
```

West	North	East	South
Pszczola	Rombaut	Rosenberg	Combescure
1NT	pass	2◇*	dbl
2♡	3◇	all pass	

After the lead of the ♡Q (king, ace, five) and a low-spade switch, it is apparent that the 1NT opener is a heavy favorite to hold the ♣Q to make up his point count; East is marked with a spade honor and the ♡QJ. After taking the ♠A and ruffing away East's ♡J, declarer still has significant handling problems, and to get home legitimately must break clubs at Trick 4. Rombaut, playing all-out for his contract with only non-vulnerable undertricks at stake, makes the essential play of the ♣J: queen, ace, low. He cashes one high heart safely, then plays his remaining heart winner, Pepsi ruffing with the ◇3 as dummy's remaining spade disappears. Passive defense — a spade continuation — would work now, but Pepsi, apparently playing Rosenberg for 4=5=2=2, exits with a club, destroying East's ten and giving Rombaut time to knock out the ace-queen of trumps for +110.

After his excellent start, Rombaut can get home against best defense only with another timely play: after cashing no more than one heart winner, he must lead a second club. If Rosenberg covers to block the suit (best, but not relevant), Rombaut returns to hand in clubs, and can play the fourth round of hearts.

West	North	East	South
Lorenzini	Moss	Quantin	Grue
1NT	pass	2◇*	dbl
2♡	3◇	all pass	

Moss, with the same information in the same contract, leads low to the ♣A at Trick 4 to take his spade discards, and can't avoid a club loser for one down, -50.

France wins the set 36-30, and at the end of the second day leads 205-186. There are 32 deals left to play.

Board 98. N-S Vul.

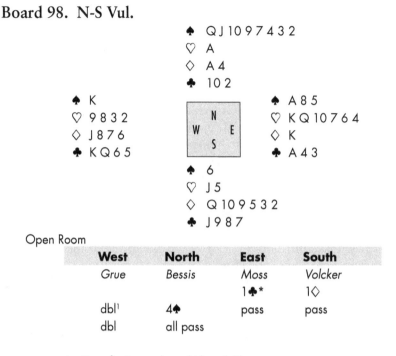

Open Room

	West	North	East	South
	Grue	*Bessis*	*Moss*	*Volcker*
			1♣*	1◇
	dbl¹	4♠	pass	pass
	dbl	all pass		

1. Game-forcing, no better bid available.

I am sure that no self-respecting strong clubber would consider opening the East hand with 1♡, but it's easy to imagine having to overbid later or risk losing the suit after starting with an artificial bid. This doesn't matter much here, as East-West can't outbid North's spades with profit. Indeed, doubling 4♠ for down two is more than satisfactory for East-West.

Moss gets the defense off to a promising start by leading the ◇K: deuce, six, ace. When Bessis advances the ♠Q, Moss is reluctant to let it slip past him when he might well have two diamond ruffs coming. The sight of Grue's king on this trick is a disappointment, but there are still prospects in hearts and clubs, and there may still be time for one or two diamond ruffs. If West has the missing ◇4, his play of the six at Trick 1 is either high suit-preference from six-four or neutral from four-six-higher. If *declarer* has the ◇4, however, the six is unambiguously suit-preference for clubs. Moss switches to the ♡Q. Bessis claims, conceding two club tricks, +790. Although it is safe to underlead the ♣A unless Grue's diamonds are six-four doubleton (not impossible), the ♣A would usually suffice; West would discourage when he held the ♡A, and would rely on East to play him for equal length in clubs and hearts.

Whether West should not send a neutral message at Trick 1, when he holds the ♡A and the ♣K, is an interesting partnership issue.

Curiously, if East leads a high heart on the go, the defense might be easier: West switches to a diamond when he wins the ♠K, and East has time to switch to clubs to get his diamond ruff.

Closed Room

West	North	East	South
Combescure	Pszczola	Rombaut	Rosenberg
		1♡	pass
2NT¹	4♣	5♡	all pass

1. Invitational or better.

South leads his spade against 5♡, essential for the defense. Pepsi follows with the ♠Q as declarer conceals the five. North wins the trump continuation and plays a second spade (the suit-preference jack). Rosenberg ruffs with the jack in front of dummy and returns a diamond. There is no further trick coming and Rombaut is one down, -100. But that's 12 IMPs for France, now 33 ahead, 219-186.

Board 99. E-W Vul.

```
              ♠ K 10 2
              ♡ Q J 8 7 2
              ◇ A
              ♣ A Q 6 3
♠ 7 4 3                      ♠ A J 9 8
♡ A 9 4 3         N          ♡ K 6 5
◇ 10 5       W       E       ◇ K 9 8 7 4 3
♣ K 10 9 5       S          ♣ —
              ♠ Q 6 5
              ♡ 10
              ◇ Q J 6 2
              ♣ J 8 7 4 2
```

Open Room

West	North	East	South
Grue	Bessis	Moss	Volcker
			pass
pass	1♡	2◇	pass
pass	dbl	pass	3♣
dbl	all pass		

Volcker's 3♣ needn't deliver much, but it's hardly obvious for Grue to take a poke at it. Denmark's Bettina Kalkerup, commenting on BBO, suggests this will prove to be a gruesome double. Joe has endured that sort of wordplay all his life, but in the right context, it still has its place. He leads the ◊10 against 3♣ doubled, which Volcker wins and calls for the ♡2. Moss is ready for this and goes in with the king, but has nothing better to do than continue hearts. Declarer ruffs, ruffs a diamond, ruffs another heart and leads a spade to the king and ace. Moss exits with the ◊K, forcing dummy as Grue discards a spade, but Volcker is in no danger. He ruffs a heart, leads a trump to the queen, cashes the ace, and leads a high heart. West gets his two trump tricks, but his last card is a spade to lead to declarer's queen. Making three, +470.

Let's suppose that after ruffing the second heart, declarer leads a club. If West follows low, as he usually will, declarer puts in the six (not really double-dummy), ruffs a heart, plays a trump to the queen, ruffs another heart, felling the ace, and leads a spade to the king. East wins but is endplayed to concede the overtrick. Curiously, if East allows his partner to win the first heart and play a second diamond (best), declarer will be held to nine tricks.

It's unlikely that Volcker is beating himself up for not negotiating a tenth trick.[††]

Closed Room

West	North	East	South
Combescure	Pszczola	Rombaut	Rosenberg
			pass
pass	1♡	2◊	pass
pass	dbl	pass	2NT[1]
pass	3NT	all pass	

1. South: 'Lebensohl'; North: 'natural'.

Rosenberg, like Volcker, is not willing to try to defend 2◊ doubled (the action touted, rather too forcefully, in my opinion, on BBO by Kit Woolsey and Karen Allison). He intends 2NT as Lebensohl, planning to pass 3♣, but Pepsi interprets 2NT as natural and constructive and raises to 3NT. Fortunately, Rosenberg has some diamond stoppers and some fitting cards, but not quite enough to overcome the bad club break and major-suit layout. Rosenberg goes down only one, -50, but France tacks on another 11 IMPs to increase the lead to 44, 230-186.

---

†† Grue's double of 3♣ reminds me of a time when England's Keith Stanley was scoring up and a similar disaster had ensued at the other table. He gently asked, 'Did you need the extra fifty points?' — *Mark Horton*

Board 100. Both Vul.

```
              ♠ Q 10 7
              ♡ 6 4
              ◇ K J 6 5 3
              ♣ K Q 6
♠ J 4                        ♠ A K 9 8 6
♡ Q J 8 7 5         N        ♡ A K 3
◇ Q 10 4 2      W     E      ◇ A 7
♣ J 9               S        ♣ A 5 2
              ♠ 5 3 2
              ♡ 10 9 2
              ◇ 9 8
              ♣ 10 8 7 4 3
```

Open Room

West	North	East	South
Grue	Bessis	Moss	Volcker
pass	pass	2♣*	pass
2◇[1]	pass	2♡[2]	pass
2♠[3]	pass	2NT*	pass
3◇[4]	pass	3♡	pass
3♠[5]	pass	3NT[6]	pass
4◇	pass	4NT[7]	pass
5♣*	pass	5◇*	pass
5♠[8]	pass	6♡	all pass

1. Artificial game force.
2. Natural, or balanced, stronger than a 2NT opening.
3. Artificial, waiting.
4. Usually 5+♡; rarely minors, emphasis on clubs.
5. Four clubs or four diamonds.
6. Which?
7. RKCB for hearts.
8. ♡Q, but no side king.

After Bessis passes his aceless 11-count, the Americans have the auction to themselves. Moss, noting that his screenmate, Bessis, has taken some extra time passing over the artificial 2◇ (and the natural 4◇), places him with some diamond strength, but enough outside to dissuade him from doubling. Backing his judgment that spades are more likely to come in if he needs that, Moss drives to the thin but playable slam.

After a club or trump lead, Moss would have to concede a club and play for all five spade tricks, using a trump and a club ruff to do so, and a diamond lead would leave declarer without resource, but Volcker, reluctant to blow a trick, leads the ♠2: jack, queen, ace. If Moss can build a diamond trick he can get home with only four spade winners, so he tries the ◇7 at Trick 2, an interesting play that bears no fruit when the ten loses to the jack. A second spade would force declarer to guess well (he *can* get home without finessing against the ♠10: ♡K, ◇A, ♡Q, diamond ruff with the ♡A, spade ruff, ♡J, with the ♣A the entry for two more spade winners — but could easily go wrong), but Bessis switches to the ♣K, forcing out the ace. Moss plays four rounds of trumps, Bessis discarding first a diamond, then a spade. When Moss calls for a spade, the ten comes up, so he can claim: five spades, five hearts and two aces, for +1430.

Closed Room

West	North	East	South
Combescure	Pszczola	Rombaut	Rosenberg
pass	1◇	dbl	pass
1♡	pass	2◇	pass
2NT	pass	3♠	pass
4♠	all pass		

Pepsi is willing to open 1◇, which seems to create some problems for his opponents. Perhaps Combescure could bid 4◇ to offer a choice of majors; his raise to 4♠ leads to a shaky contract. The lead of the ◇9 is covered all around, and Rombaut tries the effect of passing the ♠9. Pepsi wins with the ten and switches to the ♣K, which Rombaut decides to win to cash the ace and king of trumps, producing a happy result. That is +650, but it's 13 IMPs to USA 2 to reduce the deficit to 31 IMPs, 199-230.

Board 104. Neither Vul.

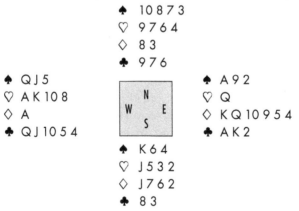

```
            ♠ 10 8 7 3
            ♡ 9 7 6 4
            ◇ 8 3
            ♣ 9 7 6
♠ Q J 5              ♠ A 9 2
♡ A K 10 8          ♡ Q
◇ A                 ◇ K Q 10 9 5 4
♣ Q J 10 5 4        ♣ A K 2
            ♠ K 6 4
            ♡ J 5 3 2
            ◇ J 7 6 2
            ♣ 8 3
```

Open Room

West	North	East	South
Grue	Bessis	Moss	Volcker
1♣*	pass	1♡[1]	pass
1♠[2]	pass	2♠[3]	pass
2NT[2]	pass	3♡[4]	pass
3NT	pass	4♠[5]	pass
4NT[6]	pass	5♣	pass
7♣	all pass		

1. 12+, not including hearts unless 5 hearts (3-3-2), when he would rebid 2♣ over 1♠.
2. Relays.
3. 6+ diamonds, no side suit, some shortness.
4. 3=1=6=3.
5. 12 3-2-1 control points (A=3, K=2, Q=1).
6. RKCB for clubs.

It's always exciting to make a natural bid in the trump suit for the first time at the seven-level on the sixth round of bidding, and I suspect that the relay guys live for these deals. Even more enjoyable when the final contract is the best, as here. Grue wins the spade lead with dummy's ace, cashes the ♣A, comes to the ◇A, draws trumps ending in dummy, sets up diamonds with a ruff and uses the ♡Q as the entry to the long cards, +1440.

Closed Room

West	North	East	South
Combescure	Pszczola	Rombaut	Rosenberg
1♣	pass	1◇	pass
1♡[1]	pass	2◇[2]	pass
3NT[3]	pass	4◇	pass
4♡	pass	4NT*	pass
5♡*	pass	5NT*	pass
6◇	pass	7NT	all pass

1. Natural: unbalanced or 17-18 balanced.
2. Artificial game force.
3. 16-18, not clear whether balanced or unbalanced.

The French auction does not seem to deal with the club fit, and the possibility that West has only one diamond. Rombaut reveals later that he could have bid 6♠ over 6◇ to offer a choice of grand slams. At first sight, 7NT is a very respectable contract, as either red jack might capitulate and there might be time to fall back on the spade finesse or a squeeze (despite some serious communication issues). However, when Pepsi chooses the ♠8 for his opening lead, the secondary chances disappear. Declarer calls for the ♠A, of course, and duly tests diamonds, discarding spades, unblocks the ♡Q, and runs clubs, but Rosenberg needn't hold on to the master diamond or the master spade and takes the last trick with the ♡J for one down, -50.

That is a cool 16 IMPs to USA 2, back within 15 IMPs, 215-230, in the blink (or three) of an eye.

If you're experiencing a bout of *déjà vu*, that's because you remember the eerily similar Board 29 in the 1964 Olympiad semifinal between Italy and Great Britain, covered in the first chapter of *Close Encounters, Book 1*!

Board 105. E-W Vul.

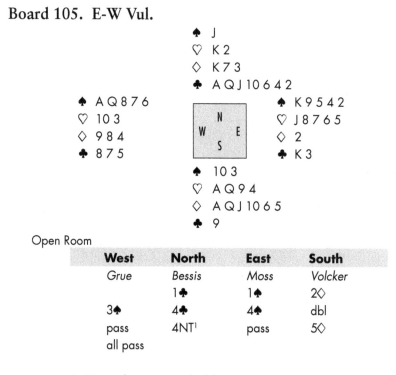

Open Room

	West	North	East	South
	Grue	Bessis	Moss	Volcker
		1♣	1♠	2♡
	3♠	4♣	4♠	dbl
	pass	4NT[1]	pass	5♢
	all pass			

1. Diamond support, mainly clubs.

West	North	East	South
Combescure	Pszczola	Rombaut	Rosenberg
	1♣	1♠	2◇
3♠	dbl[1]	pass	4♡
pass	5◇	all pass	

1. Good offensive hand, game force.

A case can be made for someone to bid six in both rooms, but what is clear is that this is not an easy deal. Volcker makes seven on a heart lead to gain an IMP, 231-215.

Board 107. Neither Vul.

```
              ♠  5 4
              ♡  A K J 10 3
              ◇  A Q 3
              ♣  K 10 7
♠ A K 8 7 3              ♠  J 6 2
♡ Q 9 6 5        N       ♡  7 2
◇ 8 7 6      W     E     ◇  10 2
♣ 6              S       ♣  A J 9 5 3 2
              ♠  Q 10 9
              ♡  8 4
              ◇  K J 9 5 4
              ♣  Q 8 4
```

West	North	East	South
Grue	Bessis	Moss	Volcker
			pass
1♠	2♡	2♠	dbl*
pass	3♣	pass	4♡
all pass			

Grue is steaming a bit now, and tries to keep the ball rolling with a light 1♠ opening in second seat. Volcker's aggressive responsive double gets him to game, and if he bids 3NT he has a chance to make it because he has an unassailable stopper on this layout. With spades raised on his right, however, he is reluctant to go in that direction. Perhaps, because he has such a poor hand for hearts (in particular), he should take his medicine that way. As it happens, 4♡ has some possibilities at single dummy. Unfortunately for France, those possibilities are dashed immediately when Grue carefully wins the spade lead with the ace to convince Moss not to duck the club switch at Trick 2: ♣A, club ruff, ♠K. Grue exits in diamonds, but Bessis finesses against the ♡Q to get out for one down, -50.

Closed Room

West	North	East	South
Combescure	Pszczola	Rombaut	Rosenberg
			pass
pass	1♡	pass	1NT
pass	2NT	pass	3NT
all pass			

Pepsi and Rosenberg cruise into 3NT uncontested and Combescure leads his fourth-best spade to the jack and queen. Rosenberg plays a diamond to the queen, cashes the ◇A and the ♡A, and finishes the diamonds: West discards first the ♡6, then his singleton club, while East plays five-deuce-three of clubs. As East might well have parted with a spade from an original jack-third, Rosenberg decides 4-4 spades is a real possibility, and plays a club rather than rely on the heart finesse. Aargghh! One down here too, -50. No swing.

Board 110. Neither Vul.

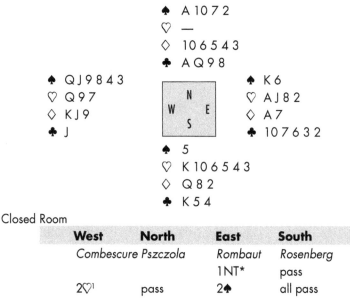

```
              ♠ A 10 7 2
              ♡ —
              ◇ 10 6 5 4 3
              ♣ A Q 9 8
♠ Q J 9 8 4 3              ♠ K 6
♡ Q 9 7        N          ♡ A J 8 2
◇ K J 9     W     E       ◇ A 7
♣ J            S          ♣ 10 7 6 3 2
              ♠ 5
              ♡ K 10 6 5 4 3
              ◇ Q 8 2
              ♣ K 5 4
```

Closed Room

West	North	East	South
Combescure	Pszczola	Rombaut	Rosenberg
		1NT*	pass
2♡[1]	pass	2♠	all pass

1. At least five spades.

Rosenberg needs more to come in over Rombaut's 10-12 1NT, then finds himself in the wrong seat to act over 2♠, as West is unlimited. He leads a heart against 2♠, which Pepsi ruffs to return a diamond. Later, after Rosenberg discards a suit-preference ♡3 on the second trump, Pepsi underleads his clubs and gets a second heart ruff in exchange for Rosenberg's natural heart trick; +140 for Rombaut.

Open Room

West	North	East	South
Grue	Bessis	Moss	Volcker
		1◇[1]	1♡
2♡[2]	pass	2♠	pass
pass	dbl	rdbl	all pass

1. 2+ diamonds, 10-15.
2. At least six spades.

Let's turn our attention to the Open Room, where Volcker considers 1♡ less dangerous than a weak jump overcall, neither side vulnerable. That may well be true, but Bessis's penalty double of 2♠ implicitly credits him with more defense. Moss does not expect to go more than one down and sees an opportunity for a big result by redoubling. Volcker does not consider himself involved here, and Bessis really has nowhere to go with any confidence, although South figures to have some length in at least one minor if he's short in spades.

Volcker leads his singleton trump against 2♠ redoubled: nine, deuce, six. Bessis ducks the trump continuation, and Moss leads the ♡2 towards dummy. Volcker follows low and Bessis ruffs the nine with the ♠10, cashes the ace, and plays the ♣A and another club. Moss takes the force in dummy, and concedes the ♡Q to Volcker's king, the last trick for the defense. The number is +840 for USA 2, a gain of 12 IMPs that leaves the teams only 3 IMPs apart — France 232, USA 2 229.

Ancient proverb: 'If system tells you to open 2NT with:

♠K Q 2 ♡K 9 8 5 ◇K Q J ♣K Q 5

a wise man pretends not to hear.' On Board 111, Combescure, left to play in his 2NT opening, goes one down, -50. Grue can open a strong club and rebid 1NT, which also yields seven tricks, +90. USA 2 adds 4 IMPs, which produces a new leader, USA 2, 233-232. It was not so long ago that France was 44 IMPs ahead.

So, maestro, what do we have for dessert?

Board 112. E-W Vul.

```
              ♠ J 7 5 4 3
              ♡ 10 9 4
              ◇ K 8 3
              ♣ Q 3
   ♠ A 8                        ♠ K Q 9
   ♡ Q 6 5 3 2      N           ♡ K 8
   ◇ 9 5        W       E       ◇ A 4 2
   ♣ 7 6 5 2        S           ♣ A J 9 8 4
              ♠ 10 6 2
              ♡ A J 7
              ◇ Q J 10 7 6
              ♣ K 10
```

Closed Room

West	North	East	South
Combescure	Pszczola	Rombaut	Rosenberg
pass	pass	1♣	1◇
dbl[1]	2◇	2NT	pass
3NT	all pass		

1. At least four hearts.

The Closed Room auction has elements of normalcy, although East's upgrade to 18-19 doesn't work too well when West is reluctant to give up on the vulnerable game bonus and watches Rombaut go two down in 3NT on the indicated lead of the ◇Q; -200 is simply a crappy result.

Open Room

West	North	East	South
Grue	Bessis	Moss	Volcker
pass	pass	1◇	pass
1♡	1♠	1NT[1]	2♠
2NT	all pass		

1. 18-19.

In the Open Room, a remarkable parlay unfolds. First, Moss also upgrades to 18-19 but opens 1◇ just to create something out of nothing. Bessis, tired of all the body blows, tries to generate something for his side at the favorable vulnerability, but his truly ugly 1♠ overcall generates only one more unpleasant result when his opponents stop at 2NT and Volcker can't find a good reason *not* to lead a spade. Moss plays low from dummy and takes the jack with his king, then tries to steal a heart trick. Volcker takes Moss's king with his ace and continues spades to dummy's ace. Now comes a club (three, jack, king). Volcker plays a third spade, not a diamond, and when the ♣A splits out the suit, Moss can claim nine tricks, +150, and 8 IMPs to USA 2 from out of the blue.

After scoring 25 IMPs on the first three deals of the set, France earns only 2 more over the remaining 13. USA 2, meanwhile, chalks up 55 IMPs in weird and wonderful ways. With 16 deals remaining, USA 2 leads by 9 IMPs, 241-232. Amazing stuff.

Session Eight (Boards 113-128)

After coming back from the dead (or dying) early in the previous session, the Americans must be more than pleased with their current position, but the margin is only 9 IMPs, and we can be sure that complacency is not going to be an issue down the home stretch. Both teams field fresh troops: Martel and Fleisher come in for Pepsi and Rosenberg, while Quantin and Lorenzini replace Rombaut and Combescure.

Board 113. Neither Vul.

```
                  ♠ J 3
                  ♡ A K 9 7 4 3
                  ◇ 9 3 2
                  ♣ 9 6
  ♠ K Q 7 6 4                    ♠ 10 9 8
  ♡ 2              N             ♡ Q 8 6 5
  ◇ K Q 6     W         E        ◇ 10 8 7 5
  ♣ K Q 4 3        S             ♣ 10 7
                  ♠ A 5 2
                  ♡ J 10
                  ◇ A J 4
                  ♣ A J 8 5 2
```

Open Room

West	North	East	South
Moss	Lorenzini	Grue	Quantin
	2◇[1]	pass	4◇[2]
pass	4♡	all pass	

1. Weak 2♡ or weak 2♠.
2. Bid your major.

It is common for exponents of this version of Multi (no strong options) to use a response of 4♣ to request a transfer into opener's long suit, but Quantin-Lorenzini's convention card reserves a 3♣ response for this task. As Quantin is willing to play game opposite either weak two-bid, he opts for preemption rather than concern himself with becoming declarer. Moss can double for takeout or take a shot at 4♠, but Quantin's bidding can conceal better support for spades than hearts and his strength is unknown. With only slow cards to offer, and the live possibility that Grue would have to pass a takeout double, Moss decides to go quietly at the prevailing vulnerability.

As he knows dummy will have adequate support for both majors, Grue attacks with the ♣10 rather than the safe-looking ♠10. Lorenzini wins with dummy's ace to pass the ♡10. East wins and switches to the ♠10, which Lorenzini wins to lead towards the concealed ♣9. Moss does the right thing by going in with the queen. He cashes the ♣Q, then switches to the ◇Q. Declarer wins with dummy's remaining ace, overtakes the ♡J to draw trumps, and leads a hopeful diamond to the jack and king. The ◇10 is the second undertrick, -100.

Closed Room

West	North	East	South
Volcker	Fleisher	Bessis	Martel
	2◇[1]	pass	2♠[2]
pass	3♣[3]	pass	4♡
dbl	all pass		

1. Weak 2♡ or weak 2♠.
2. Pass with spades; describe strength with hearts.
3. Maximum weak 2♡.

Martel takes a different approach: the South hand is much more promising if the jack-ten of hearts face a weak 2♡ bid (4-10) rather than a weak 2♠ (2-8) as secondary honors are worth more *a priori* in partner's suit(s) and primary honors more in side suits (readers who have not read Jeff Rubens' classic, *The Secrets of Winning Bridge,* will find great value in the chapter on 'In-and-Out Valuation'). He settles for a pass-or-correct bid that will get him enough information to choose the right level in hearts. Volcker, who could not act over 2♠, can double 4♡ for takeout, and finds Bessis with nowhere to go.

With no aces to contribute to the defense, Volcker sets about trying to protect his high cards by leading trumps. Martel can't afford to eat his honors, so ducks to the queen, and Bessis switches to the ◇7: four, queen, low. Volcker switches to the ♠K, which Martel wins to play three rounds of trumps, discarding a spade. Volcker discards two spades and a club, and

Martel calls for the ♣9, covered all around. When Volcker continues with two rounds of spades, declarer ruffs in dummy, and ruffs out West's ♣K, with the ◊A the entry to cash the ♣J and get out for one down, -100, and a push.

On Board 114, both North-South pairs find the best lead against a normal 3NT from different sides, which matters, albeit only a bit. France is poised to gain an IMP by holding it to three, but Quantin ducks an ace, then gives declarer a soft landing to concede two overtricks. Bessis makes four by declaring from the optimal side but France loses an IMP, 232-242. How often we naively dismiss these 2-IMP swings as part of the cost of doing business!

Board 115. E-W Vul.

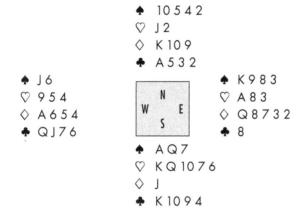

```
                  ♠ 10 5 4 2
                  ♡ J 2
                  ◊ K 10 9
                  ♣ A 5 3 2
  ♠ J 6                         ♠ K 9 8 3
  ♡ 9 5 4              N         ♡ A 8 3
  ◊ A 6 5 4        W     E       ◊ Q 8 7 3 2
  ♣ Q J 7 6            S         ♣ 8
                  ♠ A Q 7
                  ♡ K Q 10 7 6
                  ◊ J
                  ♣ K 10 9 4
```

Closed Room

West	North	East	South
Volcker	Fleisher	Bessis	Martel
			1♡
pass	1NT	pass	2♣
pass	pass	dbl	pass
2◊	2♡	pass	3♣
all pass			

Bypassing a four-card spade suit to respond with a semi-forcing 1NT is a plus for Flannery users, whose 1♡ opening denies as many as four spades unless strong enough to reverse. Bessis can't ignore this possibility when deciding whether to reopen over 2♣, especially when Fleisher will be short in hearts to pass what might (admittedly very occasionally) be a three-card suit; indeed, it is not clear why Fleisher does not offer false preference to 2♡ with three useful-looking cards. However, with 5-4 in the unbid suits and honors where they should be, double seems worthwhile to Bessis, and he succeeds in pushing North-South to 3♣, Martel converting 2♡, which would have been an easier contract. With such strong hearts, it seems certain that Martel expects Fleisher to have a fifth club or only two low hearts.

Volcker leads the ♠J: deuce, three, queen. Declarer leads a heart to the jack and ace, and Bessis switches to his singleton trump to the ten, jack and ace. Martel comes to the ♣K and reverts to hearts, discarding spades from dummy. Volcker ruffs in on the fourth round and cashes the ♣Q, but the defense has only the ◇A coming. Nine tricks for Martel, +110.

Open Room

West	North	East	South
Moss	Lorenzini	Grue	Quantin
			1♡
pass	1♠	pass	2♣[1]
pass	2◇[2]	pass	2♠[3]
pass	2NT[4]	pass	3♣[5]
pass	3◇[6]	pass	3♠
pass	4♡	all pass	

1. Natural, or most strong hands.
2. Artificial, 8+.
3. Natural, game-forcing.
4. Inquiry.
5. 3=5=1=4.
6. Ostensibly a notrump probe.

If the Open Room bidding looks particularly aggressive, that's because it is. The first four bids follow standard Gazzilli practice, but when Quantin continues with 2♠ (rather than a limiting 2♡) he is showing at least a queen more than he has. As the auction is now game-forcing, what ensues is a strain investigation that concludes in the chunky 5-2 heart fit.

It's clear that 4♡, not hopeless at single dummy, is going to be an uphill struggle with clubs lying badly, even with trumps 3-3 and the ♠K onside, but Moss adds an element of excitement by underleading the ◇A on the go, with declarer known to be short. When Quantin calls for the nine it is possible that Grue will follow low, playing declarer for singleton ace, but Grue gets it right; he wins with the ◇Q and switches to the ♠3. Quantin takes heart when his queen holds, and a trump to the jack wins; he expects to build a spade discard by taking a ruffing finesse in diamonds through East, and will need only some good luck in trumps and clubs. No, Moss takes the second diamond with the ace and exits with a spade, and Quantin must lose a late club trick and the ace of trumps for one down, -50. So 4 IMPs to USA 2, 246-232.

Board 117. N-S Vul.

```
              ♠  —
              ♡  9 7 6 4
              ◇  K 10 9 2
              ♣  K Q J 6 3
♠ Q J 9 7 5                    ♠ 8 6 4 3 2
♡ 8 5 2           N           ♡ A 3
◇ J 6         W       E       ◇ Q 4 3
♣ 10 9 2          S           ♣ A 8 7
              ♠  A K 10
              ♡  K Q J 10
              ◇  A 8 7 5
              ♣  5 4
```

Closed Room

West	North	East	South
Volcker	Fleisher	Bessis	Martel
	pass	pass	1NT
pass	2♣	pass	2♡
pass	3♠[1]	pass	3NT[2]
pass	4♡[3]	all pass	

1. Strong heart raise, unspecified shortness.
2. Where?
3. Spades.

Left alone, the main task for Martel and Fleisher is to avoid a poor slam. Despite his super-maximum, Martel pulls in a notch when he learns that Fleisher, a passed hand, is short in spades. With everything breaking, +650 is straightforward on the lead of the ♠Q.

Open Room

West	North	East	South
Moss	Lorenzini	Grue	Quantin
	pass	1♠	dbl
4♠	4NT*	pass	5◇
all pass			

Although the East hand does not look like a traditional opening bid in second seat, not vulnerable, Grue and Moss trade on their Precision style to open with any excuse, a five-card major being high on the list of excuses. The hailstorm this style can pour down on the other side is demonstrated graphically here, where Moss can raise to 4♠, a bid that can be made on many very different types of hand facing a limited opening bid. It would be unkind to point out that 4♠ can be doubled and set 800 because the North hand has too much offense to settle for a responsive double that would too often be passed for an inadequate return for the vulnerable game or slam bonus. Indeed, Lorenzini's 4NT looks like the normal action, but, unfortunately, it gets him to 5◊, where there are three unavoidable losers; adding to the French misery is the news that on the lie of the cards, both 5♡ and 5♣ would yield eleven tricks. Quantin is -100 and USA 2 gains 12 more IMPs, now ahead by 27, 259-232.

The auction would be very different if Quantin overcalled 1NT, which seems the straightforward choice unless looking for a swing: Moss would bid only 3♠ — indeed, maybe only 2♠ — and Lorenzini would have room for a responsive double or a cheaper exploratory sequence that would bring hearts into focus.

Board 118. E-W Vul.

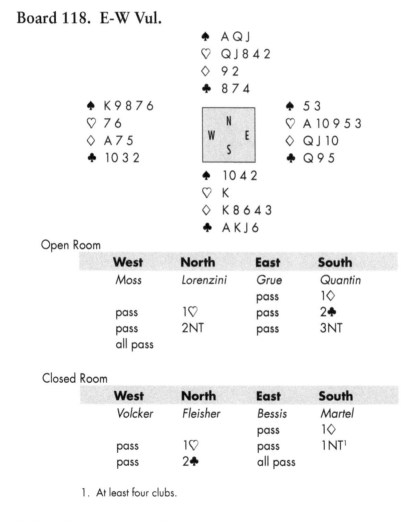

Open Room

West	North	East	South
Moss	Lorenzini	Grue	Quantin
		pass	1◊
pass	1♡	pass	2♣
pass	2NT	pass	3NT
all pass			

Closed Room

West	North	East	South
Volcker	Fleisher	Bessis	Martel
		pass	1◊
pass	1♡	pass	1NT[1]
pass	2♣	all pass	

1. At least four clubs.

Martel's 1NT rebid and Quantin's 2♣ both show clubs, but where Quantin's bid limits his hand, Martel's is intended as forcing. Not vulnerable, Fleisher takes the low road by offering non-forcing preference to 2♣, knowing opener could bid again with extra values but Lorenzini takes the other approach, continuing with 2NT, minimum for an invitation. Perhaps 2◊, not a pretty bid, would be a compromise, as South could bid again with extras. As is often the case, the lower contract fails while the more optimistic contract succeeds.

Bessis leads the ♠5 against 2♣. With the ♠3 missing, Volcker can place his partner with QJ53 or five-three doubleton, so carefully withholds his king. Fleisher wins cheaply and leads a heart, taken by the ace. Bessis switches to a trump and Fleisher wins with the ace. He crosses to the ♣A as he thinks it likely the ♠K is on his left, discards a spade on the ♡Q, and continues with the ♡J, throwing a diamond. Volcker ruffs and leads the ♠K to force dummy, Bessis parting with a heart. Declarer, in trouble now, tries a low diamond, ducked to East, who continues trumps. Although Fleisher successfully finesses the jack, he leads a second *low* diamond, so East can win and play a third club. Fleisher must concede a third diamond and is down one for -50.

To get home when he wins the ♣J, declarer must call for the ◊K, forcing West to win. West can't play a third diamond with profit, so must lead another spade; declarer discards and East is squeezed in front of dummy, though declarer is about to ruff with the king. If he throws his heart, declarer ruffs a diamond for his eighth trick; if he discards his diamond winner, declarer leads the master ◊8 to force East to ruff with the ♣Q, and declarer's ♣8 takes the last trick.

That would have been a pretty ending, but it needn't come to that. If Volcker, after ruffing the third heart, exits with a trump rather than the ♠K, declarer can neither get a diamond ruff in hand nor establish a long diamond in dummy. But, then, it needn't come to that either. If Fleisher does not try to cash the ♡J, he can get home by playing any of the other suits, including trumps (finessing the jack); he stays one step ahead of the defenders regardless of which strategy they adopt.

Against 3NT, Grue leads the ♡5. Lorenzini wins with the king (seven, discouraging, from West), and starts on diamonds: three, seven (suit preference, not Smith), nine, ten. Grue duly switches to the ♠5, but Moss puts up the king. Lorenzini wins and plays a second diamond: jack, king, ace. When Moss returns the ♡6, Grue plays the ten under declarer's queen, trying to create the impression that Moss has both the ◊Q and the missing ♡3 to lead through the jack. Not surprisingly, Lorenzini gives his next play plenty of thought before cashing his spade winners, which has the delightful effect of forcing Grue to discard the ♡3 he was doing his best to conceal. The play so far strongly suggests the actual layout, so Lorenzini finesses the ♣J and soon records +400 when clubs are 3-3. France gains 10 IMPs, its first significant pickup since Board 99 early in Session Seven. The margin is down to 17, 242-259.

If Grue started with 2=5=2=4, Lorenzini could still make 3NT as long as the ♣Q is onside; he can play a fourth round of clubs, and Grue will have to concede the ♡9 to declarer's jack at Trick 13.

Lots of boards remaining — has momentum departed the American camp, if only to sneak a Gauloise behind the French bunkhouse?

Although Board 119 is a straightforward push at North-South +620 in 4♠, I am reminded yet again that the game has changed since my playing days. Both vulnerable, Moss and Volcker are dealt:

♠ Q 8 7　♡ K 9 8 6　◇ A Q 10 6　♣ J 7

and hear 1♠ on their right. Both double for takeout. Nothing bad befalls them. I cringe. Am I a dinosaur for thinking badly of the popular black-suit flawed sub-minimum double?

Board 120. Neither Vul.

```
                    ♠ Q 3
                    ♡ J 3
                    ◇ 10 6 2
                    ♣ Q 10 8 6 5 3
      ♠ K 10 9 7 4                  ♠ J 8 6 5 2
      ♡ 9 4              N          ♡ K
      ◇ A Q 8 7 3    W       E      ◇ J 9 5
      ♣ 4                S          ♣ K 9 7 2
                    ♠ A
                    ♡ A Q 10 8 7 6 5 2
                    ◇ K 4
                    ♣ A J
```

Open Room

West	North	East	South
Moss	Lorenzini	Grue	Quantin
1♠	pass	3♠	dbl
4♠	pass	pass	5♡
all pass			

West	North	East	South
Volcker	*Fleisher*	*Bessis*	*Martel*
pass	pass	pass	2♣
2♠	pass[1]	4♠	5♡[1]
all pass			

1. Double would be penalty.

Shades of Board 117! Opening light with spades, not vulnerable, seems to be a domain belonging exclusively to Moss and Grue in this match, although this six-loser West hand would be opened by many pairs using standard systems. Not Volcker and Bessis, however, which again creates different scenarios for South at his first turn.

Grue, with some junky defensive cards, settles for a mixed raise, so Quantin can choose between doubling before bidding hearts and bidding 4♡, intending to double next if it comes to that. When he takes the more optimistic option he finds himself in roughly the same position as Martel, who was left in peace for a moment to open 2♣ in the other room. Sooner or later, the guys with spades find their total-tricks level. Both Souths are obliged to introduce their long suit at the five-level, where they are not very comfortable.

Moss keeps the defense alive by leading the 'right' black four — the ♠4: *queen* (if East covers, West might not know whether a spade is cashing), five, ace. Quantin cashes the ♡A, and plays the ♣A then the ♣J. If Moss has the ♣K, it won't matter who has the ◊A as the ♡J stands as a timely entry. Disaster! Moss carefully ruffs the ♣J and exits safely in spades, and soon gets his two diamond tricks when declarer uses the heart entry to lead towards the ◊K, -50. Moss can discard on the ♣J with the same effect, as Grue could win the king and switch to diamonds, but why create a problem for partner?

If Quantin believed that Grue's ♠5 at Trick 1, though not the lowest outstanding spade, is genuine suit-preference for clubs, he would find the winning line. As Grue should have one of the important minor-suit honors for his mixed raise — we have already seen how little these Americans need to raise a major to four — there is no good reason it should be an ace rather than a king, especially after Moss's self-raise to game.

Volcker leads the 'wrong' black four against Martel, who does not play dummy's ♣Q to give himself a potential extra entry for the trump finesse if East does not cover (the implications for the heart position accruing from whether East covers the ♣Q are of some interest). Martel wins Trick 1 with the ♣J and cashes the ♡A. When Bessis obliges with the king, declarer crosses to the ♡J to draw the last trump and leads towards the ◊K to try for an overtrick; +450. So 11 IMPs to USA 2, 1 IMP more than France had gained on Board 118 to end the long American run. The USA 2 lead is 28, 270-242.

Board 121. E-W Vul.

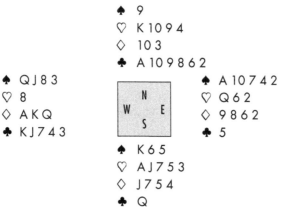

```
            ♠ 9
            ♡ K 10 9 4
            ◇ 10 3
            ♣ A 10 9 8 6 2
♠ Q J 8 3                    ♠ A 10 7 4 2
♡ 8            N             ♡ Q 6 2
◇ A K Q    W     E           ◇ 9 8 6 2
♣ K J 7 4 3     S            ♣ 5
            ♠ K 6 5
            ♡ A J 7 5 3
            ◇ J 7 5 4
            ♣ Q
```

Open Room

West	North	East	South
Moss	Lorenzini	Grue	Quantin
	pass	pass	1♡
dbl	3♣[1]	3♠	pass
4♠	5♡	pass	pass
dbl	all pass		

1. Fit-showing.

Closed Room

West	North	East	South
Volcker	Fleisher	Bessis	Martel
	pass	pass	1♡
dbl	3NT[1]	4♣	pass
pass	5♣	pass	5♡
dbl	all pass		

1. Good raise to 4♡; 4♣ would be a splinter.

It's not often that we encounter consecutive deals where the same pairs play five of a major, but here we are.

As East-West's 4♠ can be set legitimately only with a most unlikely diamond lead — North's singleton nine of trumps helps declarer considerably — it's probably just as well for North-South to push on to 5♡, although it looks like a captaincy violation for North to do so, especially with good defense in context. Fleisher can't double 4♠ to involve partner, as that would be penalty, but for Lorenzini, double would be 'Please do something', so I am surprised he would rather bid 5♡ facing a third-seat opener at favorable.

Moss and Vocker lead a high diamond and cash the ◊Q after East discourages. They switch to the ♠Q and East takes the ♠A to continue spades.

Quantin ruffs the second spade in dummy, plays the ♣A, ruffs a club (diamond from Grue), ruffs the good spade in dummy, and ruffs another club as Grue discards his last diamond. Quantin has delayed his diamond ruff too long, and now must ruff the third round with the ♡K. He ruffs another club and leads the thirteenth diamond, which is going to be ruffed by whichever defender has been dealt the ♡Q. That is East this time, and Quantin is two down, -300.

Martel wins the second spade with the king to lead the ♣Q: king, ace. On the ♣10 continuation, Bessis discards a diamond as declarer ruffs cheaply to play a diamond, ruffed safely in dummy when the king appears. Declarer ruffs another club, ruffs his losing spade, and confidently plays the ♡K and a heart to the jack to claim the last two tricks with the ace of trumps and the ◊J. Martel is down only one for -100, and earns 5 IMPs for USA 2, ahead now by 33, 275-242, with only seven deals remaining.

Chip Martel

Board 123. Neither Vul.

```
              ♠ Q 9 7 6 5
              ♡ J 10
              ◇ J 6
              ♣ K 10 9 6
  ♠ K 2                        ♠ A J 10 4
  ♡ 9 4 3          N           ♡ A 8 5
  ◇ A Q 10 7 5 4  W   E        ◇ K 8 3 2
  ♣ 4 3              S          ♣ 7 2
              ♠ 8 3
              ♡ K Q 7 6 2
              ◇ 9
              ♣ A Q J 8 5
```

Closed Room

West	North	East	South
Volcker	Fleisher	Bessis	Martel
			1♡
2◇	dbl	2♡*	3♣
pass	pass	3◇	all pass

As Fleisher's negative double does not guarantee clubs, Martel's free bid of 3♣ suggests five, so he does not compete further over 3◇ despite the favorable vulnerability, and Fleisher, with a balanced minimum, is not willing to do more. Volcker takes no chances in the play after the lead of the ♡J, and settles for +110.

Open Room

West	North	East	South
Moss	Lorenzini	Grue	Quantin
			1♡
2◇	dbl	2NT[1]	3♣
3◇	4♣	all pass	

1. Good four-card diamond raise.

By competing to 4♣, Lorenzini is going to earn a couple of IMPs for France for -50, but a funny thing happens on the way to the bank. Moss attacks with the ♠K, and continues the suit: queen, ace. If building a trump trick for Moss is Grue's plan, he can cash the ◇K, get a count, and play another spade. Instead, perhaps reading nothing into declarer's suspicious play of the ♠Q, he continues with a third spade immediately. Quantin's clubs are strong enough to handle this ruff and another to establish dummy's long card while drawing trumps, so the diamond loser goes away; he loses only to the ♡A for +130, and France gains 6 IMPs, not 2, cutting the margin to 27, 248-275. Five boards to play.

Board 124. N-S Vul.

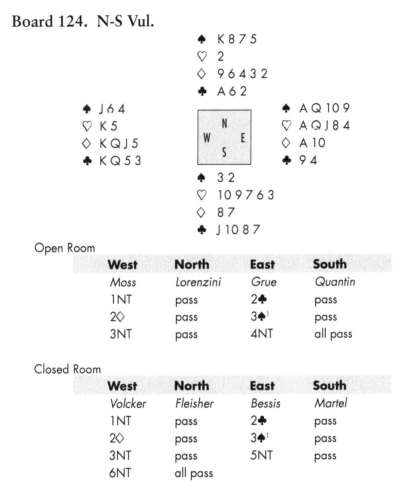

```
              ♠ K 8 7 5
              ♡ 2
              ◇ 9 6 4 3 2
              ♣ A 6 2
♠ J 6 4                        ♠ A Q 10 9
♡ K 5              N           ♡ A Q J 8 4
◇ K Q J 5     W       E        ◇ A 10
♣ K Q 5 3         S            ♣ 9 4
              ♠ 3 2
              ♡ 10 9 7 6 3
              ◇ 8 7
              ♣ J 10 8 7
```

Open Room

West	North	East	South
Moss	Lorenzini	Grue	Quantin
1NT	pass	2♣	pass
2◇	pass	3♠[1]	pass
3NT	pass	4NT	all pass

Closed Room

West	North	East	South
Volcker	Fleisher	Bessis	Martel
1NT	pass	2♣	pass
2◇	pass	3♠[1]	pass
3NT	pass	5NT	pass
6NT	all pass		

1. Four spades, five hearts, game force.

The East hand is worth more than its high-card count, West's significantly less. Moss can open a guilt-free 1NT as his range is 14(13)-16 here, but Volcker could exercise judgment to downgrade his hand. He is not keen to do so as his counterpart is sure to open 1NT at the other table, but this is the sort of hand that could generate a positive swing by doing something different that is eminently reasonable.

After showing a game force with 4-5 in the majors, Bessis does the practical thing by driving to slam, but Grue would be overbidding to do so, and settles for an invitational raise to 4NT. Although Moss could have a point or two less, his hand looks terrible, so he passes.

Against 4NT, Lorenzini attacks with a spade, but Moss finesses successfully and takes twelve tricks, losing only to the ♣A for +490.

Against 6NT, Fleisher leads a passive diamond. If the ♣A is onside and the ♠K offside, declarer can come to twelve tricks if hearts are no worse than 4-2 by playing on the 'right' black suit. If Volcker judges that Moss and Grue will also be in 6NT with the same opening lead, he can try the less obvious line of play as a sensible way to swing, with 14 IMPs the reward for being right. No, Volcker wins the ♢A, crosses to the ♡K, and passes the ♠J, repeats the finesse, tests hearts, and leads a club to the king, which is ducked ('Maybe this will create a losing option,' thinks Fleisher). Volcker eventually takes a third spade finesse for the overtrick, +1020, and 11 IMPs to France, now within 16 at 259-275.

Suddenly, there are plenty of boards remaining!

But four may not be enough, as Board 125 is a push at East-West 3NT+2. Then there are three.

Board 126. Neither Vul.

```
              ♠ A J 4
              ♡ Q 6 4
              ♢ Q 8
              ♣ 10 9 7 5 3
   ♠ 5 3                        ♠ K Q 9 8 2
   ♡ A 7 3 2          N         ♡ J 9
   ♢ K J 10 7 3    W     E      ♢ A 9 6
   ♣ 4 2              S         ♣ Q J 8
              ♠ 10 7 6
              ♡ K 10 8 5
              ♢ 5 4 2
              ♣ A K 6
```

Open Room

West	North	East	South
Moss	Lorenzini	Grue	Quantin
		1NT	pass
2♣	pass	2♠	pass
2NT	all pass		

Over the course of the match, we've seen a variety of hand types deemed appropriate for 1NT, and this effort from Grue — 14(13)-16 — is probably the opening we should expect from him. Moss can't afford to pass, as his counterpart would be moving forward facing 15-17. Quantin's best guess is the ♣A, requesting an attitude signal, and Lorenzini's ♣10 encourages. Grue wins the third club, then loses the second-round diamond finesse to North, who cashes clubs. Grue blanks the ♡A and discards a spade and the ♡9 from hand, while Quantin signals eight-five in hearts. Lorenzini switches accurately to the ♡4, and Quantin equally accurately gets his king out of the way. Grue cashes out for two down, -100.

Closed Room

West	North	East	South
Volcker	Fleisher	Bessis	Martel
		1♠	pass
1NT	all pass		

Volcker declares a level lower from the other side of the table and gets the ♣5 lead, fourth best, from Fleisher. Martel takes the ♣Q with the ace and switches to the ♡5, Volcker winning his ace immediately to lead a spade through North, who follows low. Now, when Volcker loses to the ◊Q, Fleisher can revert to clubs, and the defense takes five of those, three hearts, the ◊Q and the ♠A for four down, -200. That's 3 IMPs to USA 2, no big thing but for the fact that another precious board had left the building. USA 2 leads by 19, 278-259.

With two to play, we've entered miracle territory. Perhaps the Great Shuffler has been paying attention, for the next deal is a possible slam East-West.

Marty Fleisher

Board 127. N-S Vul.

```
                ♠ J 10 8 4
                ♥ 8
                ◊ A 6
                ♣ Q 10 9 7 6 2
   ♠ A                        ♠ K 9 7 2
   ♥ A J 10 7 3 2     N       ♥ K 9 5 4
   ◊ Q 8 3        W       E   ◊ K 9 4
   ♣ K 8 5            S       ♣ A J
                ♠ Q 6 5 3
                ♥ Q 6
                ◊ J 10 7 5 2
                ♣ 4 3
```

Open Room

West	North	East	South
Moss	Lorenzini	Grue	Quantin
			pass
1♥	pass	1NT[1]	pass
2♣[2]	pass	2◊[1]	pass
3♣[3]	pass	3◊[1]	pass
3♥[4]	pass	3♠[1]	pass
4◊[5]	pass	4♠[1]	pass
5♣[6]	pass	5♥	all pass

1. Artificial game-forcing inquiry.
2. Maximum.
3. 6+ hearts, unbalanced.
4. 1=6=3=3.
5. Nine 3-2-1 controls (A=3, K=2, Q=1).
6. ♥A or ♥K, no ace or king of diamonds.

Closed Room

West	North	East	South
Volcker	Fleisher	Bessis	Martel
			pass
1♥	pass	1♠	pass
2♥	pass	4♥	all pass

The East-West 6♥ is superb, needing only to avoid a trump loser or an unlikely ruff, but it is soon evident that this is a very difficult pair of hands to bid. East fears that his ♠K might be wasted facing spade shortage, but when West's singleton is the ace, the king might provide a valuable discard. West's unprotected ◇Q starts out as a questionable asset, but facing the king combines to prevent the defenders from taking two fast diamond tricks. Meanwhile, the ten-card trump fit makes the missing ♡Q less critical.

As Bessis-Volcker finish first, their bidding is posted before the Open Room tackles this deal. They don't even sniff at slam, and record +480, so now the only way for France to gain any IMPs is for Moss and Grue to have a disaster and bid seven off the cashing ◇A.

Bessis-Volcker have several artificial major-suit raises in their arsenal, but no game-forcing raise with at least four trumps. Although they use Gazzilli after 1♡-1♠ and feel that starting slowly gives them plenty of room for opener to describe his hand, this can still be a particularly awkward start for hands with primary heart support.

Later, I would ask Thomas Bessis about Board 127, and his response is illuminating, so I will share it with you:

'After 1♡-1♠; 2♡, we play 2NT as a game-forcing relay to learn about opener's shape. Here Fred probably would have replied 3♠, showing short spades, although he could instead bid 3♡, showing 2=6=(2-3) or 2=7=2=2, treating his stiff ♣A as a 'balanced' value.

I thought for a long time about whether to use the relay and follow up with a cuebid over partner's response, or instead just jump to 4♡. My thinking was that my partner would not in any case be able to value his cards well for my purposes, as I could have a hand like I had, or instead a 16+ HCP hand with two low hearts. For example, had I heard something like 3◇, showing three spades and a diamond fragment, and continued with a slammish 3♡, partner would probably be unstoppable with a hand like:

♠ Q x x   ♡ A Q J x x x   ◇ A x x   ♣ x

in which case slam is basically 0%, and we're already in big danger at the five-level. The point is that he would have no clue that I *don't* need good hearts, and that the card I needed him *not* to have was the ♡Q. Honestly, it was not a good hand for our system, and it was quite random whether we reached slam. Frederic told me that he would have driven to slam by himself had I made any move. Of course.'

As difficult as this combination can be for natural systems, it's the sort of deal that relay methods generally handle well. Indeed, Moss and Grue have all the room they could hope for and are in no danger of reaching a doomed seven. However, they can't get past the final hurdle, and +480 is a push.

There is always speculation about artificial auctions, and it's important to learn the truth before drawing conclusions. Here's the truth, from Joe:

'When Brad bid 5♣, I knew that he had either his actual hand, which was great for slam, or a hand where we were off two aces. But more likely, in my opinion, were hands where we were on a straight finesse. Partner was a favorite to hold the ♠A to make up his nine 3-2-1 points, but I had to consider:

♠Q ♡AQxxxx ◇Qxx ♣KQx

(we count singleton honors), or:

♠A ♡AQxxxx ◇xxx ♣Kxx

With more room in the asks I would have found out every card he had. Rather than relay, I could have used our forcing-raise scheme, but I would not have been happy to hear about the stiff spade. I thought that at the other table, if East found out his partner had short spades, they probably wouldn't reach slam. That's eventually what made me decide to go low. I could have asked again about honor location by bidding 5◇, but that would get us past 5♡.'

Joe Grue

The American lead is still 19 IMPs, 278-259 and there is only one deal to play. Grim for the home team.

Rather incredibly, Board 128 is a possible grand slam for East-West, who are vulnerable. Visions of a 19-IMP swing dance in our heads, like sugar plums.

Board 128. E-W Vul.

```
                    ♠ 9 6 5
                    ♡ K Q J 10
                    ◇ 10 3 2
                    ♣ 10 6 2
   ♠ A J 4 3                        ♠ K Q 10 8 2
   ♡ A 2              N             ♡ 9
   ◇ K Q J 9      W      E          ◇ A 7 6
   ♣ J 9 5           S             ♣ A K 8 7
                    ♠ 7
                    ♡ 8 7 6 5 4 3
                    ◇ 8 5 4
                    ♣ Q 4 3
```

Open Room

West	North	East	South
Moss	*Lorenzini*	*Grue*	*Quantin*
1NT	pass	2♡[1]	pass
2NT[2]	pass	4♡[3]	pass
4♠	pass	4NT	pass
5♡	pass	5NT	pass
7♠	all pass		

1. At least five spades.
2. Four-card spade support, the only super-accept.
3. Intended as heart shortness, slam interest.

By staying low with a big fit, the Americans can show any shortness *and* differentiate between game-invitational and slam-interest hands, but Grue bids too quickly, and forgets the scheme available to him: he intends 4♡ as a slam-try splinter. Moss remembers the system, however, reads 4♡ as a balanced slam try with a heart control but no controls in the minors (Grue would have to hold: ♠KQxxx ♡KQJ ◇xx ♣Q10x to fit the system definition, chasing a slam that would be good only opposite a perfect ♠Axxx ♡Axxx ◇Ax ♣KJx), and signs off at 4♠.

When Grue invites seven, promising all the keycards and the ♠Q, Moss knows 4♡ was a misbid, but *which* misbid? Did Grue intend 4♡ as a re-transfer, to segue into RKCB, forgetting that 3♡ would have been the re-transfer? It is much more likely (Moss says later 'about 80-90%') that 4♡ was intended as a splinter, as the system bid to show short hearts and slam interest is 3NT, an easy treatment to forget.

Moss is only too aware that there will usually be a vital extra ruffing trick in diamonds if Grue is 5=1=4=3 or 5=1=3=4, West's third club going on

East's fifth spade after drawing trumps. If Grue has a second suit he could show it via a transfer after re-transferring to spades at the three-level, but that might make it awkward to show shortness later. Although Moss has good reason to expect a sixth spade, that is hardly something to count on, as we can see from looking at the East hand. It is certainly in play to bid 7◇, but Moss does not want to risk going down in 7◇ on a 5-1 trump break. He bids 7♠ (7NT would have thirteen top tricks, too, facing 6=1=3=3 with the ♣K that he expects Grue to hold in order to keep seven in the picture after the retreat to 4♠).

But reflecting on the relative merits of 7◇ will have to wait, as Moss is in 7♠, against which Lorenzini leads a thoughtful trump. Moss sees that he must avoid a club loser, with the option of playing either opponent for doubleton queen, or finessing against the queen-ten in North. A third, somewhat obscure, possibility is to lead the jack and play South for doubleton ten if North covers, which he might not do. Moss plays four rounds of spades to see what he can learn, but gets only heart discards from both opponents; then four rounds of diamonds: ♣2, ♣7, heart. That club discard is ominous, and Moss, with one entry left in hand, leads the ♣5: six, *eight*. Quantin's ♣Q is the setting trick, -100.

Joe suggests later that, 'If Brad knew I had short hearts, he would have bid 7◇ for sure.'

But to Brad, the situation was less black and white:

'It was awkward, complicated, and I didn't want to take ten years and bid 7◇, giving Joe less flexibility to go back to spades. In retrospect, I think bidding 7◇ was the most practical bid as a bridge problem, and one that I could live with if it turned out badly. While I now believe I probably misjudged, I'm still not certain. The hand will haunt me forever. In the end, what matters on this hand is that I had incomplete facts because Joe forgot the system, and I had to make a choice.'

The door is open — if only a crack — for France to tie the match if Bessis-Volcker can find their magic 7◇.

West	North	East	South
Volcker	*Fleisher*	*Bessis*	*Martel*
1NT	pass	2♡¹	pass
3♠²	pass	4♣³	pass
4♢	pass	4♡	pass
4♠	pass	4NT	pass
5♡	pass	6♣	pass
6♠	all pass		

1. At least five spades.
2. Four-card spade support, the only super-accept.
3. Natural, slam try.

Over 3♠, Bessis has sound options. He can bid 3NT (puppet to 4♣) to show (a) shortness up the line at the four-level, or (b) 6+ spades with no shortness and a specific side ace or king at the five-level; or he can make a natural bid (4♣, 4♢, 4♡) directly. In keeping with partnership style, he shows his second suit, which can help partner appreciate a doubleton there. After two control bids, Volcker, like Moss, settles for 4♠ as his hand has not improved. When Bessis tries for seven by showing the ♣K, Volcker signs off because he can't take care of the third round of clubs, but there is more to it than that. Bessis has shown all his top cards, and stopped to show a heart control *before* checking on keycards. If East's heart control is a singleton, there is an extra ruffing trick in the 4-3 7♡; if East has the ♡K, West can count thirteen top tricks in notrump (or spades), and East can convert 7♢ to 7NT.

Indeed, 6♠ is the correct level for spades, but unfortunately +1430 brings in 17 IMPs for France, not 19. The match is over, and USA 2 hangs on to win by 2 IMPs, 278-276.

For those who might need to refer to the IMP scale, +2140 and +100 add up to 2240, which is the absolute upper extremity of 19 IMPs; 2250 would be 20 IMPs, but is virtually unattainable on this final deal. Seriously!

And then the rule to resolve a tie would come into play, and that happens to be the result of the 16-board round robin match between the teams, not their relative finish in that stage. USA 2 won that match. It is impossible to imagine how everyone in our wonderful world of bridge would have reacted if Bessis-Volcker had bid and made 7♢ to tie the match, only to discover that France would lose the tie-break despite winning the seven-day round robin.

USA 2: (l-r) Jan Martel, Joe Grue, Brad Moss, Michael Rosenberg,
Marty Fleisher, Chip Martel, Jacek Pszczola

Epilogue Lyonnaise

Much has been said and written about the effect of the slam deals on the outcome, with Boards 127 and 128 highlighting the genre rather dramatically.

There were twenty-one such deals to consider, including ten that were essentially pushes, several of which might have been bid but were not. Some of the missed slams were well worth bidding, but remarkably, not one of the slams undertaken by *both* teams was a bad one!

The winning team gained 53 IMPs on five slam deals, 34 of which could be considered lucky, and the biggest gain of 16 IMPs (Board 104) was well earned in an absolute sense, although the French were unlucky that their odds-on but undeniably inferior grand slam had to fail. Then there was Board 76, a 4-IMP gain for USA 2 rather than a 13-IMP loss when the French took a phantom save against a slam that was going to fail.

The losing team gained 82 IMPs on six slam deals, 15 of them (on Board 82) not unfortunate but quite reasonable given the evidence from the auction, 11 on a 50-50 endeavor, and, most visibly, 17 on Board 128, where the swing would have been 12 to USA 2 had Moss and Grue reached 7♢ rather than the unmakeable 7♠. You can evaluate the luck on 128 as you see fit in this context.

Thomas Bessis points to Moss and Grue's successful 6♡ on Board 100 as the pivotal point in the match. 'Had it gone down, it would definitely have changed the dynamic of the rest of the segment, and probably the match. Of course, we realize that there were many other deals where luck played a role. It was, after all, a bridge match.'

That it was.

Also Available

Close Encounters — Bridge's Greatest Matches
Book 1: 1964-2001

978-1-77140-028-2

Eric Kokish and Mark Horton

The first installment in the two-book series that describes some of the most memorable bridge matches of the last fifty years. Book 1 begins with Italy asserting its supremacy over Great Britain in 1964, and ends with Germany's dramatic Venice Cup win over France in 2001.

Contact Us

Master Point Press
214 Merton St. Suite 205
Toronto, ON M4S 1A6
(647) 956-4933

Master Point Press on the Internet

www.masterpointpress.com

Our main site, with information about our books and software, reviews and more.

www.teachbridge.com

Our site for bridge teachers and students — free downloadable support material for our books, helpful articles and more.

www.bridgeblogging.com

Read and comment on regular articles from MPP authors and other bridge notables.

www.ebooksbridge.com

Purchase downloadable electronic versions of MPP books and software.